# PRISON SYSTEMS AND CORRECTIONAL LAWS: EUROPE, THE UNITED STATES AND JAPAN

*A Comparative Analysis*

By
Günther Kaiser

Transnational Publishers, Inc.
Dobbs Ferry, New York

Original German title:
*Strafvollzug im europäischen Vergleich.*
Published by Wissenschaftliche Buchgesellschaft,
Darmstadt, 1982. Translation by Sharon Byrd.

**Library of Congress Cataloging in Publication Data**

Kaiser, Günther.
Prison systems and correctional laws.

Includes index.
1. Prisons—Law and legislation—Europe. 2. Prisons—Law and legislation—Japan. 3. Prisons—Law and legislation—United States. 4. Prisons—Europe. 5. Prisons—Japan. 6. Prisons—United States. I. Title.
LAW 344.4′035 84-16361
ISBN 0-941320-12-X 344.0435



Manufactured in the United States of America

# Contents

## PART ONE: Penal Corrections in Europe— Problems, Methods and Developments

## PART TWO: Penal Corrections in West Germany and other European Nations 13

# List of Abbreviations

| | |
|---|---|
| Art. | Article |
| BewHi | Bewährungshilfe, Bonn |
| BGBl | Bundesgesetzblatt |
| BritJCrim | The British Journal of Criminology, Delinquency and Deviant Social Behaviour, London |
| C&D | Crime and Delinquency, Hackensack/N.J. |
| ch. | chapter |
| Compte général | Compte général de l'administration de la justice criminelle, Paris |
| CorrC | Corrections Code |
| CrimJAbstr | Criminal Justice Abstracts, Hackensack/N.J. |
| CrimLR | Criminal Law Review, London |
| DPrR | Dutch Prison Rules |
| DDR | Deutsche Demokratische Republik (GDR) |
| Dept. | Department |
| DPC | Dutch Penal Code |
| DRiZ | Deutsche Richterzeitung, Karlsruhe |
| ECCP | European Committee on Crime Problems, Council of Europe, Strasbourg |
| Ed(s)., ed. | Editor(s), edition/edited |
| EGGVG | Einführungsgesetz zum Gerichtsverfassungsgesetz (Introductory Law to the Law on Court Constitution) |
| EMRK | Europäische Menschenrechtskonvention (HRC) (European Human Rights Convention) |
| et al. | et alii |
| EuGRZ | Grundrechte. Die Rechtsprechung in Europa. Europäische Grundrechte—Zeitschrift, Kehl |
| f., ff. | following page, following pages |
| FAZ | Frankfurter Allgemeine Zeitung, Frankfurt/M. |

| | |
|---|---|
| FedProb | Federal Probation, New York |
| FrPC | French Penal Code |
| GBl | Gesetzblatt |
| GDR | German Democratic Republic |
| gevangeniesstatistiek | gevangeniesstatistiek (Prison Statistics), Utrecht |
| Halsbury's | Halsbury's Statutory Instruments, London |
| HngPC | Hungarian Penal Code |
| Howard Journal | Howard Journal of Penology and Crime Prevention, London |
| HRC | Human Rights Convention |
| IntJCrim | International Journal of Criminology and Penology, London, New York |
| IntJOff | International Journal of Offender Therapy and Comparative Criminology, London |
| I.R.A. | Irish Republican Army |
| JA | Juristische Arbeitsblätter, Berlin |
| JGG | Jugendgerichtsgesetz (Juvenile Court Code) |
| JR | Juristische Rundschau, Berlin |
| JResCrim | Journal of Research in Crime and Delinquency, Hackensack/N.J. |
| Jur.Diss. | Juridical Dissertation |
| JZ | Juristenzeitung, Tübingen |
| KrimB | Kriminologisches Bulletin, Zürich |
| KrimGegfr | Kriminologische Gegenwartsfragen, Stuttgart |
| Kriminalforsorgen | Kriminalforsorgen, Prison and Probation. Ministry of Justice, Copenhagen |
| Kriminalvarden | Kriminalvården, Official Statistics of Sweden, National Prison and Probation Administration, Norrköping |
| KrimJ | Kriminologisches Journal, München |
| KrimsozBibl | Kriminalsoziologische Bibliographie, Wien |
| loc.cit. | loco citato |
| m.n. | marginal note |
| MS | manuscript |
| MschrKrim | Monatsschrift für Kriminologie und Strafrechtsreform, Köln |
| NJ | Neue Justiz, (East-)Berlin |
| NJW | Neue Juristische Wochenschrift, München, Frankfurt/M. |
| No., Nr. | number |
| NTfKrim | Nordisk Tidsskrift for Kriminalvidenskab, Copenhagen |
| ÖJZ | Österreichische Juristenzeitung, Wien |
| ÖRiZ | Österreichische Richterzeitung, Wien |

| | |
|---|---|
| p., pp. | page, pages |
| par. | paragraph |
| PolPC | Polish Penal Code |
| PolPExecC | Polish Penal Execution Code |
| Prison Statistics | Home Office, Prison Statistics. England and Wales, London |
| pub. | published |
| Research Bulletin | Research Bulletin of the Home Office Research Unit, London |
| Revpénit | Revue pénitentiaire et de droit pénal, Paris |
| ROW | Recht in Ost und West. Zeitschrift für Rechtsvergleichung und interzonale Rechtsprobleme, Berlin |
| RSCrim | Revue de science criminelle et de droit pénal comparé, Paris |
| ScandStudCrim | Scandinavian Studies in Criminology, Oslo |
| ScandStudLaw | Scandinavian Studies in Law, Stockholm |
| SchwZfStr | Schweizer Zeitschrift für Strafrecht, Bern |
| Sec. | Section |
| Sourcebook | Sourcebook of Criminal Justice Statistics. National Criminal Justice Information and Statistics Service. Washington/D.C. |
| sp.iss. | special issue |
| StGB | Strafgesetzbuch (Penal Code) |
| StrVoSchw | Der Strafvollzug in der Schweiz, Aarau |
| StVollzG | (Strafvollzugsgesetz) Corrections Code |
| SWA | Sozialwissenschaftliche Arbeitsgemeinschaft |
| SwPC | Swiss Penal Code |
| UdSSR | Union der Sozialistischen Sowjet-Republiken (USSR) |
| U.N. | United Nations |
| UNAFEI | United Nations Asia and Far East Institute for the Prevention of Crime and the Treatment of Offenders, Fuchu-Tokyo |
| Vol. | Volume |
| VollzD | Vollzugsdienst, Freiburg i.Br. |
| VR | Volksrepublik (People's Republic) |
| vs. | versus |
| WGO | Monatshefte für Osteuropäisches Recht, Hamburg |
| w/o. pl. | without place |
| ZblfJugR | Zentralblatt für Jugendrecht und Jugendwohlfahrt, Köln |

| | |
|---|---|
| ZfStrVo | Zeitschrift für Strafvollzug und Straffälligenhilfe, Saarbrücken |
| ZRP | Zeitschrift für Rechtspolitik, Frankfurt/M. |
| ZStW | Zeitschrift für die gesamte Strafrechtswissenschaft, Berlin |

# Preface

A comparative analysis of European penal corrections is both necessary and useful. Partial assimilation and the further tendency toward unity in western European correctional systems underscore this importance. Comparative analysis, however, helps to fulfill the general need for orientation. This fact apparently was recognized two hundred years ago, since the tradition of comparative observation of corrections dates back this far.

Europe certainly does not end at the Baltic Sea, at the Elbe or at the Bavarian Forest. This truth is banal but still must be kept in mind constantly. One always is faced with the danger of confining interests to Western Europe and thereby thinking one has grasped Europe in general. To the extent that information is available, Eastern Europe also is included in this comparative analysis.

Since, however, neither politics nor research in the field of penal corrections can be limited to Europe, but rather clearly encompass worldwide dimensions, it appears sensible to include these perspectives in our study. The correctional systems in Japan and the United States are appropriate for this purpose. In any European situation and trend analysis it is necessary to include the theory and practice of penal corrections in both of these countries, if one is attempting to attain a representative evaluation of corrections and correctional policy.

The relevant literature published before the end of 1981 has been considered. Only the French documentation of "Les systèmes pénitentiaires en Europe occidentale" by M. Ancel and Ph. Chemithe (Paris 1981), which first appeared in the middle of January, could not be evaluated. Although this documentation is limited to Western Europe, it is similar in organization and emphasis to this study, and it recognizes particular importance in the goal of penal corrections, the treatment of prisoners, and the organization of the correctional system.

I would like to thank Messrs. Bernhard Flümann and Ulf Köpcke for their research surveys and Ms. Jacqueline Kaspar for her production of the manuscript.

Ms. Sharon Byrd translated the text into the English language. I would like to thank her particularly for her excellent work.

Finally, I am gratefully indebted to the Wissenschaftliche Buchgesellschaft, Darmstadt, for their support and to Transnational Publishers, New York, for their interest in including an English edition of this book in their program for American publication.

Freiburg im Breisgau, February 1984 Günther Kaiser

# PART ONE

## Penal Corrections in Europe

### Problems, Methods and Development

# I. International Comparative View of Penal Corrections as a Problem and Necessity

**Citations:** Howard, J.: *The State of the Prisons in England and Wales with Preliminary Observations and an Account of some Foreign Prisons.* Washington 1774; Julius, N.: *Vorlesungen über die Gefängnis-Kunde oder über die Verbesserung der Gefängnisse und sittliche Besserung der Gefangenen, entlassenen Sträflinge usw., nebst einer Einleitung über die Zahlen, Arten und Ursachen der Verbrechen in verschiedenen europäischen und amerikanischen Staaten usw.* Berlin 1828; Lucas, Ch.: *Le système pénitentiaire en Europe et aux Etats-Unis.* Paris 1828; v.Würth, J.: *Die neuesten Fortschritte des Gefängniswesens in Frankreich, England, Schottland, Belgien und der Schweiz.* Vienna 1844; v.Holtzendorff, F.: "Nationale und internationale Elemente des Gefängnisswesens." In: *Handbuch des Gefängnisswesens,* ed. by F.v.Holtzendorff et al. Vol. 1. Hamburg 1888, pp.24–28; Hugueney, L., de Vabres, H., Ancel, M. (Eds.): *Les grands systèmes pénitentiaires actuels.* Paris 1950; Jescheck, H.-H.: "Vorwort." In: *Reform des Strafvollzugsrechts. Rechtsvergleichende Arbeiten. Materialien zur Strafrechtsreform.* Vol.8. Bonn 1959, pp. If.; Müller-Dietz, H.: "Der deutsche Strafvollzug im westeuropäischen Vergleich." In: *Grundfragen des strafrechtlichen Sanktionensystems.* Heidelberg et al. 1979, pp. 246–266; Wicks, R., Cooper, H.: *International Corrections.* Lexington, Mass. 1979; Vogler, Th.: "Bemühungen um eine europäische Strafrechtsvereinheitlichung." In: *Strafrechtsreform und Rechtsvergleichung*, ed. by H. Lüttger. Berlin, New York 1979, pp. 144–170; Kaiser, G.: *Perspektiven vergleichender Pönologie.* MschrKrim 63(1980), pp. 366–378; Blau, G.: "Einleitende Vorbemerkung." In: *Die Reform des Strafvollzugs im Lichte internationaler Reformtendenzen.* Studienberichte Vol.IV. Bochum 1981, pp. 1–6.

## 1. Initial Methods

Since the beginning of modern imprisonment in the sixteenth century, Europeans generally have been interested in comparing the various types of punishment and their execution within other nations. During the seventeenth century, for example, the Amsterdam penitentiaries were a model for the development of their corresponding German institutions, whereas later during the nineteenth century, the North American prison system was none the less influential in the remodelling of German penal execution.

Numerous European authors have been interested in comparative analysis of prison systems. The English philanthropist John Howard expanded upon his analysis of the state of English prisons by describing individual penal institutions on the continent. Over one hundred fifty years ago, Hamburg physician Nikolaus Julius, who wrote the first book on imprisonment in the German language, included in the introduction to his text vast statistical information on the development of crime and punishment in European countries and North America. According to his conclusions "the greatest advances occurred in other countries." Although Julius did not support this finding any further, his comparative data apparently were relevant enough to encourage "prison reform" and "prisoner improvement" within Germany, as the subtitle to his book indicates.

## 2. Expansion and Development of Comparative Analysis

The opinion that information concerning foreign penal execution was not only helpful but also necessary was generally adopted by the end of the nineteenth century. Comparative analysis also has been furthered through international congresses on imprisonment, which have convened in Germany since 1846 and which are now organized by the United Nations. Numerous academic treatises exist propagating the opinion that "the history of modern prison reform is simultaneously the history of common efforts by contemporary cultures toward the effectuation of ruling criminal law concepts."

"Without question, the theory and practice of imprisonment, to an even greater extent than that of substantive criminal law, involves countless elements of a cosmopolitan, international nature." One finds "the international or cosmopolitan elements of imprisonment mainly in the ethical-legal principles of penal execution and in the general causes of crime." Of course, it would be just as much a mistake "to attempt to repeat experiments that have failed at one's own costs and risks without concern for experience gained in other countries" as it would be to copy "institutions, which have succeeded abroad, without examining the exact situation." The opinion "that only relative truths exist as to the purposefulness of numerous aspects of prison control and that the legislature must often choose between the greater or lesser evil in light of existing circumstances" (v.Holtzendorff, 1888, pp.25f.), warns against the danger of making rash generalizations and demands rational and careful consideration of the situation. Nevertheless, one is convinced that one cannot avoid "applying the comparative approach by finding parallels in the experiences made by other nations." "All nations need each other for the purpose of an ever continuing, never completed prison reform. This gradual and continually increasing recognition resulted in the founding of international congresses on imprisonization and the appointment of a commission thereto in 1872: the existence of such partially periodic, partially permanent institutions is of the highest importance, not only for the enrichment of prison theory and science, but also for the improvement and refinement of prison practices in all countries, thereby creating an active balance of national and international factors in criminal justice'' (v.Holtzendorff, 1888, p.27).

## 3. New Beginnings

After the Second World War, an internationally comprehensive report written in France (see Hugueney, et al., 1950) marked the initial return to the nineteenth century tradition of the ''école pénitentiaire.'' Based on remnants of the past epoch, it again envisioned the goal of worldwide ''réforme pénitentiaire'' as a ''synthèse comparative.'' In addition, comparative legal investigations which were also based on nineteenth century traditions were initiated by the Justice Department in Germany during the 1950s, to prepare for a reform of penal execution.

''Their goals were to provide a survey of the execution of prison sentences and freedom-depriving disciplinary measures in other countries, to compare the variously applied solutions, and to obtain stimulation for our own penal execution reform. We certainly were not concerned with the mere state of law, but rather with an explanation of the actual situation in these countries. The study, therefore, extended beyond purely ''legal'' comparison . . . The spirit of international cooperation, which has influenced penal execution for centuries, proved in this instance to be very rewarding. The individual studies generally followed the accepted basic scheme of dividing countries into data units and making comparative legal cross-section analyses . . . The comparative legal studies needed for penal execution reform extended beyond their direct goal of preparation of the Federal Corrections Code and contributed to international discussion, which has always been conducted on a truly co-operative basis . . . Conscientious and sincere work has been conducted on German penal execution, but there is still much to be done by our government to attain the high level demanded not only by the new Criminal Code but also by the cultural level in Germany. Smaller and poorer nations should be an example to us!'' (Jescheck, 1959, pp.If.)

## 4. Retrospect and Interim Results

Even though the last decade appears to be a milestone in the revision of penal execution these determinations, opinions and demands are still substantially applicable today. Blau (1981, pp.1ff.) reviews this development as follows:

The strong developmental influences from other nations as well as from international conventions of researchers and academicians in criminal punishment execution were always clearly evident in any portrayal of West German penal execution reform, a reform which was instituted after World War II, which culminated in the Corrections Code of March 10, 1976, and which in the meantime has come to a standstill. Already in the nineteenth and beginning of the twentieth centuries and up until the deliberate autarchy of the Nazi period, the internationalization of reform discussions was a great deal more intensive, lively, and fruitful among the "penalists" than were the discussions with neighboring countries carried out by criminal lawyers and experts in criminal procedure, who were tied more strongly to national legal development.

The individual stages of development in German penal execution during this period are almost all characterized by expressions of foreign origin: one can consider the progressive system of Sir Walter Crofton, the solitary or social confinement of the Pennsylvanian or Auburn system, the outdoor labor model of the Italian "lavoro al aperto", or security custody according to the Swiss design of Carl Stooss . . . Neither the open nor semi-open institutions in West Germany, which were described and avidly supported at the worldwide congresses in The Hague and Geneva; nor the social therapeutic institutions, which were propagated later by the so-called "alternative" professors with express reference to the Dutch and Danish models; nor the determination of a prisoner's legal rights, which was formulated at the above-mentioned Geneva Congress of the United Nations in 1955, modified by the Council of Europe, and called "Minimum Rules for the Treatment of Prisoners" or "Minima"; nor the Corrections Board, which was set up as a tribunal integrated within the corrections system according to the Italian and French models, would have been thinkable without such international attention. On the other hand, German discussions of penal execution, which were published in the daily reports of the Attorney General's appointed Major Commission, and later in the reports of the Juvenile Corrections Commission, as so-called "alternative" draft, also prompted action in other nations and vigorously influenced foreign laws and individual institutions of penal execution.

Although much has been accomplished in reforming penal execution, remaining or continuing deficiencies illustrate the problematic situation and the necessity of academic observation and analysis from a comparative point of view. This type of attention must be given, even though any comparison of penal execution is made more difficult by the diversity of criminal laws in the individual nations and by the necessity of integrating correctional practices (Müller-Dietz, 1979, pp.248, 251ff.). Imprisonment also cannot be viewed in isolation, but rather must be seen as imbedded within the entire complex of penology and criminal justice. Only through extensive comparative perspectives can the recognition of fundamental principles, e.g. humanity, justice, freedom, constitutionality, social orientation, success and failure, and the relevance of prison statistics be judged.

## 5. Comparative Analysis of European Penal Corrections as a Responsibility

We have formulated our investigation essentially as a comparative observation of punishment execution in European countries. We also have considered the institutions involved herein. Our presentation is organized according to country and followed by a comparative analysis of solutions to individual problems. This type of research is not novel for European academicians. Only unawareness could lead to the assumption that comparative methods were almost unknown in the criminological research of Europe. (See, however, L. Shelley: *Readings in Comparative Criminology.* Carbondale, Ill. 1981, p.xxxiii.)

Comparative penology is assisted by the fact that in Western Europe, particularly by the Council of Europe, questions about punishment execution have been raised and the ''Minimum Rules for the Treatment of Prisoners'' have been accepted and applied on an increasing basis. In addition, the ''European Committee on Crime Problems'' has been especially helpful, since it already has published an impressive number of comprehensive studies on penal execution. To be sure, these reports have been limited to the results of an exchange in experiences with various penal correctional structures. They still, however, are considered to be very beneficial to comparative penology. (The opinion of Wicks, et al., 1979 is similar; academically more demanding is Hugueney, et al., 1950, p.IX, and recently Blau 1981, p.3.) Nevertheless, one should not lose track of the goal of ''European criminal law standardization'' even though it appears exceptionally limited in its possibilities. (See Vogler 1979, pp.144ff.) The newly formed ''Comité de coopération pénitentiaire'' (see J. Sacotte, ReSCrim 1981, pp. 482f.) is oriented toward this goal with its dedication to advancement in penal execution, particularly with respect to prisoners' legal rights and the adoption of the Minimum Rules for the Treatment of Prisoners. Formulated differently, it wishes to shift the movement ''from penal execution in Europe to European penal execution.''

A comprehensively designed comparison of penal execution, however, has never been undertaken. Such a comparison is difficult enough to perform on a regional or institutional level within one country since unsurmountable barriers are always present. On an international level, however, such a study seems to be more a case of wishful thinking than an attainable reality. Nevertheless, one should attempt to obtain at least an oriented survey of existing conditions. Such a comparison should not only show that recent changes in German penal execution were often based on international developments and foreign models. It also should permit an expert and objective comparison of reform results and efforts made both domestically and in other countries. The execution of punishment can fulfill its role meaningfully only if it does not become rigid and remains open to foreign and domestic innovations. (See particularly Blau 1981, pp. 3f.)

# II. Concept of Penal Corrections

**Citations:** Stefani, G., Levasseur, G., Jambu-Merlin, R.: *Criminologie et science pénitentiaire.* 4th ed. Paris 1976, pp. 259f., 298f., 308f.; Kunst, G.: *Strafvollzugsgesetz (StVG) und die den Strafvollzug betreffenden Bestimmungen in anderen Gesetzen sowie Verordnungen und Erlässe mit einer Einführung und Erläuterung des Gesetzes . . .* Vienna 1979; Wicks, R., Cooper, H.: *International Corrections.* Lexington, Mass. 1979, pp.1ff., 183ff.; Kaiser, G., Kerner, H.-J., Schöch, H.: *Strafvollzug.* 3rd ed. Heidelberg 1982, pp.1ff.

## 1. Concept and Designation of Stationary Deprivation of Freedom through Criminal Sanctions

Penal execution is the application of freedom-depriving criminal sanctions, viz., imprisonment and freedom-depriving disciplinary measures for improvement and security. This definition is derived from the development, utilization and relevance of conventional penitentiaries and prisons.

The terms "Strafvollzug", "Freiheitsstrafvollzug" and "Gefängniswesen" essentially all have the same meaning in German. They correspond to the concepts "administration pénitentiaire" or "système pénitentiaire" in Belgium and France, "prison and borstal system" in Great Britain, "corrections" in the United States, "Gevangenisvezen" in the Netherlands, and "kriminalvården" in Sweden. Most of the relevant books, journals and statistics in the various countries contain these terms in their titles.

## 2. Conceptual Consequences

Individually one can surmise from this recognition that,

a) punishment execution is mainly concerned with stationary correction or with freedom-depriving criminal sanctions;

b) punishment execution includes not only imprisonment but also criminal law disciplinary measures for improvement and safety (confinement in security custody, in a socially therapeutic institution, in an institution for alcoholics or in a psychiatric hospital);
c) punishment execution relates only to criminal sanctions, and when exactly interpreted, excludes pre-trial detention, corrective training and the non-criminal legal confinement of the mentally ill;
d) because of historical interpretation in West Germany, the topic "punishment execution" generally does not include the execution of criminal sanctions not involving confinement, such as monetary fine and conditional release. In other Western European countries, however, the alternatives to imprisonment are usually included under this topic both conceptually as well as practically.

## 3. Consequences for Comparative Analysis

As is apparent from the relaxation of conditions in prisons, from the general opening of penal institutions, from the granting of conditional release, and from the attempts toward "treatment outside the prison," contemporary law recognizes many sanctions tending toward non-confinement. For this reason, both forms of corrections often are expressed jointly, e.g., "prison and probation" in England, "Kriminalforsorgen" in Denmark, or "Kriminalvården" and "Frihetvården" in Sweden, and the limits of stationary sanctioning have become unclear. Clarity also is lacking as to the concept of penal execution. It, therefore, must be determined by convention from statutes, administrative regulations, or academic agreement. Because of the substitutability and exchangeability of individual institutions or sub-systems of penal execution, we have found it advisable to include alternatives and exceptions (confinement in a psychiatric clinic) or even evasive state strategies (committal to a concentration camp) in our analysis.

## III. Historical Development of Penal Corrections

**Citations:** Wagnitz, H.B.: *Historische Nachrichten und Bemerkungen über die merkwürdigsten Zuchthäuser in Deutschland.* Halle 1791; Mittelstädt, O.: *Gegen die, Freiheitsstrafen. Ein Beitrag zur Kritik des heutigen Strafensystems.* Leipzig 1879; Wahlberg, W.: "Die Gesammtentwickelung des Gefängnisswesens und der Haftsysteme von der Mitte des XVI. Jahrhunderts bis zur Gegenwart." In: *Handbuch des Gefängnisswesens,* ed. by F.v.Holtzendorff. Hamburg 1888, pp.I, 79–141; v.Jagemann, E.: "Das ausserdeutsche Gefängnisswesen in Europa." In: *Handbuch des Gefängnisswesens, loc.cit.,* pp.I, 206–344; Krohne, K.: *Lehrbuch der Gefängniskunde unter Berücksichtigung der Kriminalstatistik und Kriminalpolitik.* Stuttgart 1889; Leitmaier, V.: *Österreichische Gefängniskunde mit Berücksichtigung des ausländischen Gefängniswesens.* Vienna 1890; Hafner, K., Zürcher, E.: *Schweizerische Gefängniskunde.* Bern 1925; v.Hippel, R.: "Die geschichtliche Entwicklung der Freiheitsstrafe." In: *Deutsches Gefängniswesen,* ed. by E. Bumke. Berlin 1928, pp. 1–15; Radbruch, G.: "Die ersten Zuchthäuser und ihr geistesgeschichtlicher Hintergrund." In: *Elegantiae juris criminalis.* 2nd ed. Basle 1950, pp. 116–129; Suttinger, G.: *Das Gefängnis als Abschreckungs-, Erziehungs- und Verwahrungsanstalt.* JZ 1952, pp. 737–741; Hellmer, J.: *Kriminalpädagogik.* Berlin 1959; Peters, K.: *Grundprobleme der Kriminalpädagogik.* Berlin 1960; Schmidt, E.: *Einführung in die Geschichte der deutschen Strafrechtspflege.* 3rd ed. Göttingen 1965; Blau, G.: "Die Entwicklung des Strafvollzuges seit 1945—Tendenzen und Gegentendenzen." In: *Strafvollzug in der Praxis,* ed. by H.-D. Schwind et al. Berlin, New York 1976, pp.1ff.; Stefani, G. et al.: "La science pénitentiaire et son histoire." In: *Criminologie et science pénitentiaire.* 4th ed. Paris 1976, pp. 272ff.; Kaufmann, H.: *Kriminologie III.* Strafvollzug und Sozialtherapie. Stuttgart et al. 1977, pp. 209–216; Krebs, A.: *Freiheitsentzug. Entwicklung von Praxis und Theorie seit der Aufklärung.* Berlin et al. 1978; Santucci, M.: "150 ans de jurisprudence correctionnelle, fluctuation de la déviance et son contrôle." In: *Le contrôle social de la déviance.* Colloque de Vaucresson, 24–25 octobre 1978, pp.167–183; McConville, S.: *History of English Prison Administration.* London, Boston 1981; Kaiser, G., Kerner, H.-J., Schöch, H.: *Strafvollzug.* 3rd ed. Heidelberg 1982, §3 (Geschichte und Reform).

## 1. Epochs in the Development of Penal Corrections

Development in the process of executing prison sentences reveals considerable international similarities, even though it was influenced by national ideas, programs, and planning. Essentially, the history of penal execution involves three epochs:

a) the emergence of the Amsterdam penitentiaries and their imitation by other European countries during the seventeenth century;
b) the influence of the models in North America on penal execution and the debate over the "right" system during the nineteenth century;
c) the relaxation of penal execution and the legal adoption of the Minimum Rules for the Treatment of Prisoners in the second half of the twentieth century.

## 2. Origin and Initial Form of Prison Sentences

Imprisonment in the modern sense originated during the sixteenth century. The penal system of the Middle Ages included no such criminal sanction but rather employed corporal punishment and the death penalty. The most relevant factors leading to the development and later domination of imprisonment included the era of humanism; a Christianity transformed by the Reformation and Counter-Reformation; a new evaluation of human labor which was influenced particularly by Calvinism; the cessation of welfare work performed by monasteries and cloisters, many of which were closed during the Reformation; and a vast social need, resulting from the desperate economic situation of the peasants. (Kaufmann 1977, pp.209ff.) Houses of correction were developed to confine individuals who were capable of working but who were inactive or socially disturbing and to train them to work and lead steady lives. These institutions even were named according to this basic concept, since they were to be houses in which "correction," i.e. training, took place (v.Hippel, 1928; Radbruch, 1950, pp. 116ff.). Beggars, tramps, prostitutes, and criminals as well as wayward youth were sent to these institutions. The Amsterdam House of Correction was the most famous example of this type of institution, and it significantly influenced the entire development of the prison sentence. For this reason, it is often regarded as the beginning of modern imprisonment. The execution of punishment was seen as training through work and an ordered life. "Do not be afraid! I do not revenge evil, but rather force one to good. My hand is hard but my heart is loving" (original text: "Schrick niet! ich wreeck geen quaet, maer dwing tot goedt, Straf ist myn handt, mar lieflijk myn gemoedt") was the inscription located over the entrance to the Amsterdam "Spinnhaus" (1597), an institution in which along with the Amsterdam House of Corrections (1595), the first more modern prison sentences were executed. The distinct goal of this initial type of punishment execution was forced training through work in the tradition of the Calvinistic work ethic (Schöch, 1982, Sec.4, m.n.3). Religious support also was provided and the food supply was sufficient. The exact regulations in the houses of corrections were determined by the respective institutional board. Disciplinary measures were applied to those breaking the rules, particularly in cases of unwillingness to work. The Amsterdam houses of corrections were well known and copied far beyond the Dutch borders. By the second half of the eighteenth century at least sixty such houses of corrections also existed in Germany.

## 3. Expiration and Reform Beginnings

These institutions, however, degenerated during the course of the eighteenth century and became mostly houses of horror. Those persons confined were not limited to criminals, and the various inmate subgroups were not separated from one another. In addition, there were no provisions made even for the most primitive of human needs. The concept of training was replaced by beatings, mistreatment, and brutal punishments, as well as by the exploitation of the inmates as a work force. Analyses by English prison reformer John Howard and German theologist H.B. Wagnitz revealed the atrocities of the European penal institutions at this time. Howard's guiding thought for prison reform, undoubtedly influenced by Voltaire, was "make them diligent and they will be honest," an idea which in fact was reflected in the original concept of a house of correction.

## 4. Anglo-American Reform Models, their Reception and further Development in Europe

At the end of the eighteenth century, initial Quaker reform efforts in Pennsylvania were of extensive influence for the next period. The Quakers attempted to establish a system of total solitary confinement, in order to avoid criminal infection through other inmates and to initiate a process of change through reflection and tranquility. Although this attempt at resocialization was totally unrealistic, the idea did win recognition that criminal contagion could be avoided when the prisoner performed communal work in large rooms under conditions of total silence. It was the cost-reducing effects of this economic penal execution concept, however, which were largely responsible for its wide acceptance. The Pennsylvania "solitary system" and "silent system" thereby represented two different approaches to penal execution and stimulated worldwide discussion over the propriety of each system. This debate continued over the course of the entire nineteenth century.

## 5. Restoration, Stagnation and Relapse during the 19th and 20th Centuries

During the first half of the nineteenth century, prison reform was influenced by the Christian movement (e.g. Fliedner and Wichern), by the growing body of knowledge on prisons in Germany (Julius, et al.), and by the "école pénitentiaire" in France (Lucas, et al.). Particular emphasis was placed on eliminating gross abuses, remodelling penal institutions, and improving the prisoners' morals. During the second half of the century, efforts toward so-called improvement and formal regulation of penal execution increased. The English-Irish progressive system with levelled relaxation in the execution of punishment and disciplinary measures was widely discussed and acknowledged. In addition, the opposing penal goals of deterrence and security were being re-evaluated, as can be seen in Mittelstädt's treatise "Against Imprisonment" (1879), which induced criticism of the "conventional lie in punishment for improvement and in solitary confinement."

During the first half of the twentieth century, the already slow process of improving conditions of penal execution was hindered even more severely by the two World Wars and their resulting economic recessions, as well as by fascist governments which opposed humanizing and modernizing penal execution. Arbitrary arrests and inhuman prison conditions, both during protective custody and in the concentration camps, marked a general misuse of power and social decline. The number of prisoners increased accordingly. In Italy and Germany, for example, it was twice as high as in other neighboring countries (cf. MschrKrim, 1937, p.298; see also Table 16 *infra*) even when concentration camp inmates were excluded. In spite of an increased international recognition of the existing problems, the International Congress for Prison Information was only partially and temporarily capable of positively influencing penal execution during the period from 1846 to 1935. Until after World War II, the prison was seen to be an "institution of deterrence, training, and confinement" in public and academic opinion (cf. Suttinger, 1952, pp.737ff.). Critical empirical analyses, which encouraged the gathering of reliable information and experience, remained almost totally ineffective and inconsequential.

## 6. International Reform Impulses during the Second Half of the 20th Century

An important breakthrough occurred in the wake of the United Nations' 1955 World Congress on Crime Prevention and the Treatment of Offenders, during which the "Minimum Rules for the Treatment of Prisoners" (standard minimum rules) were adopted and the recommendation given to open the penal execution system. Both of these occurrences have persistently influenced the development of penal execution until the present. "After 1945 penal reform again became a worldwide movement for the first time since the significant influences of Anglo-American penology during the nineteenth century" (Blau, 1976, p.28). The "défense sociale nouvelle" movement (Ancel) also strongly encouraged reform developments (Stefani, et al., 1976, pp.291ff.), and penal correctional models in Scandinavia and the Netherlands gained no less attention. In West Germany, many of these impulses were assimilated and explored by criminal pedagogues (Hellmer, 1959; Peters, 1960). Nonetheless, the international "trend toward opening penal execution" and the general encouragement of increased prisoner contact with the outside world, attained through less restricted correspondence, more frequent visiting privileges, and even occasional prison vacations, gained only slow acceptance. Since the 1960s, reform attempts have been accelerated by public discussions of the so-called prison scandals in the Federal Republic of Germany, France, Great Britain, and Italy, as well as by several basic decisions by Austria's and West Germany's higher courts. In particular, prisoners' legal rights have been defined, determined and adopted in the laws of an entire group of European nations. These rights, as well as a prisoner's duties and limitations, are now subject to judicial review almost everywhere.

## 7. Present Crisis in Corrections through Imprisonment

Most recently, however, certain retarding influences have developed that in part seriously restrict the further reform and humanization of penal execution. One factor is a developing scepticism about the prison sentence, which even can be considered a crisis with respect to its propriety. The question arises whether individuals can be "improved" whatsoever, i.e., whether they can be taught to lead a life at liberty without committing crimes. Increased narcotic usage, within as well as outside the prison system, and the repercussions of confining terrorists have interfered with attempted resocialization processes. Increased criminality, the more recent overcrowding of penal institutions, and reductions in financial resources all have had extremely disadvantageous effects on furthering correctional reform. These observations are not limited to the Federal Republic of Germany, but are generally applicable to all of Europe.

# PART TWO

## Penal Corrections in West Germany and Other European Nations

## Penal Corrections in West Germany and Other European Nations

**Citations:** Lucas, Ch.: *Le système pénitentiaire en Europe et aux Etats-Unis.* Paris 1828; v.Jagemann, E.: "Das ausserdeutsche Gefängnisswesen in Europa seit 1830." In: *Handbuch des Gefängnisswesens,* ed. by F.v.Holtzendorff et al. Hamburg 1888, pp.206–344; Hugueney, L., de Vabres, H., Ancel, M. (Eds.): *Les grands systèmes pénitentiaires actuels.* Paris 1950; Conrad, J.: *Crime and its Correction. An International Survey of Attitudes and Practices.* Berkeley, Los Angeles 1965; Bockelmann, P.: *Bemerkungen zur Reform des Strafvollzugs, zugleich ein Bericht über den Besuch einiger westeuropäischer Vollzugsanstalten.* Munich 1972; Bertel, Chr.: *Der Strafvollzug in rechtsvergleichender Sicht.* ÖRiZ 66 (1977), sp.iss., pp.1–4; Doleschal, E., Newton, A.: *International Rates of Imprisonment.* Hackensack, N.J. 1979; Müller-Dietz, H.: "Der deutsche Strafvollzug im westeuropäischen Vergleich." In: *Grundfragen des strafrechtlichen Sanktionensystems.* Heidelberg et al. 1979, pp.246–266; Short, R.: *Care of Long-Term Prisoners.* London 1979; Wicks, R., Cooper, H.: *International Corrections.* Lexington, Mass. 1979; ECCP: Report on the Standard Minimum Rules for the Treatment of Offenders by a Select Committee of Experts to Examine the Implementation of the Standard Minimum Rules for the Treatment of Prisoners. Strasbourg 1980; Kaiser, G.: *Perspektiven vergleichender Pönologie.* MschrKrim 63(1980), pp.366–378; Blau, G. et al.: *Die Reform des Strafvollzugs im Lichte internationaler Reformtendenzen.* Bochum 1981; Sliwowski, J.: *Kara poszbawienia wolnósci we współczesnym świecie* (The Sentence of Imprisonment in the Present World). Warsaw 1981, pp.103–170; Ward, D., Schoen, K.: *Confinement in Maximum Custody. New Last-Resort Prisons in the United States and Western Europe.* Lexington, Mass. 1981.

The interest in and necessity of comparative examination of European systems of penal execution extend far into the past, as demonstrated above. The decisive *motivation* for comparative analysis was not only to *know* something about neighboring countries but also to *learn* from them in order to improve one's own circumstances. At this point, however, our interest does not lie in recapitulating historical attempts at comparing European systems of penal execution, most of which were repetitive. Instead, emphasis will be placed on portraying the modern systems of penal execution in Europe. Of course, in order to improve our understanding of the present situation, it will be necessary at times to consider the historical developments which have occurred since the first post-war period. Observation of the contemporary state of penal execution, however, is even more important since many significant changes in statute, organization and practice, which distinguish the present situation radically from that of the 1950s or even that of the pre-war period, have occurred in many European countries over the past decade. For these reasons and for the advancement of further reform development, we shall focus on current penal corrections.

In the following chapters, we *initially* shall present a *survey of corrections in the European countries.* This survey will be limited to those correctional systems of "larger" and "smaller" countries which have been relevant to German developments in penal execution. The penal execution systems in the United States and Japan also will be included because of their traditional importance and because of current discussions and developments. Furthermore, we will include a comprehensive, comparative observation of individual problems, of their solutions, and of institutional forms in an effort to achieve comparative synthesis or cross-section analysis.

# I. West Germany

**Citations:** Schüler-Springorum, H.: *Strafvollzug im Übergang.* Göttingen 1969; Baumann, J. (Ed.): *Die Reform des Strafvollzuges. Programm nach den Vorstellungen des Alternativ-Entwurfes zu einem Strafvollzugsgesetz.* Munich 1974; Schwind, H.-D., Blau, G.: *Strafvollzug in der Praxis.* Berlin, New York 1976; Kaufmann, H.: *Kriminologie III. Strafvollzug und Sozialtherapie.* Stuttgart et al. 1977; Müller-Dietz, H.: *Strafvollzugsrecht.* 2nd ed. Berlin 1977; Eisenhardt, Th.: *Strafvollzug.* Stuttgart et al. 1978; Bemmann, G.: "Über das Ziel des Strafvollzugs." In: *Festschrift für P. Bockelmann.* Munich 1979, pp.891–899; Böhm, A.: *Strafvollzug.* Frankfurt/M. 1979; Schneider, H.-J. et al.: "Corrections in the Federal Republic of Germany." In: *International Corrections,* ed. by R. Wicks et al. Lexington, Mass. 1979, pp.39–55; Kury, H. (Ed.): *Strafvollzug und Öffentlichkeit.* Freiburg 1980; Brühl, A.: *Die Rechte der Verurteilten und Strafgefangenen. Ein Handbuch mit Verhaltenshinweisen für Betroffene und ihre Interessenvertreter.* Weinheim et al. 1981; Calliess, P.: *Strafvollzugsrecht.* 2nd ed. Munich 1981; Dünkel, F., Rosner, A.: *Die Entwicklung des Strafvollzuges in der Bundesrepublik Deutschland seit 1970—Materialien und Analysen.* Freiburg 1981; Mai, K. (Ed.): *Psychologie hinter Gittern. Probleme psychologischer Tätigkeit im Strafvollzug.* Weinheim et al. 1981; Mechler, A.: *Psychiatrie des Strafvollzugs.* Stuttgart, New York 1981; Kaiser, G., Kerner, H.-J., Schöch, H.: *Strafvollzug.* 3rd ed. Heidelberg 1982.

## 1. Legal Foundation for Penal Corrections

Modern punishment execution is principally regulated by the Corrections Code (*"Strafvollzugsgesetz"* (StVollzG) of March 16, 1976 (BGBl 1, p.581). This newly unified code came into effect on January 1, 1977 and eliminated past uncertainty about the prisoner's legal position. In addition, it determined the rights and duties of prisoners and individuals in custody, the responsibilities and permissible interferences by the correctional authorities, and the organizational and personnel requirements for the execution of punishment. Furthermore, it specified the types of criminal sanctions and the methods to be used in their execution from the time of the prisoner's admittance into criminal and custodial institutions until his release.

The Corrections Code, however, contains only the regulations applicable to adult prisoners and individuals in custody. Juvenile corrections are governed by Art.91 of the Juvenile Code ("Jugendgerichtsgesetz" = JGG) in connection with *administrative statutes on juvenile corrections* ("Verwaltungsvorschriften zum Jugendstrafvollzug"), which were passed federally and adopted by the individual state justice departments to become effective on January 1, 1977. According to the intent of the legal administrative body, these statutes merely were to bridge the transitionary period before the enactment of a comprehensive legal code. A Federal Justice Department Commission, formed for the compilation of this code, presented its final report in 1979. On the basis of this report, the Justice Department presented a "Draft of the Law for the Further Development of Juvenile Correction and the Integration of Juvenile Delinquents" in 1980. During the transitionary period, some of the regulations in the adult Corrections Code, particularly those regarding a prisoner's rights, are to be applied expressly or through analogy to juvenile corrections. This application is especially relevant to those rules governing a prisoner's wages and his usage thereof (§176 StVollzG). In general, however, juvenile corrections and the execution of prison sentences for adult criminals must be distinctly separated (§92 Sec.1 JGG) except in the cases of §92 II No.1, and §114 JGG).

Before the enactment of the Corrections Code, penal correction was governed by various statutes and administrative regulations, particularly by the official corrections regulations of December 1, 1961. In connection herewith, §§ 23f. Introductory Law to the Law on Court Constitution ("Einführungsgesetz zum Gerichtsverfassungsgesetz" = EGGVG) introduced the possibility of legal protection from measures applied by the correctional authorities. Legal decisions by the criminal divisions of the state courts of appeals, responsible therefore according to §25 EGGVG, have defined more precisely the legal position of prisoners and individuals in custody and have facilitated reform over the last decade. This legal basis, however, proved to be dissatisfactory since it did not satisfy certain constitutional requirements. The March 14, 1972 Supreme Court decision concerning the question of limitations on prisoners' basic rights indicated clearly that statutory regulations on the execution of criminal punishment had become absolutely necessary.

As a result of the first two statutes on criminal law reform, the proportion of criminal sanctions denying freedom dropped to less than 10 percent in the 1970s. Past uncertainty as to the legal position of the 33,000 to 42,000 (depending on day counted) prisoners and individuals under custody (including inmates of the juvenile correction system; see Table 1) had to be clarified, and the right of intervention by the 17,000 (1970) to 24,000 (1979) penal correctional system employees in the over 120 independent and 40 non-dependent judicial correctional institutions had to be statutorily determined (cf. for individual aspects of this development the material analysis by Dünkel, et al., 1981). The Corrections Code created a foundation for solving these problems. Regulations on administrative matters, as well as on prison personnel and safety standards for punishment execution in the individual federal states, were enacted federally on January 1, 1977. They provided concrete rules and expanded upon organizational and personnel requirements. The Corrections Code clarified prisoners' rights, the permissibility of intervention by correctional authorities and the basis for secure custody of dangerous criminal actors. In content, and from a socially oriented state viewpoint, this code hardly introduced anything new. It nevertheless provided a usable foundation for the goals and responsibilities of corrections and for work performed within this system and among confined individuals. Furthermore, it did not eliminate the possibility of long range further development, since it indicated only the general direction and opened paths for many reform measures. Actual reform, however, must proceed first and foremost on a step-by-step basis.

**Table 1:** Prison Population in the Federal Republic of Germany (including Juvenile Corrections and Security Custody, and excluding Pre-Trial Detention)

| Year | Number of Prisoners | Number of Prisoners per 100,000 of respectively | | |
|---|---|---|---|---|
| | absolute** | Total Population relative** | Total Population having reached the age of criminal responsibility relative** | Index 1971 = 100 |
| 1 | 2 | 3 | 4 | 5 |
| 1963 | 48,413 | 84,0 | 106,7 | 154 |
| 1968 | 48,501 | 80,6 | 103,5 | 150 |
| 1969 | 46,745 | 76,8 | 99,1 | 143 |
| 1970 | 35,927 | 59,2 | 75,2 | 109 |
| 1971 | 33,015 | 53,9 | 69,2 | 100 |
| 1972 | 33,314 | 54,0 | 69,0 | 100 |
| 1973 | 35,974 | 58,0 | 73,8 | 107 |
| 1974 | 36,763 | 58,5 | 74,6 | 108 |
| 1975 | 34,608 | 55,3 | 69,9 | 101 |
| 1976 | 37,860 | 60,4 | 76,4 | 110 |
| 1977 | 39,918 | 65,0 | 80,2 | 116 |
| 1978 | 41,557 | 67,8 | 82,8 | 120 |
| 1979 | 42,229 | 68,8 | 83,5 | 121 |
| 1980 | 42,235 | | | |

* as of March 31 of each year

** as of January 1 of each year; Index calculations are related to the fourth column.

Sources: *Statisches Bundesamt:* Strafvollzug 1979, 20; Ausgewählte Zahlen für die Rechtspflege 1975, 37; 1978, 39; 1979, 44; 1980, 41; Rechtspflege 1963, 24; 1971, 24; 1972, 24.

## 2. Correctional Goals and Responsibilities

When a crime is committed and the state must interfere with the various legal rights and general living conditions of the culpable party and his relatives by depriving him of his freedom, then it also assumes the responsibility of achieving its goal as effectively as possible without damaging the affected citizen's individual interests any more seriously than is justified by this goal. The Corrections Code evaluates and ranks the goals and purposes of punishment to the extent necessary for securing the prisoner's legal rights and facilitating his treatment. For this reason, §2 StVollzG provides that the execution of a prison sentence should enable the imprisoned party to live a future life of social responsibility without committing crimes *(correctional goal).* In addition, penal execution also should serve to protect society from further criminal acts.

In order to attain this correctional goal, the prisoner's life within the institution should be as similar as possible to life in the outside world. The correctional system is required to offer assistance in this respect. On the other hand, the prisoner also influences the type of treatment applied and thereby the attainment of this correctional goal. His cooperation, therefore, should be inspired and encouraged. Of course, he is also subject to those restrictions on his freedom which are provided in the Corrections Code. To the extent that this code does not contain a particular restriction, however, the prisoner may be subject only to those restrictions necessary to maintain security or to avoid severe disturbance of institutional order (§4 II StVollzG). It must be possible to limit the prisoner's freedom so that life in the institution can proceed in an orderly manner and promote treatment.

The Corrections Code, therefore, has various duties and functions. In addition to securing consistent realization of a humane and rational criminal policy, being materially and formally consistent with revised substantive criminal law, and creating a unified legal basis for the execution of punishment, this code of laws also guarantees the legal rights of prisoners and others in custody. It hereby provides a constitutionally sufficient formal basis for the necessary, serious interferences with basic rights. In addition, the treatment or resocialization goal is declared to be the primary goal of correction. Although a few goal conflicts do exist, the law clearly requires that correctional authorities employ such treatment that will assist every prisoner in leading a non-criminal future life. This requirement, in light of the decision of the Supreme Court for Constitutional Matters (NJW 1977, pp.2525f.), is also expressly applicable to prisoners serving life sentences, since they too must be provided with the chance of regaining their freedom. Logically, they also should have the right of resocialization, and this right is in fact secured in the Corrections Code. The only provision for the different treatment of life termers is contained in §13. This section, however, also makes them, as other prisoners, subject to correctional treatment (Bemmann, 1979, and Schöch, 1982).

## 3. Prisoners' Legal Rights and Judicial Review of Correctional Measures

As mentioned above, the most important tasks of the revised Corrections Code were to determine the legal rights of prisoners, the right of interference by correctional authorities, and the prerequisites for judicial review.

Section 4 II of the Corrections Code provides that prisoners be subject to the limitations on their freedom as stipulated therein. To the extent that the law does not contain a particular rule, prisoners may be burdened with only those limitations which are unavoidable for maintaining security or for averting a severe disturbance of order in the institution. It appears questionable, however, whether this rule is sufficient for securing prisoners' legal rights. The courts, therefore, are called upon to provide the necessary clarity and unequivocality of law, which they have done in more recent legal decisions.

At the beginning of the incarceration period, the inmate undergoes a treatment examination. Only prisoners with long prison terms, however, have a right to this examination. According to the results, an individual correctional plan is prepared. A prisoner can be transferred to a different institution, for example, if his treatment can be furthered better elsewhere or if special treatment in a socially therapeutic institution is indicated. A prisoner also can be placed in an open correctional facility, but he has no right to demand this placement. On June 30, 1980, only 17.7 percent of all individuals sentenced to prison terms and only 10.5 percent of all juvenile offenders were in open facilities (Dünkel, et al., 1981). Correctional relaxations or vacation leaves are left to the discretion of the correctional authorities. The number of regular leavers increased in West Germany from 12,633 cases in 1977 to 17,151 cases in 1979, i.e. more than 35 percent. So-called short leaves during the same period increased 48 percent in respect to the average yearly prison population. In 1979, the average prison inmate received 2.6 vacations. According to expectation, relaxation of penal corrections occurs more often in open correctional facilities. In 1979, day leaves were granted 17 times and vacations and short leaves five times more often in open than in closed facilities. In 1979, 62.9 percent of all those released from an open institution and only 3.8 percent of those released from a closed institution were day releases. Here, of course, one must realize that practices in the various federal states vary and that women currently receive significantly fewer correctional privileges than men. In 1979, 15 percent of all men and only 3 percent of all women released from prison had been on day leaves (Dünkel, et al., 1981). On the whole, the potential for conflict reflected in such actions as suicide, suicidal attempts, self-mutilation and hunger strikes was essentially reduced in those institutions granting leaves. Surprisingly enough, however, disciplinary procedures occurred more than twice as often and accidents three times as often in open institutions as in closed facilities. Release can be prepared for through certain measures.

Prisoners, dressed in institutional clothing, work together. During rest periods, they are to be confined alone in their individual cells. In reality, however, on June 30, 1980, more than 39 percent of all prisoners were confined in multiple cells, whereas 75 percent of the inmates of open and only 33 percent of the inmates of closed institutions were communally confined (Dünkel, et al., 1981). Every prisoner has the right to receive visitors at least one hour per month and to unlimited correspondence privileges. Although correspondence with one's attorney is generally not controlled, other correspondence can be censored for reasons of treatment, security or order. Intercepting outgoing mail is also possible only under limited circumstances. The prisoner has a right to religious counsel and attendance at church services and other religious assemblies. The institution is required to provide for the physical and mental health of the prisoner. It must take adequate precautions for protecting health and securing hygiene. The prisoner is allowed to receive a normal number of magazines and newspapers through the institution and may listen to the radio and watch television together with other inmates.

The prisoner may address himself to the institutional supervisor with his desires, interests and complaints in matters that concern him. He is provided with the possibility of filing a disciplinary complaint against his supervisors just as every citizen has the right of petition. The *court may be called upon* to eliminate measures applied to control certain occurrences (§109 StVollzG). Application also can be made to require the performing of a neglected or denied measure. The Corrections Board at the District Court has jurisdiction over these matters (§110 StVollzG). Its decision may be appealed to the Penal Tribunal at the Superior Court. Appeals are permissible, however, only if necessary to further legal development or to ensure the uniformity of legal decisions. A similar provision for juvenile detention and imprisonment and for pre-trial detention is contained in §§23f. EGGVG. In cases in which basic rights have been violated and other legal remedies have been exhausted, the prisoner has the possibility of appeal to the Supreme Court for Constitutional Matters. He also can file a complaint against the violation of basic human rights with the European Human Rights Commission. The so-called Contact Prohibition Statute of September 30, 1977 imposed serious and questionable interferences upon prisoners' legal rights. According to this statute, prisoners who were in pre-trial detention or penal institutions for criminal acts according to §129a Penal Code ("Strafgesetzbuch" = StGB) or for acts of violence listed therein (primarily, the violent acts of terrorists) could be denied contact with other prisoners, with individuals in the outside world, and even with their attorneys. The courts, however, have unequivocally accepted their controlling role in matters of penal execution and have always reestablished any of the prisoner's basic legal rights infringed upon (supportive hereof, Schöch, 1982, §5ff.).

## 4. System and Organization of Penal Corrections

The prisoners' rights and duties can be maintained and the goal of corrections fulfilled only when the penal correctional system and its organization are so oriented. Treatment and resocialization, for example, cannot take place in a correctional system oriented primarily toward security. For this reason §§139ff. Corrections Code provide for the *division and differentiation* of penal execution. Accordingly, the distinction between open and closed institutions should take both treatment and security into account. Juvenile punishment must be executed in separate juvenile correctional institutions and socially therapeutic confinement in facilities separated from the other correctional institutions. Security custody cells also must be located in separate institutions or divisions thereof. Deviations from these requirements are possible, however, if indicated for more effective treatment. Women's institutions must provide facilities for mothers and their children. Transfer from closed to open institutions shall be undertaken in preparation for the prisoner's release. Facilities for employment, vocational training and work therapy must be provided. In the so-called admission facility or division, one decides on the basis of an examination which of the various correctional facilities is the most appropriate for the further treatment of the prisoner. To the extent not determined by federal statute (§138 StVollzG), however, the decision to confine an individual in a psychiatric hospital or in a withdrawal clinic is governed by state law.

Not only the differentiation in forms of penal corrections and the assignment of prisoners according to a correctional plan (§152 StVollzG), but also the internal *structure of the correctional staff* are of significance. The institutional director is a civil servant of higher authority. He represents the institution and is responsible for all correctional planning. He is assisted by civil servants employed in the administrative services. The general correctional staff is responsible for supervision, whereas civil servants in the industrial and social services and members of other vocational groups are responsible for specific individual tasks (§§154ff. StVollzG).

The *length of sentence* plays an important role in the differentiation of correctional institutions and in the classification of prisoners. For short-term prisoners, the question arises whether treatment can be effective over such a short period and whether the corresponding efforts should and could be made. On the other hand, one is more concerned with the possibility of criminal contagion among long-term prisoners and with the other undesirable effects of imprisonment, such as those occuring during confinement for life. Short-term imprisonment has been significantly reduced through the most recent criminal law reform. In the period from 1970 to 1980, the number of men receiving short-term prison sentences of less than six months decreased from 23 to 17 percent of all prison terms. On the other hand, prison terms of less than six months, resulting from revoked suspended sentences and above all from alternative prison terms, accounted for 20 percent of all prison terms being served on any one day (cf. Table 2). This percentage is composed mainly of adult males (Dünkel, et al., 1981). In this case, one must consider that a considerable proportion of short-term prisoners are released conditionally after having served two-thirds of their terms, making the average actual sentence served only a few months. For this reason, one is concerned with the question of whether short-term corrections properly can remain purely custodial. On the other hand, in long-term corrections, one is concerned with avoiding the undesirable long-term effects of confinement and with advancing socializing measures so that reentry into society is possible. Prisoners with a probable confinement period of more than one year account for approximately one-half of all prisoners and confinees. Although the number of short-term inmates has dropped one-third over the past two decades, the number of prisoners serving terms of more than five years has increased significantly (cf. Tables 2 and 3.).

**Table 2:** Inmates according to Probable Length of Prison Term

| Year | Prison Terms in General[2] | | Prison Terms of less than 6 months | | Prison Terms of 6 months to one year | | Prison Terms of more than one year | | | | | | | | | | Juvenile Prison Terms of unspecified length and security custody | |
|---|---|---|---|---|---|---|---|---|---|---|---|---|---|---|---|---|---|---|
| | | | | | | | Total | | 1–2 Years | | 3–5 Years | | 6–15 Years | | Life | | | |
| | Total | % | Total | % | Total | % | Total | % | Total | % | Total | % | Total | % | Total | % | Total | % |
| 1976 | 37,860 | 100 | 7435 | 19,6 | 10,513 | 27,8 | 18,861 | 49,8 | 8689 | 23,0 | 6684 | 17,7 | 2511 | 6,6 | 977 | 2,6 | 1051 | 2,8 |
| 1977 | 39,918 | 100 | 7446 | 18,7 | 11,128 | 27,9 | 20,338 | 50,9 | 9200 | 23,0 | 7275 | 18,2 | 2874 | 7,2 | 989 | 2,5 | 1006 | 2,5 |
| 1978 | 41,557 | 100 | 7530 | 18,1 | 11,780 | 28,3 | 21,354 | 51,4 | 9464 | 22,8 | 7765 | 18,7 | 3146 | 7,6 | 979 | 2,4 | 893 | 2,1 |
| 1979 | 42,229 | 100 | 7382 | 17,5 | 11,766 | 27,9 | 22,263 | 52,7 | 9847 | 23,3 | 7973 | 18,9 | 3476 | 8,2 | 967 | 2,3 | 818 | 1,9 |
| 1980 | 42,235 | 100 | 7229 | 17,1 | 11,697 | 27,7 | 22,517 | 53,3 | 9619 | 22,8 | 8289 | 19,6 | 3653 | 8,6 | 956 | 2,3 | 792 | 1,9 |

[1] Excluding a period of pre-trial detention which is deducted from the total term being served but including possibly suspended remaining terms; data gathered on March 31 of each of the respective years; the period prior to 1976 is not considered since corrections statistics are not available allowing this differentiation.

[2] Including individuals in security custody and inmates of juvenile penal institutions.

Source: Statistisches Bundesamt: Strafvollzug 1976, pp.28f.; 1977, pp.20f.; 1978, pp.22f.; 1980, pp.22f.; percentages figured according to data presented.

**Table 3:** Prison Inmates according to Probable Prison Term from 1961 to 1980*

| | Prison Terms in General | | Up to 9 Months | | 10 Months to 2 Years | | 3–5 Years | | 6–15 Years | | Life | |
|---|---|---|---|---|---|---|---|---|---|---|---|---|
| Year | Total | % | Total | % | Total | % | Total | % | Total | % | Total | % |
| 1961 | 39,098 | 100 | 17,151 | 43,9 | 11,721 | 30,0 | 7551 | 19,3 | 1816 | 4,7 | 859 | 2,2 |
| 1963 | 40,435 | 100 | 17,737 | 43,9 | 11,862 | 29,3 | 8007 | 19,8 | 1927 | 4,8 | 902 | 2,2 |
| 1965 | 42,541 | 100 | 18,296 | 43,0 | 12,439 | 29,2 | 8767 | 20,6 | 2073 | 4,9 | 966 | 2,3 |
| 1967 | 41,387 | 100 | 18,346 | 44,3 | 11,097 | 26,8 | 8723 | 21,1 | 2193 | 5,3 | 1028 | 2,5 |
| 1969 | 40,407 | 100 | 15,506 | 38,4 | 11,489 | 28,4 | 9796 | 24,2 | 2532 | 6,3 | 1084 | 2,7 |
| 1971 | 27,614 | 100 | 10,876 | 39,4 | 7893 | 28,6 | 5810 | 21,0 | 1997 | 7,2 | 1038 | 3,8 |
| 1973 | 29,894 | 100 | 11,564 | 38,7 | 9894 | 33,1 | 5612 | 18,8 | 1861 | 6,2 | 963 | 3,2 |
| 1975 | 28,840 | 100 | 11,356 | 39,4 | 9513 | 33,0 | 5045 | 17,5 | 1981 | 6,9 | 945 | 3,3 |
| 1977 | 33,559 | 100 | 12,358 | 36,8 | 11,316 | 33,7 | 6298 | 18,8 | 2259 | 7,2 | 989 | 3,0 |
| 1979 | 35,594 | 100 | 12,596 | 35,4 | 12,026 | 33,8 | 6842 | 19,2 | 3163 | 8,9 | 967 | 2,7 |
| 1980 | 35,537 | 100 | 12,383 | 34,8 | 11,738 | 33,0 | 7135 | 20,1 | 3325 | 9,4 | 956 | 3,7 |

* Data on prison sentences gathered on March 31 of the respective year; ———— until 1970, including penitentiaries, prisons, confinements, criminal arrest and detention and as of 1971 excluding a period of pre-trial detention deducted from total prison term.

Source: *Statistiches Bundesamt:* Strafvollzug 1979, p.20; 1980, p.20.

Whereas in many western countries the long-term prison sentence has been recommended again and applied increasingly, knowledge of the effects of such penal measures in still lacking. In spite of the many descriptions and portrayals of impressions which now exist, the observable and measurable effects of long-term deprivation of freedom by no means have been clarified.

The number of *foreign inmates* has increased over the past twenty years as a result of the increased number of sentences passed on non-German persons. These prisoners currently account for approximately 7 percent of all prisoners and individuals in custody. Sentenced foreigners appear to have had less experience with custody than the corresponding German prison population. Correctional differentiation and classification is particularly difficult when dealing with foreign prisoners because of their number, social status, specific needs and economically deficient situation. These problems are based primarily on language difficulties, educational deficiencies and sociocultural differences, which appear to be so significant that the provision of equal treatment is seriously compromised.

Although statutory preference is given to placing those prisoners suitable in open correctional facilities, in fact only 18 percent of adult and 10 percent of juvenile prisoners are confined in *open penal institutions.* In addition, only 1 percent of all imprisoned women are confined in open facilities. If one includes day leavers, who work without supervision outside the institution, in this calculation, then the average number of individuals in open or relaxed penal correctional institutions increases to over 20 percent of all individuals in custody or in prison.

**Table 4:** Execution of Freedom-Depriving Correctional Measures outside the Official Prison Institutions

| Year | | 1963 | 1965 | 1967 | 1970 | 1973 | 1976 | 1980 |
|---|---|---|---|---|---|---|---|---|
| Total[1] on Jan. of Given Year | | 4514 | 4839 | 4882 | 4749 | 4227 | 3864 | 3782 |
| New Entries[1] Within Given Year | | 1588 | 1369 | 1356 | 1243 | 1345 | 1637 | 2031 |
| Of these | Psychiatric Hospital | 1222 | 963 | 1035 | 1010 | 1139 | 1169 | 1199 |
| | Institutions for alcoholic and drug addicts | 366 | 406 | 321 | 233 | 206 | 468 | 832 |

[1]These figures include sanatoriums and nursing institutions (with temporary confinement) as well as institutions for alcoholics and drug addicts prior to 1974; as of 1976, they include psychiatric hospitals (with temporary confinement) and alcoholic and drug addiction institutions; none of the figures include work houses or asylums.

Source: *Statistisches Bundesamt:* Strafvollzug 1963, 46; 1965, 46; 1967, 48; 1970, 49; 1973, 42; 1976, 44; 1980, 36.

*Closed correctional institutions,* which are graded into various levels, mainly take security needs into account. Particularly problematic are the high security sections for politically motivated, violent criminals, for life-term prisoners and for individuals confined in security custody. Although the 208 individuals who were confined in security custody in 1980 are hardly significant in number, they often present practical difficulties because of the principle of separation required by §140 I no.2 StVollzG. To the extent that separation is not expressly required as it is for security custody inmates, the solution to these problems can be found only in the integration of the questionable group of prisoners within normal correctional facilities. Particular difficulties also are present in the confinement of individuals in psychiatric hospitals, which housed more than 3,000 individuals on the day our data were collected. The average period of confinement for these individuals is 10 years. Reform in this area is urgent because of the danger involved, the uncertainty in diagnosis and prognosis, and the actual lack of treatment. Penal corrections for women and juveniles also appear to present problems. At the end of November 1980, female inmates numbered 2,245 and accounted for barely 4 percent of the entire correctional population, with over one-third of them confined in pre-trial detention. Over the last decade, however, the number of female inmates has doubled.

*Personnel problems* in penal institutions have been seen as significant since the beginning of reform. Deficiencies exist in training and qualifications. On the other hand, a very disadvantageous personnel-prisoner ratio exists and a low social reputation is attached to vocational groups active in penal corrections. A long-term comparison, however, reveals positive changes over the last ten years. In 1979, 43.8 employees per 100 prisoners represented a significantly better ratio than the 35.1 to 100, which existed in 1970. Accordingly, the number of planned employment positions in the penal system grew by 75 percent during the 1970s. Because of reform efforts, the professional groups increasing the most since 1970 were teachers, psychologists and social workers. Nevertheless, at 72 percent, general prison personnel accounted for the largest single group of prison employees in 1980, followed by administration and technical service employees with 15 percent, workmen with 5 percent, and the entire social services with only 7 percent (on the entire complex, Dünkel, et al., 1981).

In addition, the costs of penal execution have increased significantly over the last ten years. In 1980, a 1.67 billion Mark budget for corrections was proposed in the eleven German state parliaments, as opposed to a mere 234.1 million Marks (i.e. 14.5 percent) of total income. In 1970, 26.3 percent of total costs for corrections could be covered. At that time 23 Marks per prisoner per day was the nationwide average planned expenditure. By 1979, 65 Marks per prisoner per day was being estimated. Imprisonment, therefore, has become an extremely expensive form of state-imposed punishment.

## 5. Employment and Advanced Training

*Employment* opportunities within the prison system are extremely important for resocialization, and the law, therefore, requires that prison authorities provide prisoners with economically productive employment according to their individual abilities, skills, and interests. Institutional employment facilities should approximate those in the outside world. An inherent right to work, however, does not exist. It is a prisoner's duty to work on jobs appropriate to his physical abilities, and for this work he receives a salary of approximately 5 percent of that which he would receive in the outside world.

In addition, prison authorities must provide for the prisoners' *education and advanced training.* Suitable prisoners should have the opportunity to receive initial and advanced vocational training, retraining for another vocation or other educational or developmental measures. Educational courses also are provided for prisoners who have not completed grade school. In order to avoid stigmatization, the diplomas awarded may not indicate that the graduate was a prisoner. During the prisoner's free time he should have the possibility of attending classes, taking correspondence courses, and participating in vocational seminars and other programs for educational advancement. The law also allows the prisoner to own a reasonable number of books and other materials needed for further training.

Longer periods of inmate inactivity result in a rapid increase in tension and open conflict, particularly in closed prisons. The prisoner's *lack of work or occupational activity* has proved to be especially disadvantageous, and over the past years has affected up to 17 percent of the prisoners in some institutions and regions. Other grounds for scepticism in connection with prisoner employment also exist. In light of the type of prisoners confined in these institutions and due to their extreme diversity, one must see vocational training as a part of broadly directed welfare measures. This viewpoint is particularly obvious when one realizes that over one-half of these prisoners are *untrained day laborers* (cf. Kerner, 1982, §10). Because of this widespread lack of education, every correctional measure directed toward vocational improvement is to be welcomed, since lack of training presents additional problems for the prisoner's reintegration into society. Efforts made toward prisoner improvement cannot be judged reliably with respect to the prisoner's post-release, non-criminal record. Earlier experience, however, has indicated partially encouraging results.

## 6. Assistance, Treatment and Aid to Released Prisoners

Although *welfare* includes all measures which are directed toward improving institutional life and normalizing corrections by simulating the conditions of life outside the institution, *treatment measures* are much more specific. Through therapy, they attempt to give the prisoner the ability to lead a life of self-responsibility without repeated failure in situations of conflict arising after treatment has been completed. Treatment measures include open or relaxed correctional surroundings, vacation leaves, release preparations, visitors, correspondence, as well as free-time planning and social assistance parallel to employment and training. Specific therapy and social welfare assistance are offered in the socially therapeutic institution. The goal of treatment, however, is not to be differentiated here from the general goal of corrections.

*Post-release assistance* is provided statutorily within the range of social welfare aid. Accordingly, the prisoner is to be advised concerning the organization of his personal, economic and social situation. This advice includes a listing of offices responsible for social assistance, at which he shall be assisted in finding employment, housing and available personal contacts for the period after his release. Prior to release, the prisoner shall be given financial assistance in his relocation and transition to normal life and, if necessary, in purchasing sufficient clothing. For these purposes, cooperation exists between correctional authorities and social welfare employees for post-release assistance. Although prisoners have been included in state unemployment compensation plans since 1977, they are not included under the state health and retirement plans. This inclusion, however, is being planned.

## 7. Evaluation and Developmental Tendencies

If the question arises whether the law and the actual practice of modern corrections has been successful, no single answer can be provided. Undoubtedly, over the last century there have been *successful attempts* at limiting prison confinement and improving the remaining correctional system through a more advantageous prisoner-personnel ratio as well as through increased freedom-granting measures. In addition, the legal position of prisoners has decisively improved.

*Continuing deficiencies,* however, cannot be overlooked, even though the ratio of adult male prisoners with previous criminal records dropped from 89.4 to 80.5 percent between 1970 and 1980. The rate of recidivism for released prisoners with single offense criminal records and prior prison experience is, at 50–70 percent, also significantly lower than expected. The percentage of adult female prisoners who have criminal records, which has always been lower than for the respective group of male prisoners, dropped from 73.3 to 56.7 percent. On the other hand, high recidivism rates, the frequency and length of pre-trial investigative confinement, the growing negative characteristics in prisoners, problems with narcotics and foreign prisoners, and the confinement of individuals serving short-term alternative prison sentences appear to be serious barriers to the attainment of correctional goals. Treatment groups, social therapy, and open penal corrections are still the exception even though success therewith appears to have reached its expected level. Post-release or continuous social welfare assistance, residence in half-way houses, and other forms of correctional relaxation are still unusual. Post-release observations reveal that neither the problems of social stigma and rejection nor of practical post-release assistance have been solved satisfactorily. Practical results lie far below expectations, since deficiencies exist in psycho-sociological advice and assistance due to lack of sufficient funds in the social agencies. The over 2,700 official post-release assistance offices still function independently of one another and are insufficiently coordinated. Even if one does not unrealistically overestimate the resocializing value in employment compensation, realistic compensation really has never been provided.

Prisoners are not confined individually during rest periods but rather in groups, because sufficient prison facilities are not available. Since institutional facilities were reduced significantly during the 1970s by the closing of smaller prisons, and since the number of prisoners recently has increased, it is no wonder that many institutions are overfilled and single cells occupied by two individuals. During the 1970s the average prison population increased markedly from 46,670 to 54,726. During that same period, the number of correctional institutions declined from 211 in 1970 to 163 in 1980. This simultaneous reduction in the number of institutional facilities and increase in the number of confinees led to essential changes. Of particular concern was the fact that in 1980 for the first time, prisoners in closed institutions, who numbered 51,325, exceeded the number of places available (50,934). On the other hand, during this same period, almost 500 places remained unfilled in open correctional facilities, which housed only 6,649 individuals (Dünkel, et al., 1981). To some extent, prisoners also are confined under degrading circumstances, and the courts have been forced to reaffirm the wrongfulness of this type of confinement.

With a failure rate of approximately 3 percent, vacation leaves have proved to be generally successful. The systematic integration of transition and post-release periods, however, exceeds the goals projected in the law of penal corrections, since the state's obligations with regard to the execution of prison sentences usually stops at the institutional doors. The organizational dovetailing between correctional institutions and post-release assistance offices, which is essential to avoid the problems inherent in the transitional and post-release periods, is lacking, particularly on the local level.

## II. Austria

**Citations:** Nowakowski, F.: *Strafgesetz- und Strafvollzugsreform. Juristische Blätter 1958,* pp.196ff.; Mayer, K., Kern, R.: *Strafvollzug in Linzer Gefängnissen. Ergebnisse einer Gefangenenbefragung.* Linz 1976; Bertel, Ch.: *Der Strafvollzug in rechtsvergleichender Sicht.* ÖRiZ 55(1977), sp.iss., pp.1–4; Gonsa, H.: *Rechtsschutz im Strafvollzug.* ÖRiZ 55(1977), sp.iss., pp.17–19; Jesionek, U.: *Neue Wege im Strafvollzug.* ÖRiZ 55(1977), sp.iss., pp.54–60; Pickl, V.: *Möglichkeiten der Differenzierung im Strafvollzug.* ÖRiZ 55(1977), sp.iss., pp.29–31; Sagl, Th.: *Der Jugendstrafvollzug. Sonderanstalt für Jugendliche Gerasdorf.* ÖRiZ 55(1977), sp.iss., pp.21–24; Wolf, W.: *Das Vollzugsgericht.* ÖRiZ 55(1977), sp.iss., pp.24–29; Strutz, H.: *Zur Statistik des österreichischen Strafvollzugs seit 1950;* Österreichische Zeitschrift für Soziologie 1(1968), pp.29–40; Bundesminister für Justiz (Ed.): Berufsaus- und Fortbildung im Strafvollzug. Enquête 1978. Vienna 1979; id.: *Bericht der Bundesregierung über die innere Sicherheit in Österreich (Sicherheitsbericht 1978).* Vienna 1979; id.: *Sicherheitsbericht 1979.* Vienna 1980; id.: *Sicherheitsbericht 1980.* Vienna 1981; Burgstaller, M.: "Die Strafrechtsreform Österreichs im Vergleich mit der Strafrechtsreform der Bundesrepublik Deutschland." In: *Strafrechtsreform und Rechtsvergleichung,* ed.by H. Lüttger. Berlin, New York 1979, pp.39–65; Gratz, W.: "Der Vollzug der mit Freiheitsstrafen vikariierenden vorbeugenden freiheitsentziehenden Massnahmen (§2 II und §22 StGB)." In: *Sozialarbeit und soziale Demokratie,* ed. by H. Keller et al. Vienna 1979, pp.35–70; id.: "Konsequenzen der Verknüpfung von Therapie und Freiheitsentzug." *Schriften zur forensischen Psychiatrie und Psychotherapie.* Iss. 2. Vienna 1980; Kunst, G.: *Strafvollzugsgesetz (StVG) und die den Strafvollzug betreffenden Bestimmungen in anderen Gesetzen sowie Verordnungen und Erlässen mit einer Einführung und Erläuterung des Gesetzes.* Vienna 1979; Neider, M.: "Zehn Jahre Strafvollzugsgesetz, fünf Jahre Strafgesetzbuch, fünf Jahre Massnahmenvollzug." In: *Sozialarbeit und soziale Demokratie,* ed. by H. Keller et al. Vienna 1979, pp.121–125; Sozialwissenschaftliche Arbeitsgemeinschaft (SWA): *Strafvollzug heute. Versuch einer Antwort auf die Reaktion der Gesellschaft.* Vienna 1979; Glassl, K.: *Die Gefangenenarbeit und ihre Entlohnung.* ÖJZ 35 (1980), pp.257–266; Sluga, W.: "Die Unterbringung im Massnahmenvollzug." *Schriften zur forensischen*

*Psychiatrie.* Iss.8. Vienna 1980; Schmatral, F.: *Strafvollzug und Sicherheit.* ÖJZ 35(1980), pp. 197–199; Pilgram, A.: *Zur Veränderung der Haftentlassenen-Population seit der Strafrechtsreform.* KrimsozBibl 8(1981), pp.25–37; id.: *Vom Strafvollzug zum Behandlungsvollzug. Zum Formenwandel der Kriminalpolitik.* ÖZS 6(1981), pp.19–27; Winalek, W.: *Einige Gedanken zum Strafvollzug.* ÖJZ 36(1981), pp.6–9.

## 1. Legal Foundation for Penal Corrections

The modern legal basis for corrections is contained in the *Corrections Code* of March 26, 1969, which went into effect on January 1, 1970. The draft of this code, which was open to public discussion in 1965, has been changed repeatedly. During the major reform of criminal law, one basic change occurred in the Amendment to the Law of Penal Corrections of July 11, 1974. At present, a further amendment is being prepared (Winalek, 1981, p.8).

Two factors essentially influenced the legislative course of events. To the vast majority, the necessity of statutorily defining correctional rules and their administration appeared to be constitutionally mandatory (Kunst, 1979, p.4., remark). In addition, the entire criminal law reform was influenced by widespread basic scepticism concerning the prison sentence as a form of punishment. In the revised law, central attention was given to the basically recognized principle that corrections be oriented primarily toward social reintegration and individual treatment. On the other hand, the legislature was faced with solving existing practical problems. The adópted code has been criticized as being quite typical of classical correction law (Pickl, 1977, p.30, remark).

## 2. Correctional Goals and Responsibilities

According to §20 Austrian Corrections Code, there are three purposes of penal corrections. The imprisoned individual should "be assisted in adopting a lifestyle which adheres to the laws and demands of society." Secondly, he should be prevented from pursuing dangerous criminal activities. Finally, he should be shown "the unworthiness of his behavior as condemned in the criminal judgment." Not only special prevention through resocialization (Kunst, 1979, p.49) and general protection of society from dangerous criminal offenders are considered, but also the "reprimanding function" of punishment is included as a third purpose of corrections in Austrian law. In addition to special prevention and deterrence, therefore, particular attention should be paid to compensation for blameworthiness (retribution) and general prevention (Kunst, 1979, p.51). Today, the *primary importance of resocialization* is generally recognized in connection with overlapping legislative intents (Jesionek, 1977, p.55; SWA 1979, p.12).

According to an investigation conducted in three prisons in Linz in the spring of 1975, the importance of resocialization hardly was reflected in the subjective experiences of the prisoners. Apparently, the resocializing nature of the prison term is recognized more in situations in which the prisoners' relationship to the institutional authorities is better than the prisoners' relationship to each other (Mayer, et al., 1976, p.7).

Although the short-term prison sentence was successfully abolished during the Major Criminal Law Reform (Bundesregierung 1975, p.97; 1979, pp.103f.), long-term sentences of more than one year increased during the 1970s. Accordingly, the average total length of penal terms has increased (Pilgram, 1981, pp.32f.). Unlike the German Corrections Code, corresponding Austrian law provides for *correction in levels* (§136–143 CorrC). All prison sentences of more than one year, therefore, are divided into three consecutive time periods. The prisoner must spend at least one-fourth of his total term in each of the lower and middle levels (§137 II). The different levels, which are characterized by increased privileges, play an important role in the daily execution of punishment. Prisoners on the highest level are permitted to spend their prison salary for certain items for their own personal use. They are permitted to receive visitors more frequently, and as a reward for good behavior, they increasingly receive more personal freedom, such as permission to wear non-prison clothing, to watch television, to participate in practical art classes, and to have lights on later in their cells (Bertel, 1977, p.1).

The legislature assumed that this levelled system would gradually adjust prisoners to free life (§136 II). This assumption, however, has been strongly criticized (cf. Bertel, 1977, p.1) and the socializing function of this system questioned, as was the case with the German levelled system in the 1920s. One problem with this type of system is that the different levels and privileges are granted mechanically rather than according to the individual prisoner's progress. On the other hand, one must admit that the Austrian Corrections Code in no way overestimates the value of a levelled system for treatment purposes (cf. Kunst, 1979, m.n.2 on §§136 and 227).

## 3. Prisoners' Legal Rights and Judicial Review of Correctional Measures

The necessity of adopting a unified corrections code had been emphasized in Austria since 1958 (Nowakowski, 1958, p.196). It was seen to be particularly important that correctional decisions be controlled statutorily and that they be made through a legally defined procedure in which the affected party were guaranteed certain legal rights. The diverse rules which existed at that time contradicted constitutionally guaranteed rights that should not have been diminished through a criminal verdict. The *convicted party's rights* were essentially contradictory to the state's demand for punishment. Accordingly, the Supreme Court for Constitutional Matters declared all correctional regulations, prison rules, etc. to be unconstitutional, since they were lacking statutory basis (cf. Neider, 1979, p.121).

Regulations on personal ownership, vacation privileges, employment compensation, written correspondence and visiting privileges, as well as on security, order and legal protection, contained in the Austrian Corrections Code are actually similar to those of a conventional correctional system.

Prisoners in the lower or middle levels may receive visitors only every three to four weeks (§§138 I and 139 I). They may carry on written correspondence with individuals other than immediate relatives only if these individuals are expected to influence the prisoner positively, to assist in his post-release integration or to provide some other benefit (§86 III). These restrictive regulations are justified in part by the argument that most long-term prisoners come from a criminal milieu and that contact therewith cannot be advantageous to treatment. For this reason, institutional directors, relying on §86 III, sometimes request police records on individuals with whom the prisoner is corresponding. The isolating effect of these types of regulations is criticized strongly. (cf. Jesionek 1977, p.56) Investigations of visitor frequency have revealed that two groups of prisoners, each comprising about 38 percent of the total prison population, exist, one of which receives visitors on an average of at least twice a month, and one of which receives no visitors at all. Approximately one-third of all prisoners do not have any steady immediate family relationships. (Mayer, et al., 1976, pp.45, 58).

Contacts with the correctional commission are regulated differently. While exercising their official duties and control functions, the members of this commission always have the right to communicate with prisoners. According to §96 II, this communication cannot be supervised in any manner, as can the prisoner's contact with other visitors.

Prisoners may receive newspapers and magazines but may not own their own radios (§§33, 60 and 132). They may purchase books only if they serve further development and only if they are financed by means other than those available through the correctional system (§ §33 and 60; criticism of §132 Bertel, 1977, pp.1f.; Jesionek, 1977, p.56).

Contrary to the original draft of §122 (hereto, Wolf, 1977, p.26; Kunst, 1979, p.5 on §99, pp.165f.), Austrian correctional law permits no vacation leaves. An interruption of a maximum of eight days during the prison term (§99) is permitted. This type of prison leave, however, is not permitted for prisoners sentenced to more than three years. Regardless of the length of prison term being served, prison leave is also denied those prisoners who present a particular danger for the security of the state, for other individuals, or for property. Dangerousness can be inferred from the type of crime committed, from the motive behind the crime, or from the prisoner's general lifestyle. When granted at all, leave is only permitted for special reasons (e.g. death or serious illness of a family member). Leave also can be granted for economic reasons, but then only to prisoners sentenced to a maximum of one year (Wolf, 1977, p.27). Although the number of permissible leaves within one calendar year is not determined statutorily, leave must be in harmony with the purposes of corrections as stated in §20 I (Kunst, 1979, p.1 on §199, pp.164f.). Paragraph 147 permits one to two releases of a maximum of three days each in preparation for the prisoner's release if no danger of misuse exists and if the prisoner's expenses are covered for the release period. At 4.5 percent, the quota of misusage is very low (Wolf, 1977, p.24).

Protection of the prisoner's legal rights, which is considered to be sufficient and effective, includes the petition for legal remedy (§119), complaint (§§122f.), appeal the disciplinary board (§122), and, after exhaustion of all other stages of appeal, appeal to the Supreme Court for Constitutional Matters and to the European Supreme Court (Gonsa, 1977, pp.18f.). Important decisions regarding corrections are reserved to the jurisdiction of correctional courts (§§16f. and 162f.). These decisions usually concern a conflict between the prisoner's elementary basic rights and public security. Such a decision may be requested through official channels or through petition by the institutional director, but it may not be requested by the prisoner himself. In such a case, the prisoner must be heard in response to the testimony given by the plaintiff and the institutional director. The prisoner, however, then can file a complaint against the decision of one of these courts (§17 I and IV). The Court of Corrections has jurisdiction over the ordering or maintaining of particular security measures, over compliance with relaxed correctional rules, and over prison leaves, stays of execution, and conditional releases (Wolf, 1977, p.24). The Court of Corrections also decides on matters involving freedom-depriving, precautionary measures applied during the correctional period according to §§21f. of the Austrian Penal Code. These decisions concern the period of confinement in disciplinary facilities and the conditional or unconditional release from one of these facilities (Wolf, 1977, p.28). On the administrative level, the legal protection available to a prisoner is exhausted after appeal to the institutional director, correctional authorities and superior correctional authorities.

## 4. System and Organization of Penal Corrections

According to §§8f. Austrian CorrC, penal facilities are either *correctional institutions* or *judicial houses of incarceration.* Prison sentences of more than one year are executed in the correctional institutions. Sentences of three months to one year can be executed in either of the two types of facilities, and sentences of three months or less are executed in the houses of incarceration.

Correctional institutions include general and special institutions. In §8 III special institutions are reserved for first offenders (§127), negligent offenders (§128), offenders with tuberculosis, juvenile offenders (§58 Juvenile Court Law) and, in general, offenders who are not suited for general correctional facilities because of psychiatric pecularities (§129). Since the Major Criminal Law Reform of 1975, preventive measures in conjunction with prison terms are provided for in §§ 21ff. of the Austrian Penal Code and expressly regulated in §§158f. of the Austrian Corrections Code. It must be pointed out, however, that until spring 1979, not one special institution as described in §8 III had been opened (Kunst, 1979, p.3 on §8, p.32; SWA, 1979, pp.20f.). On the contrary, the Oberfucha Institution for First Offenders, which had existed since 1960, was closed in the middle of the 1970s (Pickl, 1977, p.31). Special sections within general institutions, however, have been opened for the groups of prisoners listed in §8 III (Kunst, 1979, p.3 on §8, p.32; SWA 1979, pp.20f.). According to §134, the assignment of prisoners to the appropriate type of institution is the duty of the Justice Department (classification). This procedure, however, is applicable only for prisoners with a sentence of more than one year, and it is somewhat controversial. The utility of special institutions in light of their insignificant actual distinction from general facilities appears less questionable. The total lack of multi-discipline diagnostic teams for the preparation of appropriate correctional plans, however, definitely is viewed to be a weakness in the system (Pickl, 1977, p.31).

Another object of criticism is the lack of a sufficient number of semi-open and open institutions, particularly since this type of institution is not given statutory precedence (Pickl, 1977, p.30; SWA, 1979, p.29). In 1979, a daily average of only 5.12 percent of all prisoners were *in relaxed correctional facilities,* even though §129 III provides for deviations from statutory requirements if adherence thereto would "damage" the prisoner. This statute, however, must be interpreted in its limited sense, i.e. deviations from statutorily controlled corrections can be made only if they are "unavoidable" for the individual prisoner (Kunst, 1979, p.2 on §§and 216). Accordingly, in the Mittersteig Special Correctional Facility, for example, prisoners are permitted to have more personal possessions than in other institutions. In addition, they are not punished for minor rule infractions and are not completely subject to the tri-level correctional system (Kunst, 1979, p.4 on §§129 and 217).

In 1979, a *total of 29 correctional institutions* existed in Austria (See Bundeminister für Justiz, 1980, p.3, for further details.):

| | |
|---|---|
| correctional institutions for adult males | 6 |
| correctional institutions for females | 1 |
| special institutions for juveniles | 1 |
| special institutions for treatment | 3 |
| judicial houses of incarceration | 18 |

The total population in these institutions was:

| Year | 1969 | 1973 | 1980 |
|---|---|---|---|
| Number | 9603 | 8812 | 8102 |

(Kunst, 1979, p.9; Bundesregierung, 1981, pp.112f.)

In 1979, for example, the 7,956 incarcerated and detained persons were composed of 5,512 prisoners, 2,205 pre-trial detainees, 171 confinees and 68 other detained persons (Kunst, 1979, p.9).

The personnel ratio in 1980 was 1:2.62, with a total of 3,280 correctional employees in institutions and conditional release offices. Of these employees, 66 were social workers (Bundesregierung, 1981, p.113; cf. also Kunst, 1979, p.9, with further evidence). When calculating the real personnel ratio, however, the 190 full-time conditional release officers who were in charge of more than 4,600 releasees (cf. Bundesregierung, 1981, p.104) should be deducted.

## 5. Employment and Advanced Training

*Employment* also is stressed (§§44–55, 61, 151 CorrC) in the Austrian correctional system. All prisoners capable of working have the duty to do so (§44). Paragraph 45 I even requires that every prisoner be provided with useful employment (Glassl, 1980, p.258). The efficiency of penal institutions, however, is limited by the requirement (§46) that private enterprise not be competitively threatened. Day-release employment is permitted in exceptional cases (§126), and it is also a permanent part of release preparations when experiences therewith prove to be positive (Glassl, 1980, p.259).

Prison wages are paid at the end of each month. One-half of the wages are paid to the prisoner in cash for his own personal use within the institution. The other is credited to his account for use after release. Although general wages are low (2.20 to 3.60 Austrian Schillings per hour), §§53 and 55 provide that exceptionally industrious prisoners can be awarded more. An increase in prison wages to correspond with the normal wage rate is not planned in Austria. Such an increase would not correspond to the principles of frugality, efficiency, and practicality in prison administration, and it would not be feasible in the foreseeable future because of the general economic situation (Glassl, 1980, pp.265f.). Nevertheless, the 1980 Amendment Draft provides for expansive changes in employment conditions, e.g. a 50 percent increase in prison wages, an appropriate interest rate for those prisoners' wages which have been credited for release, inclusion of prisoners in the state unemployment compensation program, and support payments for the prisoners' dependent children.

Vocational *training* within the institution now is being directed toward short-term training programs for skilled vocations. This emphasis is not a result of institutional needs, but rather is geared to the open job market. Prisoners are trained to be mechanics, locksmiths, painters, bakers, cooks, masons, carpenters, and tailors. Three types of vocational training are available: basic training, retraining, and advanced training. This effort is considered to be promising only if supported by continued assistance after release and during the period of social reintegration (Bundesminister für Justiz, 1979, pp. 14f.,17f.,36f.).

## 6. Assistance, Treatment and Aid to Released Prisoners

In Austrian corrections, the modern tendency toward treatment, humanization, and liberalization resulted from practical experiences within a few special correctional facilities. Particularly influential was the Mittersteig Special Correction Center. This facility is for prisoners who are not suitable for normal institutions because of their psychiatric problems (Kunst, 1979, p.4 on §§129 and 217; statutory support for such an institution is contained in §8 III no.4, §129 Austrian CorrC). The individuals confined here are similar to those confined in German socially therapeutic institutions (cf. Gratz, 1979, pp.43ff.).

Although *conditional release* has been possible under Austrian law for some time, it accounted for only a mere 9.5 percent of all releasees even by the end of the 1970s (Kunst, 1979, p.9; Winalek, 1981, p.7). Every second conditional releasee has been placed under a release assistance officer. The Austrians plan to increase this percentage by expanding conditional release assistance. One basic weakness is the fact that the correctional courts responsible for conditional release hardly ever hold the generally required hearings of prisoners (cf. §152 I no.2). For this reason, this decision-making responsibility may be transferred to the institutional director in the future (critically, Winalek, 1981, p.8). The necessity of providing release assistance to complement correctional treatment is indisputable. Accordingly, numerous release initiatives have been made over the past years, and a central office for this purpose was founded in Vienna in 1979. The improvement of institutionalized post-release assistance and control is seen as absolutely imperative for a portion of the releasees (Pilgram, 1981, p.34).

## 7. Evaluation and Developmental Tendencies

It is unquestionable that a basic humanization of correctional institutions occurred through the penal corrections reform (SWA, 1979, pp.14f.). Criticism has arisen, however, since this improvement has not resulted in any observable decline in the rate of recidivism. Austrian law provides for only limited judicial control over prisoners' legal rights and the protection thereof. For this reason, the legal position of prisoners is relatively weak. Relaxation of corrections through open institutions and conditional release also plays a seemingly insignificant role, even when one recognizes the valuable function of these institutions and especially that of day release. As in other countries, it appears questionable whether the Austrian practice of levelled penal corrections is anything more than an instrument of discipline and whether it has any favorable effect on resocialization. The regulation of vacations, or more specifically of punishment interruption, is extremely restrictive. It has been pointed out that an overly secure correctional system lacking the courage to make sensible relaxation only postpones problems both internally and externally until after the time of release (Schmatral, 1981, pp.198f.). It remains to be seen whether the departmental system containing three different treatment models (full, partial, and stationary rehabilitation), such as the one utilized in the Stein Correctional Institution since 1972, will prove to be promising and applicable for the entire correctional system. Although this system is generally seen to be a positive one (Jesionek, 1977, p.57; SWA, 1979, p.25), it has received criticism for applying a seemingly superficial form of therapy in a traditional institutional setting in which basic passive-defensive prisoner behavior rarely is altered and therapy hardly effective (Pickl, 1977, p.31). Furthermore, the freedom-depriving measures applied according to §§ Austrian Penal Code have been criticized for prohibiting meaningful vocational training in the various institutions. The work performed by prisoners thereby usually involves only simple, repetitive, mechanical activities (Bundesminister für Justiz, 1979, pp.70f.). It also has been pointed out that the level of disturbance caused by therapeutic confinees is not significantly higher than normal for inmates in a correctional facility (Gratz, 1979, p.40).

## III. Switzerland

**Citations:** Hübin, J.: *Die Einzelhaft und ihre Einwirkung auf den Verbrecherstand, auf die Rückfälligkeit und Disciplin, sowie auf die physische und geistige Gesundheit der ihr unterworfenen Sträflinge.* SchwZfStr 13(1900), pp.20–25; Kurt, V.: *Die Aufgaben des Bundes im Strafvollzug.* SchwZfStr 70(1955), pp.325–346; id.: *Der Strafvollzug nach dem revidierten Strafgesetzbuch.* StrVoSchw 87(1974), pp.4, 1–9; Weiss, I.: *Schweizerischer Straf- und Massnahmenvollzug der Gegenwart in der Perspektive moderner poenologischer Behandlungsmethoden.* Zürich 1970; Aebersold, P.: "Der Zweck des Strafvollzugs und die Rechtsstellung der Gefangenen." In: *Festgabe zum Schweizerischen Juristentag 1973,* ed.by Faculty of Law of the University of Basle. Basle 1973; id.: *Ausbildung wozu? Personalausbildung im Strafvollzug darf kein Alibi werden.* SchwZfStr 92(1976), pp.225–248; Binswanger, R., Brandenberger, W.: *Zum Problem langdauernder Untersuchungshaft.* SchwZStr 91(1975), pp.406–420; Brenzikofer, P.: *Strafanstalt Saxerriet, Anstalt für erstmals Bestrafte.* Kriminalistik 29 (1975), pp.131–134; id.: *Weiterbildung im Strafvollzug.* StrVoSchw 111 (1980), pp.128–135; Murbach, R.: *Strafvollzug—heute.* Zürich 1975; Burren, E.: *Moderne Tendenzen im Strafvollzug.* SchwZfStr 92(1976), pp. 258–274; id.: *Der Vollzug der Zuchthaus- und Gefängnisstrafe gemäss Art.37 StGB in den schweizerischen Strafanstalten.* SchwZfStr 94(1977), pp.482–489; Korth, J.: *Vertrauensvollzug—ein neues Strafvollzugskonzept.* Göttingen 1976; Schultz, H.: *Halbfreiheit und Halbgefangenschaft.* StrVoSchw 93(1976), pp. 1–10; id.: *Einführung in den Allgemeinen Teil des Strafrechts.* 3rd ed. Vol.2. Bern 1977; Stratenwerth, G.: "Übersicherung im schweizerischen Strafvollzug." In: *Begleittext zur Reihe "Der Schweizerische Strafvollzug".* Aarau et al. 1976, pp.11f.; Stratenwerth, G., Bernouilli, A.: *Der Schweizerische Strafvollzug. Ergebnisse einer empirischen Untersuchung.* Aarau et al. 1983; Baechtold, A.: *Die Aufgabe der Strafrechtspflege und des Strafvollzugs in der Schweiz.* KrimB 3(1977), pp.40–51; id.: *Eine schweizerische Strafvollzugspolitik?* KrimB 4(1978), pp.23–33; Bertschi, M.: *Strafvollzug—Utopie und Realität.* StrVoSchw 101(1978), pp.1, 6–12; Bundesrat: *Stand und Reformen des Straf- und Massnahmenvollzugs in der Schweiz. Der Bundesrat beantwortet eine Interpellation aus dem Nationalrat.* StrVoSchw 101(1978), pp.154–163; Kosubeck, S.: *Praxis der Straffälligenhilfe.* Stuttgart 1978; Schubarth, M.: *Zur Rechtsnatur des vorläufigen Strafvollzuges.* SchwZfStr 96(1979), pp.295–311; Rehberg, J.: *Strafrecht II. Strafen und Massnahmen, Jugendstrafrecht.* 3rd ed. Zürich 1980.

## 1. Legal Foundation for Penal Correction

Swiss law and correctional regulations are adopted on four different levels, viz., federal, concordat, cantonal and institutional. According to Art.64 of the Swiss Federal Constitution of 1874, the execution of punishment and the administration of penal institutions are under the auspices of the cantons. They are responsible, therefore, for effectuating the principles of penal execution as stated in Art.37–47 of the Swiss Penal Code ("Schweizerisches Strafgesetzbuch" = SwPC) and the concordats (Kurt, 1955, pp.325ff.; Baechtold, 1977, p.46; Bundesrat, 1978, p.155; Rehberg, 1980, pp.18f.).

Federal legislative competence in the field of corrections essentially is limited to those rules required for the effectuation of material-legal criminal law specifications. The Swiss Penal Code and its related ordinances, therefore, contain regulations on the various types of institutions to be administered by the cantons and on the levels and forms of corrections. It also includes specifications on employment, compensation, correspondence, and visiting privileges. In addition, the legislature has the authority to oversee the execution of punishment and disciplinary measures. It must observe the official measures taken by the cantons and may intervene if public interests are seriously damaged or endangered by incorrect application of federal law. Accordingly, the institutions are required in Art.46 (2) SwPC to apply measures and provide the surroundings suitable for the emotional, mental and physical welfare of the confined individuals. Violations of this requirement, which are not based on orders or decrees, may be appealed to the legislature through a supervisory complaint. An administrative complaint may be filed with the Supreme Court if the violations are based on orders and decrees of the cantons (Rehberg, 1980, p.18). Legislation on corrections, however, is reserved to the cantons. The Swiss Penal Code provides only a framework for the execution of prison sentences and correctional measures.

Since 1971, Swiss correctional law has distinguished between first offenders and recidivists, but no longer between those sentenced to prisons and those sentenced to workhouses. Both these categories of prisoners, however, are subject to the same correctional norms and thereby serve their terms under the same situations. One can question, therefore, the usefulness of retaining such a distinction (Schultz, 1977, pp.61f.). Swiss criminal law also recognizes the conditional suspension of sentence, which corresponds to German conditional release. Conditional release from partially served sentences is also possible. In addition, the Swiss Penal Code recognizes the following correctional measures: detention of habitual criminals, hospitalization and confinement of mentally disturbed delinquents, confinement or treatment of alcoholics and drug addicts, and assignment to a vocational training institution (Art.42ff., 100 SwPC). Currently, Swiss correctional experts also are promoting the following reforms of present law: abolition of short-term prison sentences or their substitution by other sanctions, expansion on the conditional sentence, and improvement of socially therapeutic facilities, particularly for recidivists (Burren, 1977, pp.484ff.; Schultz, 1977, pp.62ff.).

The legislature (Bundesrat, 1978, 162) has expressed the viewpoint that the problems existing in the execution of punishment and other correctional measures cannot be solved through the issuance of a federal law on corrections, and that, therefore, such a measure should not be forced. The Federal Government is also constitutionally limited in its powers over penal correction to the setting up of a general legal framework. Essentially, this task has been completed in Art.35ff., 82ff., 374ff. and 397 of the SwPC. For this reason, the proposal to create a special law on punishment execution which was made during the Penal Code revision in 1971 was rejected after thorough examination. On the other hand, it is considered to be desirable that the initiated process of unifying basic correctional specifications be continued. The main responsibility of the federal government is to support the cantons in their effectuation of federal law and to encourage them to realize relevant improvements in the execution of prison sentences and correctional measures. In correspondence with federal regulations on budgetary support of correctional and penal institutions, governmental priorities lie in financial and personnel contributions to the training programs and in the improvement of institutional facilities.

Although no unified correctional law exists in Switzerland, the above-mentioned regulations in the Swiss Penal Code, with respect to criminal sanctions and their enforcement, do provide a minimum of unity (cf. Weiss, 1970, pp.33, 36). The revisions introduced in the 1970s involving semi-freedom or semi-incarceration (Art.36 (3), Art.43 (3) SwPC) are also nationwide and correspond to open corrections and day leave (cf. Baechtold, 1976, pp.3, 5). Daytime imprisonment is also possible, if the sentence does not exceed two weeks. The cantons can apply these correctional forms, if so desired.

## 2. Correctional Goals and Responsibilities

According to Art.37 Swiss Penal Code, a prison sentence shall be executed in such a manner that it disciplines the prisoner and prepares him for social reentry (Kurt, 1974, pp.1, 5ff.). The *idea of discipline* for adult corrections, however, has been criticized as being obsolete (Burren, 1977, pp.483f.). In order to attain this goal, the legislature and concordat conferences have provided for a four-level *progressive system.* Considered to be the most effective method for avoiding recidivism, the disciplinary influence on the prisoners is exerted in particular by the requirement of steady employment (Kurt, 1974, pp. 4f.).

According to the directives issued by the concordat conference, the range of progressive corrections includes solitary confinement, group confinement, open institutional forms, and conditional release (cf. Kurt, 1974, pp. 3f.; Burren, 1976, pp.270; Schultz, 1977, pp.52f.). Until the beginning of the 1970's all prison privileges and relaxations had to be earned gradually, according to the old progressive system. Today, however, they are granted at the beginning of the incarceration period. The right to communicate with the outside world, for example through written correspondence, visiting privileges and the freedom of owning a radio, newspapers and magazines, is one of the first privileges typically given. Written correspondence, however, still may be censored (opposed to abolishing censorship, Bertschi, 1978, pp.1, 9). Prisoners do not have the right to receive vacation leave, but may earn this privilege through good behavior and if it is indicated on closer examination of the circumstances (Burren, 1976, p.267). The types of disciplinary measures used for prisoners have changed. Food reduction, sleeping on boards, and solitary confinement as forms of punishment have become passé even though they are not considered to be in violation of the principle "that a punishment must be kept in proportion to the offense" and they are, therefore, still permissible (Bundesrat, 1978, p.158). According to federal law, the prisoner has no formal right to employment compensation (Art.376 SwPC). However, the right to partial employment compensation—at least on good conduct and satisfactory efficiency of work—is approved by virtue of cantonal legislation. (As to the difficulties of providing employment and financial compensation thereof, see Bertschi, 1978, pp.1, 10f.) The concordat conferences, however, have increased funds for this purpose (Burren, 1976, p.263; Bundesrat, 1978, p.160).

## 3. Prisoners' Legal Rights and Judicial Review of Penal Corrections

Although Swiss corrections correspond to the European Minimum Rules for the Treatment of Prisoners, there is still no statutory basis for judicial review of administrative files involving correctional measures. "The legal, and especially the procedural, possibility of penetrating the correctional system in Switzerland is deficient and the legal protection of prisoners insufficient" (Aebersold, 1973, p.173). Review still is reserved to internal administrative control. Presently in canton Zurich, for example, complaints may be made to the judicial director. The judiciary, however, is of the opinion that treatment of these complaints would not change if it were made by regional or superior courts. "One who maintains otherwise perhaps should review a representative sample of these complaints'' (Bertschi, 1978, p.10).

More recent federal court decisions on incarceration, however, have begun to influence daily prison life more effectively (Bundesrat, 1978, p.163). According to *decisions of the Supreme Court,* the prisoner's contact with the external world can be restricted only if necessary for purposes of confinement or for institutional order. In the last instance, a complaint against the ordinance of an institutional director or the correctional service's can be made to the Supreme Court. In this case, the HRC is directly applicable. During the last ten years, unlike previously, the Supreme Court very often had to take decisions in matters concerning the legal position of prisoners.

## 4. System and Organization of Penal Corrections

Although the Swiss correctional system is difficult to see as a totality because it has been relegated to the individual cantons and significantly reorganized over the last ten years, the following criminal law *Rules of Organization* for corrections are determinant:

a) the two-part sanctioning system of punishment and disciplinary measures,
b) the basic differentiation between first offenders and recidivists,
c) the various correctional levels from closed to open penal execution.

The most recent reform movements have been directed toward further *institutional differentiation,* which would require increased cooperation among the various cantons. Primarily, concern is directed toward the secure confinement of dangerous criminals, but interest in developing open institutions for non-dangerous prisoners also has been expressed (Bundesrat, 1978, p.168).

According to a 1977 inventory, the Swiss correctional system included 15 prisons, 7 disciplinary facilities, and 127 regional, administrative and pre-trial detention centers. (KrimB 1978, p.150)

On the basis of federal specifications in the Penal Code, the following *institutional forms* have been set up: the prison (Art.39), the institution for first offenders (Art.37), the ''other institution'' (for recidivists, socially dangerous criminals, those susceptible to drug addiction, and those prone to inducement, Art.37), the work-training institution (Art.100), the sanatorium (Art.43), and the institution for alcoholics or drug addicts. (Art.44; Schultz, 1977, pp. 51ff.; Murbach, 1975, pp.44ff., gives a survey of existing institutional forms in light of the correctional system in canton Zurich.) In addition, according to a federal legislative order of November 13, 1972, day-confinement and semi-incarceration are also possible forms of corrections. During semi-incarceration, the prisoner continues working at his place of employment and is confined only during the remaining period (Art.4 of the first ordinance to the SwPC). Penal corrections with semi-freedom are provided for in Art.37 and 42 No.3 (2) SwPC. Under this system, the prisoner is confined in open institutions or institutional divisions. Employment is sought in consultation with the correctional officers and performed outside the institution. Semi-freedom may be granted only after at least one-half of the prison term has been served. (See Schultz 1976, pp. 1, 1ff. on semi-freedom, semi-imprisonment.)

Since it would be impossible for the smaller cantons and inefficient even for the larger cantons to provide all of the institutional forms which are prescribed by federal law, all cantons have united into *three regional penal correction concordats* (Rehberg, 1980, p.19). This union primarily involves agreements among the cantons for the coordination and assignment of the various correctional duties. These concordats also could be considered to be correctional communities.

The penal correction concordat for eastern Switzerland includes the cantons Schaffhausen, Zürich, Glarus, Graubünden and all cantons east thereof. This concordat maintains the institutions Saxerriet (St.Gallen) and Gemünden (Aarau) for first offenders, the institution Regensdorf (Zürich) for recidivists, the vocational training institutions for young adults in Uttikon (Zürich) and Kalchrain (Thurgau) as well as the special institution in Cazis (Graubünden).

The remainder of the German-speaking Swiss cantons are united in the penal correction concordat of northwestern and middle Switzerland. In this area, the institutions Witzwil (Bern), Oberschöngrün (Solothurn) and Wauwilermoos (Luzern) are available for first offenders, and Thorberg (Bern), Lenzburg (Aargau) and Bostadel (Zug) for recidivists. The vocational training institutions in Arxhof (Basel) are for young adults and two special institutions exist, viz., the so-called Special Measures Center in St.Johannsen (Bern) and the Women's Correctional Facility in Hindelbank (Bern).

The penal correction concordat for western Switzerland includes the canton of Tessin. It maintains institutions in Bellechasse (Fribourg) and La Chaux- de-Fonds (Neuchâtel) for first offenders and in Orbe (Vaad) for recidivists. In addition, it maintains the special facility of Crêtelongue (Valais) for all correctional forms involving semi-freedom, the vocational training institution Pramont (Valais) for young adults, and the mixed institution in Cadro near Lugano. The administrative regional or pre-trial detention facilities in which prison terms of less than three months are served have not been included in the above listings.

The cantons agreed not only to confine their own residents who have been sentenced to prison terms in appropriate institutions in their concordat district, but also to accept prisoners from other cantons into their own institutions if these other cantons were members of the same concordat. Since penal correctional regulations differ from institutional regulations, however, the need to unify penal corrections through correctional laws and executional forms, at least within the concordat borders, has been observed. This unification usually involves regulations on visitors, vacations, contacts with the outside world, employment compensation and social security (Baechtold, 1977, pp.44ff.). The Corrections Commission for the central and northwestern Swiss concordat, for example, published guidelines for granting vacations in the concordat institutions (pub. in KrimB, 1978, pp.146ff.). On June 23, 1944, the federal legislature approved a concordat corrections budget, on which most of the other concordats also have agreed (Rehberg, 1980, p.19).

Although correction statistics encompassing all of Switzerland are in training or just being developed, one assumes that a yearly average of 3,000 to 3,500 individuals are confined in correctional facilities on any one day. Of these, only 2,000 to 2,500 are serving criminal sentences and the others, i.e. one-third of all confinees, are in pre-trial detention. The proportion of foreign prisoners is approximately one-sixth, and women account for hardly more than 5 percent. The vast majority of these prisoners are serving relatively short sentences. As evidenced in a special evaluation of prison statistics in 1975, only 9 percent of those individuals sentenced unconditionally were serving sentences of more than one year. For this reason, one needs not wonder that the rate of imprisonment in Switzerland, at only 50–55 prisoners per 100,000 population, ranks in the lower middle of European prison rates (Baechtold, 1977, pp.46ff.; further, Table 16), and that the problem of overcrowding also does not exist in the Swiss penal institutions.

Although the *number of prisoners* on any one day in Switzerland is relatively low, the yearly movement of prisoners, with 35,000 total admissions, is relatively high. Of these yearly admissions, 87 percent are confined in regional facilities, 11 percent in state prisons and 2 percent in institutions employing some form of disciplinary measures (KrimB, 1978, p.150). Two-thirds of these admissions, however, are pre-trial detainees, 31 percent are sentenced prison inmates and 3 percent are confinees in disciplinary facilities. Twenty-five percent of all penal corrections are executed in state prisons, 73 percent in regional prisons and only 2 percent in disciplinary facilities. Only 22 percent of all disciplinary measures prescribed are actually performed in disciplinary facilities. The remainder is executed in the state prisons and particularly (58 percent) in the regional prisons.

Swiss penal and correctional institutions employ 1,410 full-time personnel for the 3,500 inmates confined, of which 59 percent are in state prisons, 27 percent in regional correctional facilities, and 14 percent in institutions applying disciplinary measures (KrimB, 1978, p.150). Although the rate of personnel-to-prisoners is 1 : 2.5, only approximately 7 percent of the full-time employees have received any training specifically oriented toward correctional work (Stratenwerth, 1983, p.267). The empirical study of Swiss corrections conducted during the 1970s, which was initiated by Stratenwerth et al., revealed that no full-time psychiatrists and hardly any full-time psychologists were employed in those penal institutions studied, and that the only "welfare" assistants available were usually religious ministers. A study conducted in 1975 revealed that in 28 different penal institutions, an average of 7 percent of the prisoners were allowed to work under supervision outside the institution. Of the 7 adult prisons, 5 had open divisions, and an average of 12.6 percent of all prisoners had been granted semi-freedom (Brenzikofer, 1976, pp.13ff.).

## 5. Employment and Advanced Training

Although the prison population has changed considerably over the past decade (cf. Baechtold, 1977, 47), when compared to the general population it still can be characterized as suffering from a considerable educational deficit, evidenced, for example, by a lack of any completed schooling. According to Stratenwerth's (1983, p.267) findings, however, no effort has been made to correct this basic weakness in the correctional system. Neither the possibility of receiving a complete basic education nor vocational training is available. Another study on "Advanced Education during Penal Correction" indicated that employment "is clearly of the most significance, whereas advanced education and therapy are unimportant" (Brenzikofer, 1980, p.133). In this regard, however, one must consider that difficulties exist in the infrastructure of the institutions in that the confinees do not all speak one language, the period of confinement is relatively short, and many prisoners are lacking the stamina required to complete such training.

## 6. Treatment and Social Assistance

According to Stratenwerth's (1983, p.267) publication, the Swiss correctional system in its present form is incapable of fulfilling the resocialization responsibilities assigned to it through statute. Nevertheless, in the past few years, various Swiss penal institutions have created the prerequisites for increased therapeutic treatment of their inmates. They have formulated correctional plans on the basis of information gathered concerning the personal and social relationships existing within the institution, and have hired the specialists necessary for the implementation of these plans. In addition to the already existing vocational training facility for young adults, Switzerland opened the St.Johannsen Special Measures Center (canton Bern) in 1978. This facility was constructed especially for the treatment of adult prisoners and has employed the personnel needed for such treatment. It is hoped that the experiences gathered in this institution will be applicable to the other correctional facilities in Switzerland (Bundesrat, 1978, p.159). Significant problems also are presented by the high number of imprisoned drug addicts who require special and time-consuming treatment.

In general, Swiss law recommends that the negative effects of corrections on the prisoner and his relatives be kept to a minimum and that the prisoner be prepared for his release through counselling, welfare assistance, and treatment. Criminal corrections, therefore, must be practiced in light of this criminal policy responsibility, which is incorporated into release preparations (Baechtold, 1978, p.28). Statutory release assistance (protectionary surveillance) is a part of penal and disciplinary correctional measures, and in connection with voluntary release assistance, it is one of the most important tools for the released prisoner's reentry into society. Since its importance was not recognized adequately for some time, however, financial and personnel support for this assistance are generally inadequate. Some cantons, e.g. Zurich, however, have found new methods of fulfilling their responsibility to prepare prisoners for their release. They have introduced so-called prisoner continuous assistance, which begins immediately during pre-trial detention, and have provided a "rehabilitation bank" to assist prisoners in repaying their previously incurred debts. For the whole country the "Swiss Foundation for Aid to Offenders and their Families" was established in 1981 with a capital of more than 600,000 Swiss Francs. Its main purpose is to grant repayable financial support to clear the debts of released prisoners. It is hoped that other cantons will follow these examples after seeing positive results. The "Federal Law on International Legal Assistance in Criminal Matters," which was introduced on March 8, 1976, attempted to provide foreign prisoners with the possibility of receiving release assistance from their native countries (Bundesrat, 1978, p.161.)

After its completion in 1981, the special measures institution St.Johannsen included a semi-open custody section for 20 inmates with facilities for the application of special measures according to Art. 42 Swiss Penal Code (custody of habitual delinquents), a therapy home for the application of measures according to Art.43 SwPC (assistance and custody of the mentally abnormal), an addiction center for 30 individuals for the application of measures according to Art. 44 SwPC (alcoholics and drug addicts) and an employment facility for 24 individuals for administratively assigned employment (StrVoSchw, 1978, p.169).

The open penal institution Saxerriet, in which prison sentences for first offenders are executed, is also of particular interest. In this institution, group therapy discussions are mandatory. Twelve part-time therapists are employed at this facility, to converse with select prisoners on their present problems, social relationships and adaptability, and their general life style (Kosubeck, 1978, pp.130ff.).

## 7. Evaluation and Developmental Tendencies

Although Switzerland has given much consideration to the effects and positive results of corrections (cf. Hübin's investigations, 1900, pp.20ff.), and has incorporated many future-oriented innovations (cf. the Saxerriet and St.Johannsen facilities), any evaluation of this system is still unreliable. For this reason, the Swiss Justice Department, in its guidelines of March 22, 1976 on detention centers for particularly difficult juvenile delinquents, required that "a systematic and scientific study and efficiency control of this special center be undertaken," and that the results of this study be made available on completion (StrVoSchw, 1978, pp.139f.). In addition, Swiss prison and recidivist statistics are being reorganized in an attempt to provide more information on the successes and failures of the Swiss correctional system.

The more recent internal and external opening and relaxation of the correctional system did not seem to be accompanied by any particular security problems. As Stratenwerth (1983, p.267) reports, less than 5 percent of the more than 2,500 vacations granted resulted in non-return or non-voluntary return to the correctional institution. In light of the low danger potential from prison inmates, the authorities also have received criticism for overemphasizing security precautions. Although the main differentiation made between first offender and recidivist institutions seems to have been correct, the question remains whether levelled corrections are appropriate. In an evaluation of first offender corrections in Saxerriet, it was positively noted that over a five-year period, only 21.3 percent of those released had become recidivists (Kosubeck, 1978, pp.130ff.; see also Korth, 1976). Nevertheless, it must be recognized that the so-called first offenders in this institution were a rather select group.

New methods, accompanied by academic discussion thereof, have been applied successfully in the Swiss correctional system, and their further application can be anticipated. Such efforts could be particularly beneficial, not only in the custody facilities which house recidivists, generally dangerous criminals and prisoners presenting escape risks. Improvements have been hindered somewhat by unfavorable working conditions, by language difficulties with incarcerated foreigners, and by prisoner drug consumption. Although no right to vacation leave or employment compensation exists in Switzerland, in practice, conditions are often more favorable than in other European countries, e.g. allowing private ownership of a television within the prison cell. On the other hand, the Witzwil institution has been recently criticized since provisions for the sensible use of one's free time are "in practice almost completely lacking." Correspondingly, it has been noted that "corrections in Witzwil should facilitate the resolution of blameworthiness, the making of atonement and the furthering of achievement, and it also should provide the individual with the chance for a new beginning" (StrVoSchw, 1980, pp.146f.).

## IV. England and Wales

**Citations:** Grünhut, M.: *Englisches Gefängniswesen.* ZfStrVo 6(1955), pp.321ff.; Wolff, M.: *Prison. The Penal System of Britain.* London 1967; Hall-Williams, J.: *Zwanzig Jahre Strafrechtsreform in England und Wales.* SchwZfStr 84(1968), pp.1ff.; Cross, R.: *The English Sentencing System.* London 1975. 2nd ed. 1981; McConville, S. (Ed.): *The Use of Imprisonment. Essays in the Changing State of English Penal Policy.* London, Boston 1975; Schüler-Springorum, H.: *A Critical Comparison of the British Detention Centres and the German "Jugendarrest" System.* IntJCrim 3(1975), pp.202–211; Banks, Ch., Fairhead, S.: *The Petty Short-Term Prisoner.* London 1976; Gibson, H.: *Der Strafvollzug in Grossbritannien.* VollzD 4(1975), pp.339ff.; Huber, B.: *Neue Wege zur Kriminalitätsbewältigung in England.* ZfStrVo 24(1977), p. 225; id.: *Die lebenslange Freiheitsstrafe—Rechtsgrundlage und Praxis in England.* JZ 1977, pp.16–19; id.: *Die Freiheitsstrafe in England und Wales.* Unpubl. MS. Freiburg 1981; Home Office (Ed.): *Prisons and the Prisoner—The Work of the Prison Service in England and Wales.* London 1977; id.: *Inquiry into the United Kingdom Prison Services.* 2 vol. London 1979; Jones, S., Cornes, P.: *Open Prisons.* London et al. 1977; Sobel, L.: *Political Prisoners. A World Report.* New York 1978; West, D.J. (Ed.): *Problems of Drug Abuse in Britain.* Cambridge 1978; Ingraham, B.: *Political Crime in Europe. A Comparative Study of France, Germany and England.* Berkeley et al. 1979; Radzinowicz, L., Hood, R.: *The Status of Political Prisoner in England: The Struggle for Recognition.* Virginia Law Review 65(1979), pp.1421–1481; id.: *Incapacitating the Habitual Criminal: The English Experience.* Michigan Law Review 78(1980), pp.1305–1398; Schneider, M.A.: *Problems in Short-Term Correctional Settings.* IntJOff 23(1979), pp.164–172; Short, R.: *The Care of Long-Term Prisoners.* London 1979, pp.90–150; Smith, D. (Ed.): *Life-Sentence Prisoners.* London 1979; id.: *Reducing the Custodial Population.* Research Bulletin 9(1980), pp.18–20; Stockdale, E.: "The Correctional System in England and Wales." In: *International Corrections,* ed. by R. Wicks et al. Lexington, Toronto 1979, pp.5–20; Thomas, D.: *Principles of Sentencing,* 2nd ed. London 1979; Baldock, J.: *Why the Prison Population has Grown Larger and Younger.* Howard Journal 19(1980), pp.142–155; Bottoms, A. et al. (Eds.): *The Coming Penal Crisis.* Edinburgh 1980; Bucknell, P.: *Addicts in Prison.* Justice of the Peace 1980, p.660; ECCP: *Report on the Standard Minimum Rules for the Treatment of Prisoners.* Strasbourg 1980; King, R., Morgan, R.: *The Future of the Prison System.* London 1980; Rutherford, A.: *Report of the Inquiry into the United Kingdom Prison Services.* BritJCrim 20(1980), pp.166ff.; Thomas, J., Pooley, R.: *The Exploding Prison. Prison Riots and the Case of Hull.* London 1980; Walker, R. et al.: *The English Legal System.* 5th ed. London 1980; Wright, K.: *A Re-Examination of Correctional Alternatives.* IntJOff 24(1980), pp.179–192; Wright, M.: *Cutting Prison Overcrowding in Great Britain.* C&D 26(1980), pp.10–21; Pease, K.: *The Size of the Prison Population.* BritJCrim 21(1981), pp.70–74; Zellick, G.: *The Prison Rules and the Courts: A Postscript.* CrimLR 1982, pp.575–579.

## 1. Legal Foundation for Penal Corrections

The legal framework for present day corrections in England and Wales is contained mainly in the Prison Act of 1952 and in a few other criminal statutes of the post-war period. The groundwork was laid by the Criminal Justice Act of 1948, and changes were incorporated into the Criminal Justice Acts of 1961, 1967 and 1972 (cf. for the early development Hall-Williams, 1968, pp.3, 7ff.; more recently Huber, 1981). The legal framework has been expanded upon by administrative regulations enacted according to the power granted by the Prison Act of 1952. Existing regulations are based on the Prison Rules of 1964, which replaced those of 1949, on the Borstal Rules of 1964, and on the Detention Center Rules of 1952 (reprint of text in Halsbury's Statutory Instruments, vol. 18, London 1976; exact record in Huber, 1981).These statutes on corrections were revised repeatedly between 1968 and 1976 and were oriented toward new developments.

English correctional reform after World War II developed gradually. Essentially promising and realistic solutions to existing problems were found, which could be tested first and then effectuated. During this period, the English Parliament adapted itself to the developments in administrative practices and remodelled these developments into statutes rather than trying to exert its independent influence. For this reason, the principles of criminal law, on which the whole system is based, are never explained clearly (Hall-Williams, 1968, p.2), and the resulting system is differentiated and oriented toward the experiences and needs of the correctional system rather than according to rigidly defined legal categories (Grünhut, 1955, p.323).

## 2. Correctional Goals and Responsibilities

According to No.1 of the Prison Rules of 1964, the goal of training and treatment is to encourage and support prisoners to lead good and useful lives:

"The purpose of the training and treatment of convicted prisoners shall be to encourage and assist them to lead a good and useful life" (Halsbury's, 1976, p.13).

This goal orientation toward treatment has been altered as a result of a general change in attitudes. High rates of recidivism, secondary analyses of Anglo-American treatment research, and criticism of non-specified confinement periods all led to a departure from the treatment ideal and to a preference for "humane containment." According to the Home Office formulation (1977, Sec.13), the three main responsibilities of the correctional system are to serve the court, to provide "humane and secure containment" and, to the extent possible, to offer treatment and training. Prison escapes are to be prevented with all measures available (Home Office, 1977, p.17). This general change in attitude and the practical problems existing in the British correctional system, e.g. overcrowding and other deficiencies, have stimulated efforts to find a new position and goal for criminal corrections. (See, King et al., 1980, pp.28ff.) The report of the Committee of Inquiry into the United Kingdom Prison Services (Home Office, 1979, I, p.67) outlined the following correctional responsibilities:

a) an atmosphere should be created for the prisoner which facilitates his future adaptability to society;
b) the prisoner's sense of self-respect should be protected and encouraged;
c) damaging effects resulting from a separation from normal life outside the correctional institution should be reduced as much as possible in light of the security required for the individual;
d) the prisoner should be prepared for his release and should continue to be assisted after release.

One criticism of this report maintains that a "justice model" should be preferred to this "treatment and training model." (King et al. 1980, p.34; see also, Bottoms et al., 1980, p.25.) Accordingly, the primary responsibility of corrections should not be punishment and resocialization, but rather protection of the prisoner's human rights and his rights as a citizen during the confinement period. This goal can be attained only through a "minimum use of custody," a "minimum use of security" and a general "normalization of prison." (See K. Wright, 1980, pp. 179ff. for further discussion of the meaning and purpose of corrections.)

## 3. Prisoner's Legal Rights and Judicial Review of Correctional Measures

A recent report of the *European Council* (ECCP, 1980, p.37) indicated that the basic concepts of the United Nations, such as those expressed in the Minimum

Rules for the Treatment of Prisoners, also are incorporated into the correctional statutes of England and Wales. A comparison of the United Nations Standard Minimum Rules with the Prison Rules of 1964 reveals almost unanimous agreement. Only with respect to prisoner accommodation and particularly to the overcrowding of cells (ECCP, 1980, p.42) do these countries, as well as many other European nations, not meet the minimum standards.

The basis for protection of prisoners' legal rights is contained in No.8 of the Prison Rules of 1964. This rule reads as follows:

8. Applications

(1) Every request by the prisoner to see the Governor, a visiting officer of the Secretary of State or a member of the . . . Board of Visitors shall be recorded by the officer to whom it is made and promptly passed on to the Governor.
(2) But every day, other than a Sunday or public holiday, the Governor shall hear the applications of prisoners who have asked to see him.
(3) When a prisoner has asked to see any other such person as afore-said, the Governor shall ensure that that person is told of the request on his next visit to the prison (pub. in Halsbury's, 1978, pp.15f.).

Although England does not recognize the right of a prisoner to petition for judicial review of administrative records, inmates with complaints are not completely without legal alternatives, since every confinee can:

a) demand to see the prison director, a priest or minister, or the medical civil service employee, all of whom must visit those prisoners requesting to see them on the same day the request was made;
b) demand to speak with a member of the Board of Visitors (prison advisory board);
c) demand to see an officer of the Prison Department (supreme correctional office);
d) address an uncensored written petition to the Secretary of State. The prison director may decide on the petition only if he in fact provides the remedy sought;
3) write to a member of Parliament if the grievance made already has been the subject of a refused petition, of an address to the Board of Visitors, or to a prison employee;
f) file a complaint with the European Human Rights Commission (Home Office, 1977, p.51).

Statistics on the types and frequency of these complaints or on their success are not available. Individual complaints by English prisoners to the European Human Rights Commission, however, did increase during the 1970s. (As to their influence on English correctional practices, see King et al. 1980, pp.167f., 174ff.)

More recently, legal remedies through the English courts have become available to a limited extent. Although for some time the English courts were reserved in their observation and control of penal institutions, since 1979 the English Superior Courts have opened their doors at least for review of procedural mistakes (fair trial). (In support hereof see Huber, 1981, p.111.) Since the Court of Appeal has explained the legal nature of the Board of Visitors and entry to official courts has been opened, one expects this organ to proceed fairly and regularly. Reform proposals to change the present legal situation have very little hope of success regardless of contrary demands.

## 4. System and Organization of Penal Corrections

Since 1963, the Prison Department in England and Wales has been administered by the Home Office. The Prison Department is headed by a "General Director," who is responsible not only for penal corrections but also for parole, probation services and the social welfare of prison inmates and releasees. The Prison Department is run by the Prison Board, which is composed of the General Director and the directing administrative civil servants. The entire Prison Department is divided into four regions (North, Midlands, South-West, South-East of England). Each of the regions is headed by a Regional Director who remains in close contact with the individual prison administrators.

In 1978, the English correctional system included 112 institutions containing a total of 41,745 inmates (Home Office, 1979, II, p.83). The *number of institutions* has increased almost continually since the first half of the 1960s (cf. Table 5). The *types of institutions* include local prisons, remand centres, prisons, and borstal and detention centres (cf. Table 6).

**Table 5:** Development of Correctional Population, Personnel and Institutions in England and Wales from 1965 to 1979

| 1 April Year | Total Number of Inmates | Total Number of Prison Personnel | Total Number of Correctional Facilities |
|---|---|---|---|
| 1965 | 30,452 | 11,759 | 95 |
| 1966 | 32,848 | 12,230 | 100 |
| 1967 | 35,164 | 13,089 | 103 |
| 1968 | 32,507 | 14,093½ | 105 |
| 1969 | 33,832 | 15,117 | 107 |
| 1970 | 38,329 | 15,954½ | 108 |
| 1971 | 40,312 | 16,774 | 108 |
| 1972 | 37,735 | 18,188 | 110 |
| 1973 | 37,299 | 18,942 | 111 |
| 1974 | 36,914 | 18,986 | 112 |
| 1975 | 39,360 | 20,075½ | 109 |
| 1976 | 41,579 | 21,072 | 110 |
| 1977 | 41,783 | 21,704 | 111 |
| 1978 | 41,745 | 22,146½ | 112 |
| 1979 | 42,220 | | |

Sources: *Home Office:* Inquiry into the United Kingdom Prison Services. Vol. II. 1979, 9, 83; Prison Statistics England and Wales 1979, p.9.

**Table 6:** Average Daily Population in 1979 of Penal Institutions in England and Wales according to Actual Population and Available Space

| Type of Institution | Average Actual Population | Available Space |
|---|---|---|
| Male Institutions | | |
| Remand centres | 1,773 | 1,881 |
| Local prisons | 17,461 | 11,664 |
| Open prisons | 3,089 | 3,508 |
| Closed training prisons | 11,412 | 12,468 |
| Open borstals | 1,507 | 1,873 |
| Closed borstals | 3,617 | 3,860 |
| Senior detention centres | 1,265 | 1,322 |
| Junior detention centres | 638 | 657 |
| Female Institutions | 1,458 | 1,261 |
| Total Institutions | 42,220 | 38,494 |

Source: Prison Statistics England and Wales 1979, p.9.

The so-called *local prisons* always are connected to a particular court. They are closed institutions, usually in category "B" (cf. infra) (Home Office, 1977, p.116). Although they have several responsibilities, their main function is to confine adults during investigative procedures. If the confinee is found guilty and sentenced, the local prison puts him into one of four security categories. According to this classification, he is transferred to a "training prison." In addition, prisoners serving short term prison sentences also are placed in the local prisons (Home Office, 1979, I, p.133).

*Remand centres* serve the same function as local prisons for young adults under twenty-one years of age. They were created between 1961 and 1965 to avoid the undesirable consequences of mixing young prisoners with adult confinees. Because of the low number of female confinees, however, this separation of young and older inmates cannot be effected for females (Home Office, 1977, 97f.). The *training prison* is the normal form of correctional institution and is divided into open and closed facilities. In 1977, 50 of these prisons were in existence (Home Office, 1977, p.22).

The English correctional system also includes the so-called *dispersal prisons* to house category "B" prisoners, who are classified as being the second most dangerous group of inmates. A small number of category "A" prisoners (most dangerous group) is "dispersed" among these prisons (For more complete information, see Home Office, 1979, II, pp.183–203.) This mixing of "A" and other prisoners began in 1968, since the concentration of these dangerous individuals in one or two institutions seemed inappropriate for security reasons. Past experience with agitation in category "A" prisons also led to this decision.

*Borstals* and *detention centres* are provided mainly for young prisoners between the ages of fourteen and twenty-one. Borstal training lasts for six months to two years and is followed by a mandatory period of conditional release, which also lasts for up to two years. In 1975, the average confinement period in these institutions was less than one year (Cross, 1975, p.68). The Secretary of State decides the actual duration of confinement in borstal training institutions based on the recommendations of the Board of Visitors (Home Office, 1977, p.80). The purpose of borstal training, as for the entire correctional system, is to teach those juveniles confined to lead good and useful lives after their release. The best possible conditions shall be provided to strengthen the juvenile's character, to teach him to recognize his abilities, and to further his feeling of self-responsibility (Halsbury's, 1976, p.4). Before a juvenile is assigned to a particular borstal, his abilities are thoroughly tested in order to determine which institution would be the best suited. Borstal training consists of work, education, and vocational training (Home Office, 1977, p.82).

The detention centres are divided into junior (up to 17 years of age) and senior (17–21 years of age) inmate centres. With the exception of two senior centres, these institutions are closed facilities and are provided for young offenders serving short prison terms. They are similar to the German juvenile detention facilities (cf. Schüler-Springorum, 1975, pp.201ff.). The normal confinement period in a detention centre is three months. This period can be extended to six months and, in exceptional cases, to nine months. The actual confinement period, however, may not be less than thirty-one days. Vacation leaves are granted under special circumstances. The detention centres were introduced in the 1950s in an effort to provide an effective and lasting sanction through short periods of confinement. The primary purpose of these institutions today, however, is to offer a positive influence toward resocialization (Home Office, 1977, p.76). The eight-hour work day in the senior centres is intended to assist the confinees in adjusting to regular employment. In addition to working, these juveniles may also participate in educational programs. A probation officer is available to assist the juvenile in preparing for his release, and this contact can be maintained for up to twelve months (Home Office, 1977, p.77).

In the 1950s, so-called levelled corrections were practiced in English prisons. This type of corrections was based on a classification system which divided prisoners into a "star class" or an "ordinary class" (See, Gibson, 1973, p.3.) Privileges were granted according to the recipient's status as a "star" or an "ordinary." After 1948, the open institutions were filled primarily with stars in order to keep security risks as low as possible. Later, ordinaries also were assigned to these open institutions. Finally judged to be obsolete, this classification system, with its rigid distinctions between stars and ordinaries, was abolished.

Although the classification system here and in other European countries traditionally was introduced to facilitate treatment (cf. Home Office, 1977, p.27), security goals became of prime importance by the middle of the 1960s. Since that time, security precautions have been used as the guideline for determining classification. Furthermore, because of several spectacular escapes after 1966, the so-called Mountbatten Plan was introduced to *classify prisoners* into four categories upon their admission into the institution (Home Office, 1979, p.134):

- A = prisoners whose escape poses the most danger for society, for the police, or for the state security;
- B = prisoners whose escape must be hindered, but who do not require top security;
- C = prisoners who cannot be assigned to open correctional institutions, but who do not have the capability or possibility of attempting to escape;
- D = prisoners who can serve their terms in open correctional facilities without excessive restriction.

In 1979, one percent of all prisoners were in category "A," 30 percent in category "B," 49 percent in category "C" and 20 percent in category "D," ( as to absolute numbers in 1978, see Home Office, 1979, I, p.108 with reference to Table 9). Overcrowding in the English prisons, however, resulted in significant dilution of the four-step classification system.

The assignment of prisoners as one type of institution or another according to the criteria of the Mountbatten Plan is based on the assumption that open prisons are available only for those prisoners who present a low security risk and who can be trusted not to misuse the greater amount of freedom given them (Home Office, 1977, p.116). These open institutions either do not use high level security measures or use them in a very limited form (Wolff, 1967, pp.50f.; Jones et al., 1977, p.2). Because of the relatively inflexible criteria used in this classification and the introduction of parole and suspended sentences in 1967, the number of prisoners in open institutions remained low in comparison to the number in closed institutions, and even this number has declined since that year (Jones et al., 1977, p. 3 with table). The prison population in open facilities dropped about one-third to 10.9 percent between 1965 and 1975. In absolute numbers, a significant drop also occurred over the last decade. As a result, five open training prisons were closed by the middle of the 1970s (Home Office, 1979, II, p.83). The population of prisoners in open institutions continued to drop to 3,089 persons by 1979, although the 1,507 inmates of open borstal institutions were not included in this figure (cf. Table 6). Since all prisoners are placed in open institutions toward the end of their term in preparation for release and social reentry (Home Office, 1977, p.67), it remains unclear how many of the prisoners located in open institutions are there only because of their approaching release. Generally, open institutions are now viewed as being relatively insignificant. According to Jones et al. (1977, p.12), this evaluation is well founded since improved preparation for social reentry, which is supposed to occur in open institutions, never has been illustrated decisively. In addition, his investigation showed (1977, p.219) that, in actual practice, the open institutions are not essentially different from the closed facilities except that security measures are more relaxed. (On the development and system of open institutions, see Wolff, 1967, pp.50–60.)

On March 31, 1978, the entire prison population of 41,745 inmates (and approximately 43,000 in the spring of 1981) was matched by 22,146 prison personnel (Home Office, 1979, II, pp. 81, 83), thereby resulting in a personnel quota of approximately 1:2. A longitudinal analysis thereof reveals that between 1965 and 1978 prison personnel almost doubled, and that during the 1970s alone it increased by 50 percent. This increase affected all employee groups with the exception of medical doctors, who decreased in number by one-third after 1971. (See Table 5.)

Confinement conditions in the English correctional institutions are considerably below the minimum standards set by the United Nations (No.9–14); (Home Office, 1979, p.130). Similar to the situation found in other countries, problems in England also result from the continued use of old Victorian institutions which cannot fulfill modern needs (Huber, 1977, p.226). Sixty percent of the presently existing prisons were built during the 19th century. Twenty percent of these institutions are old military barracks, and only twenty percent of them have been rebuilt since 1945 (Stockdale, 1979, p.7). The main problem, however, is permanent overcrowding in these prisons (Home Office, 1979, I, p.134). In particular, the local prisons are filled to one-third above their capacity (cf. Table 6). The institutions for women also are overcrowded, although not to the same excessive degree (Prison Statistics, 1979, p.9). The majority of the institutions are built with cells for one person. In 1975, however, 4,746 prisoners lived three to a cell and a further 11,008, two to a cell (Short, 1979, p.94). In 1977, approximately 4,000 prisoners were still living at a rate of three prisoners to a one-person cell. As a result of this overcrowding, sanitary conditions were almost intolerable (Home Office, 1977, p.30; Short, 1979, p.95). For this reason, training and treatment has long ceased to exist in local prisons, and custody is even being questioned for its humaneness (King et al., 1980, pp.25ff.). In 1976, these deplorable conditions led to increased unrest and tumult in the English prisons. Prison personnel also went on strike because they were overburdened by the problems of prison overcrowding, personnel shortages, and confrontations with drug addicts, alcoholics and psychopaths, who could not be placed in appropriate institutions (Huber, 1977, p.226). The number of inmates has doubled over the past three decades, increasing between 1948 and 1978 from 19,700 to more than 41,700 (cf. Gibson, 1973, p.3; Home Office, 1979, II, p.83). This increase has been attributed to the greater severity of judicial verdicts and to the improved control and selection procedures performed by the public, the police and the judiciary (here, Baldock, 1980, pp.149, 153). The drastic increase in the number of crimes committed certainly also played a role in these higher rates.

## 5. Employment and Advanced Training

According to the purpose of punishment execution as stated in the correction regulations (prison rules, etc.), prison employment, which is mandatory for all prisoners, shall serve above all as an aid to resocialization. In 1977, however, 8,400 of the 42,000 inmates were not employed (Prison Statistics, 1977, p.93). Prison work also does not require much pre-training of the inmates. Most of the prisoners were employed on production lines, were doing odd jobs in the institution, or were engaged in agricultural work. The unemployed inmates were usually either on vacation, confined to the hospital, attending court procedures, or being transferred to another institution (Prison Statistics, 1979, p.120). Institutional educational training programs, in which approximately 2,000 inmates participate, are conducted by institutional instructors in cooperation with the local education authorities outside the prison. Local educational facilities are selected and remunerated by the institution director (Home Office, 1979, p.37; Short, 1979, p. 108).

## 6. Assistance, Treatment, Release and Aid to Released Prisoners

Although special release-preparation measures, such as the home-leave-system or the hostel scheme, were developed in the 1950s (Hall-Williams, 1968, p.25), conditional release (remission) after serving two-thirds of the prison sentence was introduced initially with the modified Prison Rules of 1964. At the same time, previous efforts to relax corrections were continued and expanded upon.

According to present law, conditional release is possible for all prisoners who are serving a prison term of more than eighteen months. After a review of certain criteria, which closely correspond to those contained in the West German regulations, release is possible after one-third of the prison term has been served, but not before the individual has been confined for at least twelve months. This decision is not made by the court but rather by each institution's local review committee. If this committee decides against release, their decision is reviewed by the parole board (Home Office, 1977, pp.64f.). The Criminal Law Act of 1977 expanded the scope of early release to include those individuals who have served only one-fourth of their sentences. This broadened use of early release, however, can be applied only to prisoners convicted for six months to two years (Thomas, 1979, p.156).

Different rules apply to the so-called life-termers, who accounted for approximately 1,350 inmates in 1977 (Smith, 1979, p.8; cf. Chart 1). Previously, a determination on the early release of those sentenced to life imprisonment was obligatory after seven years. This practice, however, created the mistaken assumption that early release always would be granted at this time. Today, therefore, these inmates are evaluated after three to four years, and a date for the first decision on early release is fixed for each individual (Home Office, 1977, p.66). In 1977, the average term served by life-imprisoned inmates was nine years and eight months (Huber, 1977, p.19; Smith, 1979, p.7).

**Chart 1:** Average Number of Individuals Serving Life Terms in England and Wales from 1967 to 1977

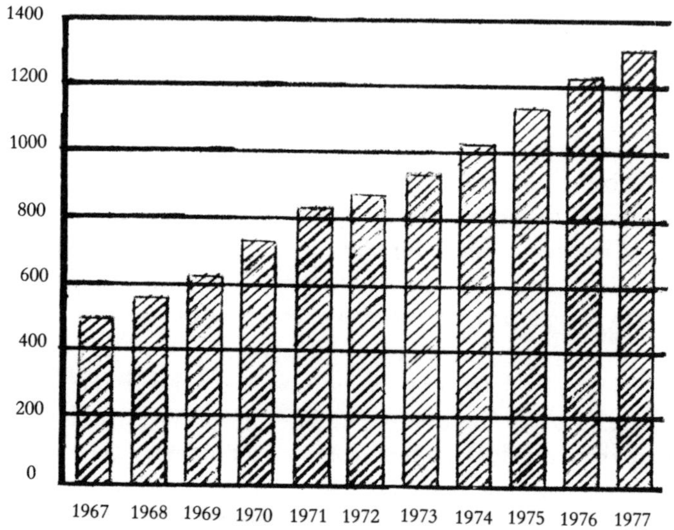


Source: *Smith,* D.: Life-sentence Prisoners. London 1979, p.5.

In England and Wales, as in other countries, release preparations are directed toward helping the prisoner intensify or establish contact with his family and the local setting in which he wishes to live and work in the future. The state unemployment office offers assistance by sending its employees to the prison to advise the inmates on employment possibilities. The inmate also has the possibility of making contact with prospective employers outside the institution. This preparation is supportive of the so-called pre-release employment scheme. Accordingly, everyone who has been confined at least four years should spend the last six months of his term working outside the institution. During this period, he does not continue to live with the other prison inmates, but rather is assigned to a separate part of the institution or to a hostel set up as a transitory dwelling place. A prisoner, therefore, is relatively free during this period.

Home-leave is granted to encourage family contact (Home Office, 1977, p.68). The first attempts herewith were carried out in the early 1950s for important family events. All prisoners serving a term of more than three years may go home twice during the last nine months of their term. Prisoners serving a sentence of two to three years may go home once during this nine-month period. In addition, the inmate may go home for two days at some time before his release on a so-called pre-parole leave. The legal basis for these vacations is found in the very liberal No.6 of the Prison Rules of 1964. Accordingly, every prisoner may be granted an unlimited number of vacation leaves, each for an unlimited period of time. The corresponding regulations in the Detention Centre Rules of 1952 and in the Borstal Rules of 1964 are equally permissive (Halsbury's, 1978, pp.8–12). In addition to these vacations which are designed to assist in preparation for release, the prisoner also may be granted temporary release for special reasons, e.g., for a family funeral or for educational training purposes (Home Office, 1977, p.77; Halsbury's, 1978, p.15).

## 7. Politically Motivated Violent Criminals and Drug Addicts as Special Correctional Problems

Until the end of World War II, political prisoners in England received special correctional treatment. The Criminal Justice Act of 1948, however, limited the application of this special treatment to prisoners serving sentences for subversive activities. This rule also was adopted by the Prison Act of 1952. The Criminal Justice Act of 1967, however, cancelled all special treatment within the relaxed, less severe correctional system. Today in England and Wales, therefore, all prisoners are treated equally (Ingraham, 1979, p.309; Radzinowicz et al., 1979, pp. 1480f.).

The Prevention of Terrorism Acts of 1974 and 1976 were adopted to effectively combat the IRA activities in North Ireland. In the early 1970s, the practice of confining some suspected terrorists over a longer period of time without a trial and verdict developed (detention without trial; Sobel, 1978, p.198). This practice, which had led to imprisonment without indictment or trial since 1971, was abolished in 1975. In February 1976, an official government statement was made to the effect that special treatment of politically motivated criminals no longer could be made (Sobel, 1978, p.200).

Although narcotics also present a significant problem for the English correctional system, this problem hardly ever has been addressed in the official or semi-official reports. The 1979 Home Office comprehensive report on English corrections included neither information on this problem nor any recommendations of approach. The 1977 Home Office report on prisons and the prisoner (p.35) merely commented laconically that "the Health Department is developing methods for drug addicts." The report of the Advisory Council on the Misuse of Drugs at least (Bucknell, 1980, p.660) remarked that directed treatment of drug addicts within the correctional system can be carried out only to the most minimum extent, if at all, because the prerequisites thereto are lacking. Treatment facilities actually exist in only two institutions, and post-release assistance and directed further treatment are completely lacking. Voluntary assistance organizations even are prohibited entry into the institution, thereby making impossible the pre-release contacts necessary to prepare for further treatment. In addition, hostels often refuse to accept drug addicts. (See, West, 1978, pp.206ff.) The number of drug addicts in the English correctional system was reported to be between 600 and 1200 in 1978/79. (See, Bucknell, 1980, p.666; Pease, 1981, p.71.) The reports on the work of the Prison Department from 1968 to 1979 indicated that the number of drug addicts at the time of admission to prison varied between 1,200 and 2,100.

## 8. Evaluation and Developmental Tendencies

English corrections through the late 1960s were characterized by future-oriented improvements such as the initiation of open institutions, the home-leave system, the hostel scheme, and the far-reaching humanization of institutional life, which included the abolishment of corporal punishment under the Criminal Justice Act of 1967. Other developments encompassed the expansion of conditional-release programs and the abolishment of benefits under the old progressive system. When seen in light of these developments, the prognosis by Hall-Williams (1968, p.35) seems to be confirmed that more and more barriers between the prison and free society are falling, and that the prison wall is slowly losing its meaning as a wall of separation.

On the other hand, the rapid increase in the prison population, which has doubled since World War II, terrorist and drug addict problems, and the limitation of financial resources have presented the English correctional system with problems which are often insurmountable and which even destroy much of that which was optimistically planned in the 1950s. Even the therapeutic institution Grendon Underwood, which was started in the early 1960s and which is similar to the German socially therapeutic institution, has lost much of its innovative power and significance because of doubts about the "treatment ideology." Post-release assistance through voluntary probation officers, as is common in Sweden and the Netherlands, also is lacking in England. Finally, protection of the prisoners' legal rights has not been guaranteed adequately, and judicial review is limited to a few exceptional situations. The expansion of community service, which was required by the Criminal Justice Act of 1972, and the broadened application of probationary release did little to reduce burdens on the correctional system. Criminal policy efforts, therefore, now are being directed more toward other possibilities of reducing the prison population. In particular, the courts are being encouraged to impose fewer and shorter prison sentences. Future development, however, is difficult to predict, since both criminality and the fear thereof are increasing.

# V. France

**Citations:** Amor, P.: *La réforme pénitentiaire en France.* RSCrim 1947, pp.1–30; id.: "Le système pénitentiaire de la France." In: *Les grands systèmes pénitentiaires actuels. Exposé systématique du régime appliqué dans les différents pays,* ed.by L. Hugueney et al. Paris 1950, pp.155–186; Tiedemann, K.: *Die Rechtsstellung des Strafgefangenen nach französischem und deutschem Recht.* Bonn 1963; Ancel, M.: *Der Strafvollzugsrichter in Frankreich.* ZStW 79(1967), p.901; Jescheck, H.-H.: *Moderne Kriminalpolitik in Deutschland und Frankreich.* ZStW 79(1967), p.878; Schmelck, R., Ricca, G.: *Pénologie et droit pénitentiaire.* Paris 1967; Chavanne, A.: *Chronique législative.* RSCrim 1971, pp.145–154; Marc, G.: "L'exécution des mesures en milieu fermé." In: *Les techniques de l'individualisation judiciaire,* ed.by G. Levasseur. Paris 1971, pp.233–254; Nicot, X.: *Les dispositions de la loi du 17 juillet 1970 relatives au régime des peines.* RSCrim 1971, pp.621–648; Léauté, J.: *Criminologie et science pénitentiaire.* Paris 1972; Sessar, K.: *Die Entwicklung der Freiheitsstrafe im Strafrecht Frankreichs.* Bonn 1983; Grebing, G.: *Die Untersuchungshaft in Frankreich. Entwicklung, Praxis und Reform.* Bonn 1974; id.: "Die Strafrechtsreform Frankreichs im Vergleich mit der Strafrechtsreform der Bundesrepublik Deutschland." In: *Strafrechtsreform und Rechtsvergleichung,* ed.by H. Lüttger. Berlin, New York 1979, pp.86–114; Picca, G.: "Les méthodes de traitement de courte durée des délinquants adultes." In: *Traitement de courte durée des délinquants adultes,* ed.by Council of Europe. Strasbourg 1974, pp.70ff.; Vérin, P.: *La prison: comment s'en débarrasser?* RSCrim 1974, pp.910ff.; Légal, A.: *Les pouvoirs du juge de l'application des peines et leur évolution.* RSCrim 1975, pp.311–325; Pinatel, J.: *Philosophie carcérale, technologie, politique et criminologie clinique.* RSCrim 1975, p.757; Stefani, G., Levasseur, G., Jambu-Merlin, R.: *Criminologie et science pénitentiaire.* Paris 1976; Dutheillet-Lamonthézie, B.: *Evolution statistique de la semi-liberté.* Revpénit 1977, p.391; Santucci, M.: "150 ans de jurisprudence correctionelle, fluctuation de la déviance et son contrôle." In: *Le contrôle social de la déviance.* Colloquy at Vaucresson, 24–25 October 1978, pp.167–183; Teufel, G.: *Reformen zur Ersetzung der kurzen Freiheitsstrafe in Frankreich.* Jur.Diss. Freiburg 1978; Gassin, R.: *Die Strafrechtsreform in Frankreich.* ZStW 91(1979), pp.163–179; id.: *La criminologie et les tendences modernes de la politique répressive.* RSCrim 1981, pp.265–279; Marx, Y., Nicot, X.: "The

French Penal System.'' In: *International Corrections,* ed.by R. Wicks et al. Lexington, Mass. 1979, pp.57–69; Ministère de la Justice: Rapport général sur l'exécution de l'exercice. Paris 1979; Gerety, P.: *A French Program to Reduce Pretrial Detention: Contrôle judiciaire.* C&D 26(1980), pp.22–34; Hagedorn, E.: *Die richterliche Individualisierung der Strafe in Frankreich.* Jur.Diss. Freiburg 1980; Pfeffer, H.: *Strafvollzug in Frankreich.* ZfStrVo 29(1980), pp.147–152; Dablanc, Ch.: *Rapport.* Revpénit 105(1981), pp.55–96, 187–250.

## 1. Legal Foundation for Penal Corrections

France has no special correctional code and does not plan to adopt one in the near future (cf. Grebing, 1979, 110). The execution of freedom-depriving criminal sanctions is governed by Art.717ff. of the Penal Code (''Code de procédure pénal''), adopted on March 2, 1959, and by numerous other regulations (''décrets''). The Fifth Book of the French Penal Code (FrPC), however, is so expansive that it can be considered a code in itself, viz. a ''véritable code de l'exécution des peines'' (Stefani et al., 1976, p.293) or a ''code pénitentiaire'' (Tiedemann, 1963, p.48).

This body of law generally has been criticized as being static and non-innovative in most aspects other than its introduction of personality tests, conditional release and a special correctional court (Grebing, 1979, p.101). It is not surprising, therefore, that it is in need of reform. The Reform Law of July 17, 1970 (see Chavanne, 1971, 145.), with its development of semi-open institutions (Nicot, 1971, pp.623ff.), the law of July 11, 1975, and numerous other regulations enacted the same year all attempted to modernize the correctional system or to unburden it by proposing non-freedom-depriving alternatives to imprisonment. Since 1970, semi-open correctional confinement (semi-liberté) has been recognized as a form of punishment and also can be imposed by the competent court (Nicot, 1971, p.621).

## 2. Correctional Goals and Responsibilities

Ever since the 14-Point Program was adopted by the 1944 Correctional Commission (see Amor, 1950, p.161, re-printed in Sessar, 1973, p.130.), corrections and reform programs were directed toward avoiding recidivism and furthering resocialization (cf. Marx et al., 1979, p.57). The goals also were included expressly in Art.33-2-21 of the legislative draft (''avant-projet de code pénal'').

Correctional life is supposed to be as similar to life outside the institution as possible. Confined persons should become capable of living normal lives within society. In the institutions in which longer prison terms are being served, treatment plans are proposed in consultation with the inmate. Correctional goals should be furthered through employment, vocational training, education and athletic activity (Picca, 1974, p.63). Particular emphasis is placed on teaching the prisoner a sense of responsibility. He is to learn to respect the rights of others in a situation involving a complex of inter-personal relationships (Vérin, 1979, p.495).

One cannot overlook the extensive material deficiencies and problems in the French correctional system. They resulted in prison revolts and disturbances in the summer of 1974 and finally in a crisis of previously unheard of proportions (cf. Marx et al., 1979, p.59). The numerous local prisons are particularly desolate. Although an amnesty granted in 1974 successfully reduced the number of prisoners (Revpénit 1977, p.180), the prison population increased significantly over the next six years to more than 40,000 (cf. Table 7; RSCrim, 1981, p.141). Since only 19,540 individuals were confined in 1955 (Schmelck et al., 1967, p.210), the prison population actually doubled by 1980. This increase was particularly prominent in the number of inmates serving long-term sentences. The placement of prisoners in appropriate institutions also has become more difficult as a result of this increase, and general institutional capacity is entirely too low. Overcrowding, with more than 7,500 excess inmates as of January 1, 1980 (Revpénit, 1981, p.96), presents one of the greatest problems for correctional treatment, since the workload is entirely too high for the prison staff available. The principle of individualization and the goal of improvement and re-socialization, especially with respect to release preparations, however, should be maintained. (Conseil supérieur de l'administration pénitentiaire, l'exécution des peines extrait du rapport général, 1979, RSCrim, 1980, pp.309ff.; cf., however, Hagedorn, 1980, pp.309ff. on the period before the last government change 1981.)

The re-socialization program provided for in Art.D 440 FrPC should strengthen the prisoner's will and his social adaptability, so that after release he will be able to follow the law without sacrificing the satisfaction of his own needs. In addition, this program should offer assistance in solving the prisoner's social and family problems. The fulfillment of these responsibilities, however, is confronted with extreme difficulties. Prison staffs are usually overworked, and coordination within the prison system is generally deficient. Opposing attitudes as to the value of this resocialization lead to conflicts between institutional directors and training staffs, particularly with respect to the importance of maintaining security and order. In 1979, only 135 individuals were employed in the entire closed correctional system to carry out these resocialization programs. Each of these individuals was responsible for approximately 280 prisoners at that time. (RSCrim 1980, p.178) The number of social workers employed also is insufficient and social facilities are sometimes completely unavailable. The most significant problem existing, however, is overcrowding in the correctional institutions.

**Table 7:** Extent and Development of Correctional Population in France 1970–1980

| Year | Men | | Women | | Combined | | Women in % |
|---|---|---|---|---|---|---|---|
| | Number Confined on Jan. 1 | Index | Number Confined on Jan. 1 | Index | Number Confined on Jan. 1 | Index | |
| 1970 | 28,088 | 100 | 938 | 100 | 29,026 | 100 | 3,23 |
| 1971 | 28,626 | 101,9 | 923 | 98,4 | 29,549 | 101,8 | 3,12 |
| 1972 | 30,717 | 109,3 | 951 | 101,4 | 31,668 | 109,1 | 3,00 |
| 1973 | 29,451 | 104,8 | 855 | 91,2 | 30,306 | 104,4 | 2,82 |
| 1974 | 26,389 | 93,9 | 711 | 75,8 | 27,100 | 93,3 | 2,62 |
| 1975 | 25,328 | 90,1 | 704 | 75,1 | 26,032 | 89,6 | 2,70 |
| 1976 | 28,759 | 102,3 | 723 | 77,1 | 29,482 | 101,5 | 2,46 |
| 1977 | 29,660 | 105,5 | 851 | 90,7 | 30,511 | 105,1 | 2,79 |
| 1978 | 31,289 | 111,3 | 970 | 103,4 | 32,259 | 111,1 | 3,01 |
| 1979 | 32,334 | 115,1 | 981 | 104,6 | 33,315 | 114,7 | 2,94 |
| 1980 | 34,534 | 122,9 | 1,121 | 119,5 | 35,655 | 122,8 | 3,14 |

Source: Revpénit 1981, p.59.

**Chart 2:** Extent and Development of Correctional Population in France 1970–1980

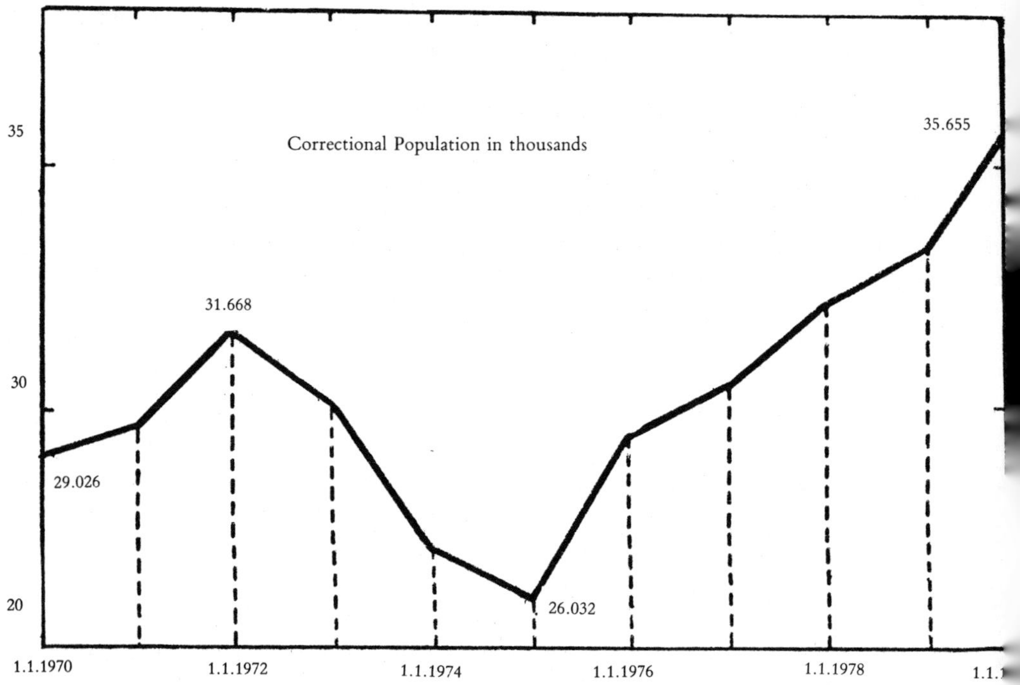


Source: *Ministère de la Justice:* Direction de l'Administration Pénitentiaire, « Rapport Général sur l'Exercice 1979 ». Melun 1979, p.12.

## 3. Prisoner's Legal Rights and Judicial Review of Penal Corrections

The United Nations Minimum Rules for the Treatment of Prisoners have been adopted verbatim in the FrPC regulations. Since the French subscribed to the European Human Rights Convention (HRC) in 1973, the French constitution (Art.55) also demands that the principles of this convention be treated as normal statutory law (cf. Marx et al., 1979, pp.74ff.). Article 122 FrPC, which prescribes the separation of long-term prisoners from other prisoners according to the principles of individualization and differentiation, does not contradict Art.6 HRC. Although the long-term prisoners are subject to greater institutional restrictions, they are not treated unfairly. According to a decision of the Supreme Court, equality under law is provided when every individual can receive the same correctional measures after he has fulfilled the necessary statutory requirements.

The prisoner is permitted to receive information and to have contact with the outside world. Every inmate can have visitors at least once a week and pre-trial confinees three times a week. The inmate's relatives do not need special visiting permission as long as institutional security and order are not adversely affected and their visits seem to have a positive effect on the inmate's resocialization (Art.D 403–412 FrPC). The prisoner has an inviolable right to carry on non-censored written correspondence with his attorney. Inmates of the "centres de détention," may have written correspondence with anyone, but this correspondence is censored. The prisoner's written correspondence with family members may not be restricted even for reasons of security and order (Art.D 413–419 FrPC). Prisoners may read any magazine or book they choose and may own and use radios (Art.D 444 FrPC).

Every prisoner has the right to work and, as is the case with other citizens, must exercise this right. Article 720 FrPC, therefore, imposes a general duty to work on every prisoner.

According to the stated goals of corrections, life in the institution should be so similar to life outside that no limitation is placed on the inmates other than their physical confinement. Since the 1974 prison revolts, however, emphasis has been placed on securing peace and order within the institution. New, extensive security provisions were introduced, particularly in the smaller prisons. The inmate must receive written notice of any disciplinary violations explaining the exact meaning of the claims made against him. He also must be heard in his own defense (Art.D 249 FrPC). Disciplinary measures are ordered by the institution director and cannot be challenged (Art.D 250 FrPC). Possible sanctions range from a warning with written record thereof in the prisoner's files to forty-five days' arrest (Art.D 167–169 FrPC). Arrest, however, can be ordered only if all other sanctions have been unsuccessful or if the extreme severity of the violation so warrants.

The duty of the judiciary traditionally ends with its verdict, and the execution of punishment is the responsibility of the corrections administration. In order to attain the goal of resocialization, however, it is necessary to observe the prisoner's personality and to determine appropriate measures for his reintegration into society. This process requires individualization and judicial control. For this reason, since the new FrPC was adopted in 1959, French law recognizes the *Institution of Correctional Judges* (''juge de l'application des peines''). These judges fulfill both a judicial and administrative function and have considerable influence on the correctional system. Article 722 FrPC determines their responsibilities and powers as follows:

> ''In every penal correction facility, the correctional judge determines the essential modalities of every inmate's treatment in the institution including the possibility of working outside the institution, of living regular day leave or of having any type of leave from the institution. Except in particularly urgent cases, this judge will make his decisions after considering the opinion of the Correctional Commission. The composition and duties of this commission will be delineated statutorily.''

The correctional judge grants vacations, pre-term releases, and in conjunction with the court, he decides on admissions to semi-open institutions. He reviews the limitations imposed to secure institutional order and the disciplinary measures awarded by the institutional director. He is also responsible for providing assistance and imposing control within the conditional release system. As director of the Conditional Release Assistance Organization, he can exert direct influence on the probationer's legal position by modifying the requirements placed on him (Teufel, 1978, p.23). The criminal policy implications of the Institution of Correctional Judges vastly exceed these concrete functions (cf. Ancel, 1967, pp.901ff.; Légal, 1975, p.312). Within the closed correctional system, their decisions are considered a part of administrative law (Nicot, 1971, p.625). Within the open correctional system, however, the attitude recently has been expressed that these decisions are more similar to legislative acts, since they are usually subject to judicial review (Légal, 1975, pp.315ff.). Of course, decisions made in closed correctional institutions are not subject to administrative court review, since as internal measures, they are traditionally non-challengeable (Teufel, 1978, p.99). The correctional judge's decisions are also non-challengeable (Marx et al., 1979, p.67). The Law of November 22, 1978, however, reduced the correctional judge's range of competence. Accordingly, two members of the Correctional Commission also have decision-making power (Marx, 1978, p.139). One of the resulting limitations on the correctional judge was the removal of his sole power to grant prison vacations. The Correctional Commission also must be consulted when a prisoner who is serving a long prison term is granted any form of day leave. Decisions made by the correctional judge are subject to review by the Grand Jury. In the 1976 draft ("avant-projet"), the sanctioning system is subjected to increased judicial review. The assignment of such functions to the correctional sanctioning judge and court is one main indication of reform efforts toward placing the correctional system under judicial domain.

## 4. System and Organization of Penal Corrections

After the number of prisoners had increased so radically to over 40,000 within a five year period, they could no longer merely be assigned to one of the 160 correctional institutions (cf. Dablanc, 1981, p.86). Instead they had to be placed and, if necessary, treated according to their degree of dangerousness and resocialization needs under the FrPC correctional program. On December 1, 1980, *40,800 inmates were under the administration, control and care of only 13,400 correctional staff members* (RSCrim, 1981, p.141). The number of prisoners shown in Table 7 is always related to the first of January of any one year and is only an approximation of the average occupancy in the penal institutions (Dablanc, 1981, pp.59ff.).

French law, similarly to that in other countries, assigns prisoners to open or closed institutions essentially according to the length of their prison term and the danger they present to society. In contrast to the open institutions ("milieu ouvert ou semi-ouvert"), the closed facilities ("milieu fermé") are oriented toward security and are supervised constantly. Prison cells must be thoroughly searched at regular intervals (Art.D 290 FrPC). The prisoners are guarded through the night, and their presence is checked four times each day. Depending upon the results of entrance examinations conducted in the special selection institutions, prisoners serving long prison terms (except life terms) are assigned either to the central institutions ("maisons centrales") or to the detention centers ("centres de détention"). More dangerous prisoners are assigned to the central institutions, less dangerous to the detention centres (Stefani et al., 1976, p.375).

Corrections can be relaxed by assigning the prisoner to one of three open correctional programs, by permitting him to be employed outside the institution, and by granting him day leaves. Placement in an open institution ("établissement ouvert") entails very few control measures. The prisoner can move about freely within the institution, his contacts with the outside world can be more frequent, and his work situation is more like that in free society. Although assignments to open facilities previously were made as a reward for good behavior, today they depend on the existence of particular personality criteria, e.g. age, health, vocation, and prison term. The largest open detention center, which has a capacity of 180 prisoners, is on Corsica (Stefani et al., 1980, p.480). The supervised employment of prisoners outside a closed institution (Art.723 (1) FrPC) is another form of relaxed corrections (Schmelck et al., 1967, p.247). The only difference between this correctional form and closed corrections is that the prisoner may temporarily leave the institution and engage in more profitable employment.

Day-leave according to Art.723 (2) FrPC (''semi-liberté'') is an even more relaxed correctional form. The day-leaver may work unsupervised outside the institution during the day but must return to the institution in the evening, on the weekends and on holidays (Schmelck et al., 1967, p. 249; Revpénit, 1981, p.281). Prisoners serving long terms can be granted day-leaves toward the end of their term to facilitate their reentry into society. This possibility was first included in the Code of Criminal Procedure in 1959. Day-leave originally was introduced because the required reform of closed local institutions was impossible over any foreseeable time period. The investments of personnel and material necessary for such a reform appeared to be insurmountable (Picca, 1974, p.70).

Day-leave is granted in two types of cases. In one case it is granted for the transition period before release (''semi-liberté de transition''), and in the other it is granted immediately for persons serving short sentences (''semi-liberté ab initio''). Over the past few years, the French prison administration has made many attempts to expand on the availability of day-leave positions. This effort also has been criticized and the question raised as to whether the available positions actually are filled (Dutheillet-Lamonthésie, 1977, p.391). Several problems exist for the day-leave employment of prisoners. One problem is the location of the institution, since it should be as close to the place of employment as possible. The high level of unemployment in general also has hindered the development of day-leave as a transitory measure, since it has become more difficult to find suitable jobs for those prisoners (cf. Dablanc, 1981, p.66). On the other hand, day-leave ''ab initio'' has increased in frequency since 1970. By 1979, it was granted for 5,080 persons, which represented an increase of 41.3 percent. Day-leave ''de transition,'' however, decreased in frequency and was granted to only 2,140 persons in 1979.

The organizational and structural requirements for day-leave are being improved continually. Ten independent correctional centers are now in existence for this purpose. By 1978, 48 percent of their total capacity was filled. Prison administration has decided to use the excess day-leave capacity more effectively for transitory inmates, since almost 30 percent of the day-leave permits are granted to short-term prisoners. In 1977, revocation of day-leaves ''ab initio'' occurred in 6.5 percent, and of day-leaves ''de transition'' in 10.4 percent of all cases. Although in comparison, revocations of initial day-leaves are not particularly high, they still are high enough to warrant improvement through offers of group therapy and social rehabilitation (Pfeffer, 1980, pp. 147ff.; cf. also RSCrim, 1980, p.185). Pre-trial detention has not proved to be a suitable situation for day-leave, since during this detention period jobs usually are lost.

As we have mentioned above, the French correctional system is divided into nine regions. In addition to special facilities, three types of correctional institutions exist, viz., central institutions, detention centers, and improvement facilities (cf. Marx et al., 1979, pp. 60ff.). The improvement facilities ("maison d'arrêt et de correction") are used as pre-trial detention centers and for prisoners with a sentence of one year or less. Pre-trial detainees are separated from the other inmates. Article 719 and Art.D 83 (1) FrPC, also provide for the solitary confinement of these prisoners twenty-four hours a day. Contact among these inmates should occur only at institutionally organized events such as church services. Many of these regional prisons, however, are fully antiquated and continually overfilled. Individual treatment is inhibited by the constant change of inmates, as a result of the short-term sentences served in these institutions, and by the resulting lack of sufficient time for effective treatment. A sensible treatment program, therefore, usually does not exist in these institutions and most of these inmates are totally inactive. Separate divisions have been formed in some of the facilities for inmates serving particularly short terms, and in some centers, it is possible for these prisoners to be employed outside the institution. Since suitable offers of employment are so scarce, however, only a few hundred prisoners can take advantage of this opportunity. In addition, the jobs which are available are usually given to those individuals who have qualified for day-leave. Day-leave is a preferred correctional measure, since the prisoner can work at his place of employment during the day-time without supervision (RSCrim, 1980, p.181). Although prisoners are to be confined individually, cells usually are occupied by several inmates, resulting in a particularly corrupt form of group corrections. (Léauté, 1972, p.762; also see Stefani et al., 1976, p.393.) Pre-trial detainees cannot always be separated from convicted prisoners (Stefani et al., 1976, p.409) and a deficiency even exists in trained correctional employees. As a result, improvement facilities are usually repressive and do not attain any of the stated goals of punishment (Teufel, 1978, p.63). Not surprisingly, the recidivism rate at 60 percent is particularly high. Over the past few years, even prisoners serving longer prison terms have been assigned to the "maisons d'arrêt" since other penal institutions also are overcrowded. In some cases, more than 30 percent of the inmates in improvement facilities are from these other institutions, resulting in overcrowding of up to 150 to 200 percent (RSCrim, 1979, p.608). Efforts have been directed, therefore, toward using those substitution possibilities for short-term prisoners provided in the 1975 Reform Act more intensively, in order at least to reduce overcrowding in the maisons d'arrêt to some extent.

According to Art.718 FrPC, prisoners serving terms longer than one year on national territory are to be assigned initially to the *Centre d'orientation* in Fresnes.

These prisoners are to be observed here, and depending upon their evaluation, assigned to a suitable penal institution. Since this selection facility is limited in capacity, however, many prisoners are assigned to institutions on the basis of pre-trial confinement reports alone. These premature assignments have been sharply criticized. The determination that an inmate is "incompatible," for example, means that he will serve his entire sentence in the "quartier de sécurité" without ever receiving any resocialization treatment. Once the assignment has been made, the prisoner usually is not reevaluated, although under altered circumstances his placement in another institution might have been indicated. In 1978, 2,157 prisoners were assigned to the "centres de détention," 756 to the "maisons centrales," and 2 to the "quartiers de sécurité" (RSCrim, 1980, p.168). Appropriate assignments often cannot be made because the choice of institution depends more on overcrowded conditions than on a correct evaluation of the prisoner. The effectiveness of this assignment also is reduced by the fact that prisoners sometimes must wait several months before receiving an assignment.

The "maisons centrales" are state correctional facilities for inmates serving longer prison terms. They include divisions specified as "quartiers de sécurité renforcée," which are small, high-level security units or so-called top security units. Prisoners are assigned to the "quartiers de sécurité renforcée" when their presence in a normal institution would endanger security and order or when they are judged to be particularly dangerous because of personality, previous life style or behavior. These top security units are provided to lower the risk of escapes, to avoid aggression toward other inmates and prison personnel, and to eliminate disturbance in the institutions. Since 1977, this type of security unit has been the subject of protest. Particularly since the "Mesrine affair," the top-security units have been criticized because confinement therein represents a serious infringement on the prisoner's interests and does not fulfill security needs. In 1979, 61 prisoners were confined in the "quartiers de sécurité" and 2,211 in the "maisons centrales" (RSCrim, 1980, p.168).

Although the high security measures generally applied in the central institutions are not intended to prohibit the prisoner's social reentry (Art.717 and Art.D 70-1 FrPC), the system practiced in the detention centers is designed mainly to encourage resocialization (Art.D 70-2 FrPC). Less dangerous prisoners are assigned to these centers (Stefani et al., 1976, p.375). They are confined individually at night and must work in groups during the day (Sessar, 1973, p.131). Overcrowding again often results in violation of this requirement. In contrast to the "maisons centrales," which are oriented toward security, the "centres de détention" are directed toward relaxation of penal corrections. These centers can be either closed or semi-open. It is possible for a prisoner to be reassigned from the "maisons centrales" to the "centres de détention." Regulations on vacations, free-time activities and institutional employment are more relaxed in these centers than in the other French penal institutions. In 1979, 3,380 prisoners were confined in detention centers. Since Art.722 FrPC gives neither definition nor criteria for deciding whether a prisoner should be confined in the "maison centrale" or in the "centre de détention," this decision is dependent on the personality judgment made by the selection institution and the correctional judge.

The French correctional system also includes special institutions for juveniles, women, the mentally ill, and the aged. In Rennes, the only large women's prison in existence houses women serving longer prison terms. Otherwise, women are confined in small, separate divisions within the normal correctional facilities. As is the case in other countries, the low number of female prisoners in France (cf. Table 7) makes treatment almost impossible, and the tendency has developed to send all women to cross-regional prison centers.

Juveniles between thirteen and eighteen years of age are separated from adults and confined in divisions of the "maisons d'arrêt." Since these institutions usually are overcrowded, however, separation cannot be guaranteed. Special juvenile correctional facilities also exist. These facilities are oriented primarily toward education and job training and permit the juveniles confined therein to participate in day-leave programs.

## 5. Employment and Advanced Training

As is the case almost everywhere in the world, employment in France is used to assist the prisoner's social reentry. Article D 101 (2) FrPC provides that employment should not be selected for the individual prisoner on the basis of his abilities and interests but rather in light of the influence this work has on his improvement and social reentry. Accordingly, Art. 720 FrPC makes employment mandatory for all prisoners. On the other hand, employment opportunities in the French prisons are very limited because of the generally poor economic conditions. Since jobs are insufficient, many prisoners are unemployed (Stefani et al., 1976, p.161). Two of the greatest problems confronting the French correctional system are locating suitable employment and providing acceptable salaries. Generally, inmates work within the institution for private employers and wages are low and unstable.

In July 1979, 16,840 prisoners were employed: 5,500 in state-owned businesses, 8,500 in private companies, 1,500 in industrial plants, 200 on construction sites, 700 on day-leave and 500 in vocational training courses (RSCrim, 1980, pp.171ff.). 15,000 prisoners, however, were unemployed.

Although this high level of unemployment leads to an unfavorable climate in the penal institutions, the possibilities of finding employment for the increasing number of sentenced persons almost are exhausted. Institutional overcrowding also interferes with the organization of employed prisoners. Employment outside the institution and day-leave, e.g. at construction sites, also present the correctional judge with problems of selection, since it is difficult to supervise these prisoners at their place of employment and the risk of escapes, therefore, is higher. Since 1976, however, extreme efforts have been made to improve job assignments, employment offers and wages. A delegate ("délégué") has been assigned to each correctional region to find jobs for prisoners in local businesses and to assist prison directors in assigning these jobs. These "délégués" have become an almost established institution and are providing a direct public service (RSCrim, 1980, p.182).

Prisoners' salaries have increased considerably since 1976. Although individuals on day-leave receive normal salaries, salaries from state-run businesses for work performed in the institution, at 17 French Francs per day (RSCrim, 1980, p.172), are still relatively low. Approximately 30 percent of the prisoner's salary is deducted as a contribution to his real expenses (Art.D 112 (2), (3) FrPC), another 20 percent is deposited by the prison director into a savings account for the prisoner's later use during his transition period (Art.D 113 FrPC), and a maximum of 10 percent can be deducted to pay the prisoner's damages, court costs or monetary fines (Art.D 113 (2) FrPC). The prisoner may use the remaining 40–50 percent of his wages as he chooses while he is in the institution, either spending the money on his personal needs or using it to support his family. The prisoner on day-leave must be given a regular employment contract (Art.103 (2) FrPC), and his salary must be the same as for anyone else performing the same job (Art.D 134 FrPC). These wages, however, are paid to the prison director, who credits them to the prisoner's account (Art. 111ff., 134 (2), D 140 FrPC).

The prisoner is free to participate in all educational and advanced training programs offered by the institution. Because many prisoners have not completed grade school, elementary education is offered in all of the penal institutions (Art.D 452 FrPC). With the institutional director's permission, inmates also may attend more advanced education classes during non-working hours (Art.D 453 FrPC), and many may participate in correspondence courses (Art.D 454 FrPC). Although the number of teachers employed in correctional facilities continually has increased, this process has slowed during the past few years because of insufficiency of funds. The educational standard in these institutions, however, has increased considerably (RSCrim, 1981, p.135f.). During the 1978–1979 school year, 18,847 prisoners completed some form of education (RSCrim, 1980, p.175).

Vocational training within the institution is oriented as much as possible to that offered in the outside world, so that prisoners can continue this training without added difficulties after release. Development in vocational training programs was promoted a great deal by high government subsidies and the opening of new vocational training divisions in many institutions. Vocational training should promote the prisoner's social stability by giving him job skills (Stefani et al., 1976, p.467), and according to Art.D 457 FrPC, it should be offered in special institutions.

## 6. Assistance, Treatment, Conditional Release and Aid to Released Prisoners

Social workers are responsible for the prisoner's *social welfare.* Upon his admission to the institutions, they must inform themselves of his financial situation and of that of his family (Art.D 464 FrPC). They visit the prisoner and offer him advice and assistance during the incarceration period (Art.D 465 FrPC), and help prepare him for release by assisting him in finding employment, residence and suitable clothing (Art.D 466 FrPC). Close contact, therefore, is absolutely necessary between social worker and prisoner. The French social workers, however, also are overburdened in their workload. In 1973, one social worker was responsible for 130 prisoners (Stefani et al., 1976, p.472). For this reason, they receive assistance from voluntary and honorary correctional officers (Art.D 472 FrPC).

During the confinement period, the prisoner is insured against accidents occurring on the job. Since 1975, the prisoner and his family also are insured under the State Health Insurance Plan for both the confinement and post-release periods during which the prisoner is seeking employment (Art.D 380 FrPC). The prisoner is included in the State Social Security Program for the period of his prison employment. The Decree of March 1977 gave the prisoner the possibility of receiving unemployment compensation after release, although this possibility is denied those individuals who have committed "serious crimes." During the prisoner's vocational training or employment periods he also is included in the State Retirement Plan.

Article D 349–401 FrPC provides for the prisoner's medical care during his confinement, and requires that athletic training and other free-time activities be made available. In case of hunger strikes, prisoners may be force-fed and medically treated. No special provisions have been made for the treatment of alcoholics, but a therapy program is offered for drug addicts. Since this program has had very low success rates, however, demands have been made for some other type of treatment.

According to Art.D 143 FrPC, a prisoner may be granted *leave* to look for employment, to take any type of examination, to care for his family, and in general, to adjust to reentering society. This type of correctional relaxation has been the subject of considerable criticism from the general public, even though only 1.5 percent of these leaves are misused and the total number of leaves granted have decreased. The Law of November 22, 1978 made leaves for all prisoners who are serving terms of more than three years dependent upon the evaluated degree of danger they present to society. These individuals may be granted leave only by the unanimous vote of the Corrections Commission. The number of leaves granted, therefore, has declined by more than 20 percent since the adoption of these new regulations (RSCrim, 1980, pp.181f.), and it appears to be stagnating further (RSCrim, 1981, p.130). Between September 1, 1978 and September 1, 1979, 4,067 leaves were granted, whereas only 2,723 have been granted since January 1, 1979. The number of prisoners not returning from the leaves granted also is declining, particularly in the central institutions, where the number of misused leaves was previously the highest. Four percent of all leaves granted from a central institution and less than 2 percent of those granted from a detention center are misused. The number of crimes committed during prison leaves also has dropped significantly to only 1 percent of the more than 12,000 leaves granted. Of the 36,000 prisoners who were granted day-leave in 1978, only 1 percent attempted an escape (RSCrim, 1979, p.613 and 1980, p.182).

Conditional release ("libération conditionnelle") is permitted under Art.729 (1) FrPC after the prisoner has served at least three-fourths of his sentence, has exhibited good behavior and has a favorable prognosis. Life termers may be conditionally released after serving at least fifteen years in prison. Conditional release may be accompanied by particular stipulations, and the individual released may be required to fulfill certain requirements. The Justice Department is responsible for conditional releases. Its decision is based on the recommendations of the correctional judge, the institutional director, the responsible public prosecutor, and the magistrate. The number of prisoners conditionally released dropped from 72 percent in 1974 to 51 percent in 1979 (RSCrim, 1980, p.168). This decline can be explained by the fact that long-term inmates have more difficulty adjusting to release than do short-term inmates, and that they, therefore, appear to require "treatment in freedom" rather than conditional release. The shortage of release assistants also is responsible for this decline (so, Hagedorn, 1980, pp.239f.). An individual on conditional release, therefore, is not assigned automatically to a release office, since as of 1979 the workload for these individuals at 135 cases each (cf. RSCrim, 1980, pp.187f.) is entirely too high.

According to the Law of December 22, 1972, which is incorporated in Art.721 FrPC, the correctional judge may grant a reduction in punishment ("réduction de peine") for good behavior if the prisoner's total sentence exceeds three months (cf. Hagedorn, 1980, p.232f.).

In 1979, 41,107 prisoners (95 percent) were granted reductions in punishment. These reductions were recalled in only 571 cases (1.4 percent, as compared to 1.9 percent in 1977) (Ministère de la Justice, 1979, p.155). Since 1973, the number of maximum reductions in punishment permissible (up to 3 months per year and up to 7 days per month of punishment term) continually increased, reaching 69 percent in 1979, even though this measure originally was planned to be a form of individualization and not to be the general rule. This practice has resulted in higher reductions of the longer prison terms. A prison term of twenty years generally is reduced by 40 percent (Ministère de la Justice, 1979, p.177), and the president can exercise clemency rights and grant conditional release at an even earlier date. It is possible for a prisoner serving a twenty-year term, therefore, to be released for good behavior after 7 or 8 years (cf. Hagedorn, 1980, p.236).

The two special forms of punishment reduction, viz., "réduction de peine exceptionelle" (Art.721 FrPC), which is granted prisoners who have passed an examination, and "réduction de peine supplémentaire" (Art.729 FrPC), which is granted to long-term prisoners who exhibit "exceptional proof of possible social reentry" (proof of a permanent place of employment, of a permanent residence, and of assistance through a suitable release organization), are granted relatively infrequently but appear to be increasing in number more recently. In 1979, 1,371 persons were granted "réduction de peine exceptionelle" and 2,198 were granted "réduction de peine supplémentaire," which represents an increase of 39 percent in relation to 1978 (Ministère de la Justice, 1979, pp.155ff.).

Like German law, French criminal law provides for the surveillance of recidivists. Penal guardianship ("tutelle pénale"), which was introduced into French law in 1970, can be ordered for prisoners who have been multiple recidivists (Art.58 (1) FrPC; Art.D 497f. FrPC; Art.176, 80 FrPC), and it is exercised after completion of their prison term. It may not exceed ten years during which time the prisoner may, or may not be confined in an institution. Two closed and two semi-open institutions exist for this purpose in France. The application of this measure, however, is relatively insignificant in frequency. At the end of 1974, only 219 persons were under penal guardianship (RevPénit, 1977, p.197).

## 7. Evaluation and Developmental Tendencies

Influenced by international trends and the défense sociale nouvelle movement, French law has taken a large step toward the accommodation of existing problems and toward future innovation in its 1959 Penal Code. This development is particularly revealed in France's establishment of the Office of Correctional Judges and in the more recent provision of day-leaves and prison vacations. After a decade of stagnation, which resulted partially from Algerian problems (see, Marx et al., 1979, p.58.), the French began to adapt corrections to modern needs during the 1970s. The reform impulses of the new social defense movement guided this development within a criminal legal system which never had been concerned particularly with dogmatic problems (Tiedemann, 1963, p.196). The creation of the Correctional Court, which was intended as an expansion upon judicial control, did not ensure the future development of corrections but did contribute to the establishment of prisoners' legal rights. One also must realize that France rejected the appeal of the European Human Rights Commission until October 1981. (See *Le Monde* No.11399 of September 23, 1981, p.10.)

On the other hand, the poor physical conditions of many institutions, the increasing number of prisoners, and the resulting partial overcrowding of prison facilities still are causing serious problems. A total correctional staff of 13,400 persons is also too meager for the more than 40,000 prisoners incarcerated. Any improvements in these conditions through conditional release, which still is inadequate in scope, are limited. Recidivism also continues to present a serious problem regardless of several legal improvements made during the 1970s. The abolition of the progressive system in 1975 has not been criticized (cf. Marx et al., 1979, pp.62f.). In France as in other European countries, however, one is convinced that the solution to difficult correctional problems lies in the further reduction of the number of short prison terms and in the development of alternatives to confinement. One effort which was made in this direction was the general relaxation and opening of the correctional system. Regardless of the exceptional selection center in Fresnes, however, the French correctional system still appears to remain behind its potential. By the middle of 1981, development appeared to stagnate, if not decline (cf. Dablanc, 1981, pp.137f.; further, RSCrim, 1981, p.147).

A phase of "rapid liberalization of corrections" seems to have begun more recently. In addition to the parliamentary abolition of the death penalty, an amnesty was granted which resulted in the release of some 6,000 prisoners. The "high security divisions" of several institutions, in which 50 individuals convicted of serious crimes were confined in complete isolation, also were abolished. In its final report, a reform commission set up by the Justice Department under the direction of J. Léauté recommended a whole series of further measures directed toward the liberalization and humanization of French corrections (cf. report in the "Badische Zeitung" No.262, November 12, 1981).

# VI. Netherlands

**Citations:** Cirpka, E.: *Das System der Straf- und Massregeln und der Reclassering in den Niederlanden.* Bonn 1962; Zentralinstitut für Anwerbung und Ausbildung—Gefängniswesen und Psychopathenfürsorge (Ed.): *Das Niederländische Gefängniswesen.* 3rd ed. The Hague 1971; Buitelaar, W.: *Gevangen in de gevangenis.* Meppel 1972; Bindzus, D., Schärer, H.: *Holländischer Strafvollzug auf neuen Wegen?* ZfStrVo 23(1974), pp.187–195; Bishop, N.: "Aspects of European Penal Systems." In: *Progress in Penal Reform,* ed.by L. Bloom-Cooper. Oxford 1974, pp.83–100; Heijder, A.: *Recent Trends Toward Reducing the Prison Population in the Netherlands.* IntJOff 18(1974), pp.233–240; id.: *Can we Cope with Alternatives?* C&D 26(1980), pp.1–9; Baring, J.: *The Recent Trends Toward Reducing the Prison Population in the Netherlands: An English Viewpoint.* IntJOff 20(1976), pp.89–96; Brinkmann, P.: *Organisation, Verwaltung und Sicherheitsfragen an der Sozialtherapeutischen Anstalt.* Psyche 30(1976), pp.585–588; Pompe, W.: "Das niederländische Strafrecht." In: *Das ausländische Strafrecht der Gegenwart,* ed.by E. Mezger et al. Vol.V. Berlin 1976, pp.17–247; Sansone, J. (Ed.): *Sentencing, Corrections and Special Treatment Service in Sweden, Denmark and the Netherlands.* Hartford, Conn. 1976; Doleschal, E.: *Rate and Length of Imprisonment. How Does the United States Compare with the Netherlands, Denmark and Sweden.* C&D 23(1977), pp.51–56; Nagel, W.: *De funkties van de vrijheidsstraf.* Alphen aan de Rips 1977; Schaffmeister, D.: *Das niederländische Strafgesetzbuch.* Berlin, New York 1977; id.: *Kriminalität und Strafrechtsanwendung in den Niederlanden.* ZStW 90(1978), pp.309–349; id.: *De korte vrijheidsstraf als vrijetijdsstraf.* Leiden 1982; Fiselier, J. et al.: "Strafrechtspflege in den Niederlanden—Strafrecht, Kriminalität und Gefängniswesen." In: *Das Erste Internationale Mönchengladbacher Seminar für vergleichende Strafrechtspflege,* ed.by G. Kirchhoff et al. Bochum 1979, pp.46–99; Short, R.: *The Care of Long-Term Prisoners.* London 1979; Steenhuis, D.: *Developments in Criminal Law and Penal System 1978—Holland.* CrimLR 1979, pp.645–648; Steenhuis, D. et al.: *The Penal Climate in the Netherlands: Sunny or Cloudy?* The Hague 1982; ECCP: *Report on the Standard Minimum Rules for the Treatment of Prisoners.* Strasbourg 1980; Goudsmit, W. et al.: "Sozialtherapie schwerst gestörter Delinquenten auf psychoanalytischer Grundlage. Erfahrungen in den Niederlanden." In: *Therapie* *sexueller Störungen,* ed.by V. Sigusch. 2nd ed. Stuttgart 1980, 247–265; Hauber, A.: "Modelle für den sozialtherapeutischen Strafvollzug in den Niederlanden." In: *Strafvollzug und Öffentlichkeit,* ed. by H. Kury. Freiburg 1980, pp.179–203; Bierheuvel, M., Peters, J.: *Rechten van Gedetineerden.* Nederlands Juristenblad 1981, pp.1045–1054.

## 1. Legal Foundation for Penal Corrections

The Dutch correctional system is governed by the "Law of December 21, 1951 for the Determination of a New Basic Code for Penal Institutions" (German translation in Materials on Criminal Law Reform vol.9, Bonn, 1960, pp.208–217), by the Corrections Code of May 23, 1953, and by the Psychopathic Control Code of September 28, 1928. Specifications on conditional and supervised release are contained in the Reclassification Rule of December 9, 1969. In addition, the Dutch Penal Code of March 3, 1886 (see Schaffmeister, 1977.) contains a few statutes affecting penal corrections.

Similar to German law, Art.10 Dutch Penal Code (DPC) specifies that a prison term can be either for a certain limited time period or for life. Life sentences in the Netherlands, however, are imposed very infrequently. In the period from 1959 to 1973, only two life terms were handed down, one in 1962, and one in 1969 (Schaffmeister, 1978, p.331). Confinement (Art.18 DPC) as a form of punishment may be awarded for a minimum of one day and a maximum of one year. It is intended to be a less severe deprivation of freedom than imprisonment. In practice, however, this difference in severity of punishment lies only in the fact that confinement is carried out in a pre-trial detention center rather than in a prison. (cf. Art.8f. of the Law of 1951; see Pompe, 1976, p.116.) According to Art.37ff. DPC, psychopaths are to be accommodated and treated in an asylum or treatment center. The court may order this treatment for a maximum of one year only. The treatment period, however, can be extended repeatedly if the so-called psychopaths are placed at the "disposal of the government." (As to possible violations of the European Human Rights Convention, see Trechsel EuGRZ, 1980, pp.520f.) This form of custody is designed to protect society from serious offenses committed by these individuals and to provide treatment for these offenders (Bindzus et al., 1974, p.188; Fiselier, 1979, pp.57f.; Hauber, 1980, p.191). In the Netherlands, as in West Germany, individuals who may not be held responsible for their crimes are placed in a psychiatric hospital if they are considered dangerous (Bindzus et al., 1974, p.188.).

## 2. Correctional Goals and Responsibilities

The goal of penal corrections is stated in the Dutch Penal Code and in the 1951 Law on Penal Institutions. Art. 12 DPC provides:

> "To the extent possible, every prisoner shall be confined in the institution best suited to his personality, whereby both the length of the punishment and the possibilities for resocialization shall be considered."

According to Art.26 of the "Law of December 21, 1951 for the Determination of a New Basic Code for Penal Institutions," and in observance of the character of the punishment or disciplinary measure, corrections should assist in preparing prisoners for their reentry into normal social life.

Contrary to prevailing opinion in the Scandinavian countries, *confinement and treatment are not seen to be contradictory* in the Netherlands (Sansone, 1976, p.34). Much attention is given to the continuous care of the prisoners during their confinement, in order to avoid the disadvantages of imprisonment and to facilitate social reentry (Zentralinstitut, 1971, p.5; ECCP, 1980, p.63). Individual treatment is designed in consideration of the prisoner's social background and personality, and it is intended to intensify his contact with the outside world in order to avoid the negative effects of isolation (Hauber, 1980, p.182). The extremely good personnel ratio in the Netherlands' correctional system (4 correctional employees to 3 prisoners; for the Mesdag-Kliniek Brinkman, 1976, p.585) facilitates the effectuation of this type of treatment. Although efforts are being made to provide humane and personal treatment, the opinion that prisoners cannot be improved through confinement is gaining acceptance in the Netherlands (Bindzus et al., 1974, p.187; Hauber, 1980, p.183). For this reason, considerable attention is being given to possibilities of avoiding prison confinement (Sansone, 1976, p.33; Steenhuis, 1979, p.645) and, as the statistics show, with recognizable success.

## 3. Prisoners' Legal Rights and Judicial Review of Correctional Measures

The prisoner's legal status in the Netherlands largely corresponds to that required in the "Minimum Rules for the Treatment of Prisoners." The official position taken in 1979 by the Netherlands to the ECCP (1980, pp.35ff.) also reveals that this country is one of the few nations in which these rules not only are maintained but even surpassed (Doleschal, 1977, p.56). Vacation leave for prisoners, for example, has had statutory basis since 1951 (Art.47 of the Law in conjunction with §97 Dutch Prison Rules or DPrR). In addition, provisions have been made for the prisoner's confinement and employment in open and closed correctional institutions.

The only ECCP requirement which is not met in the Netherlands is that every prisoner be allowed to go outside at least one hour daily. Paragraph 41 PrR provides for only one-half hour of outside activity, although most internal institutional rules extend this period to one hour when possible. Regular athletic programs (ECCP, 1980, p.44) in which the prisoners participate more than compensate for any deficiency in fulfilling this rule. The only other deficiency in the Netherlands with respect to prisoner's rights is that their wages have not been determined adequately.

Although it is self-understood that the Dutch prisoner is able to file *complaints* within the institution, his right to request judicial review is limited. Every prisoner has the right to make an administratively internal appeal to the Department of Prisons at the Central Council concerning his assignment or transfer to a particular institution. This department issues orders in consultation with the Justice Department, which is responsible for effectuating these orders (§§123–129 Dutch Law on Penal Execution). The prisoner may file a complaint with an independent supervisory board regarding any disciplinary measure which has been ordered by the prison director (§§8–15 PrR). This board must report the complaint to the Justice Department. The supervisory board also handles complaints on violations of the prisoner's mail, on questions of visitor supervision, and on any other order of the prison administration which could violate the prisoner's rights. Correspondence with this board may not be censored. In addition, every prisoner has the right to make petition to any responsible administrative office and to demand to speak with the prison director (ECCP, 1980, p.51). The only correctional decision subject to judicial review is the decision not to grant, or not to immediately grant, conditional release. The prisoner may appeal this decision within thirty days to the Arnheim Court (Art.15cff.DPC).

## 4. System and Organization of Penal Corrections

*Prison administration* is directed by the Justice Department, which heads all of the individual prison sectors (Art.22f. Law 1951). Each penal institution is supervised by a commission, the members of which are appointed by the Justice Department in consultation with the Central Council for Incarceration (§8 PrR). This commission is responsible for overseeing the prisoner's treatment and the provisions relevant thereto (§10 DPrR). An institutional council also exists which advises the prison director on treatment methods and relevant measures for individual inmates (§§16ff. DPrR).

Since adoption of the Law of 1951, the *principle of differentiation* must be applied in the penal institutions and in the assignment of prisoners to one of these institutions. Accordingly, the Dutch correctional system is divided into prisons and pre-trial detention centers. In the prisons, only prison terms may be executed. In the pre-trial detention centers, pre-trial detainees, individuals sentenced to "confinement," and in exceptional cases, individuals sentenced to not more than three months imprisonment are confined (§111 DPrR).

In 1977, 15 prisons with a total capacity of 1,044 and 19 pre-trial detention centers with a total capacity of 2,163 existed. In addition to these two *types of institutions,* combined facilities also exist, e.g. the womens' prison in Rotterdam, which has a further capacity of 440 inmates. The total capacity of all Dutch penal institutions, with the exception of 30 places in the prison hospital at The Hague, is 3,767 (Gevangenisstatistiek, 1977, p.24). Only 3,040 of these available places, however, are filled presently.

The total *prison staff* includes 4,006 individuals (Gevangenisstatistiek, 1977, p.14). The number of personnel employed per prisoner in the Netherlands, therefore, is three times higher than in Switzerland, which has about the same number of incarcerated persons (see, Table 8).

The *structure* of the Dutch prison system, which is segregated according to the prisoner's age, sex, and length of sentence is as follows:

a) 2 juvenile prisons, one for men and one for women;
b) 3 prisons for male prisoners under 23, sometimes only under 25 years of age;
c) 10 prisons for male prisoners not fitting into the above categories who have sentences of more than 3 months;
d) 17 prisons for male prisoners not fitting into the above categories who have sentences of less than 6 months.

**Table 8:** Prison Population and Correctional Staff in the Netherlands Extent and Development 1950–1977

| Year | Total Number of Prisoners* | Total Number of Correctional Employees |
|---|---|---|
| 1960 | 19,757 | 2751 |
| 1962 | 19,121 | 2542 |
| 1964 | 19,283 | 2655 |
| 1966 | 18,436 | 2648 |
| 1968 | 22,023 | 2947 |
| 1970 | 21,775 | 3293 |
| 1972 | 23,180 | 3309 |
| 1977 | 26,955 | 4006 |

*Prison population is for the entire year rather than for any given day of the year

Source: Gevangenisstatistiek, 1968, p.12; 1977, p.14.

In addition, several special institutions exist, such as a military prison, a psychiatric observation clinic (Fiselier, 1979, p.74), and a state selection institution at Utrecht (see, Hauber, 1980, pp.191f ). Two state facilities (e.g. the Dr. Henri-van-der-Hoeven-Kliniek in Utrecht) are reserved for the confinement of individuals with mental or emotional abnormalities, and feeble-minded prisoners.

All correctional institutions are divided into open, semi-open or closed facilities, depending upon the security risks posed by the individuals confined therein (Bindzus et al., 1974, p.188; ECCP, 1980, p.39). For the last few years, however, no exact information has been available as to the extent of open or relaxed correctional facilities in relation to the total correctional system. Statistics are also unavailable on fluctuations in the prison population since 1977. The only information provided is that the *prison population* increased by one-third between 1975 and 1977 (cf. Gevangenisstatistiek, 1977, p.14), thereby for the first time reaching again its 1946 level (Gevangenisstatistiek, 1968, p.12).

The increase in prison population probably would have been greater if the Dutch government had not granted multiple collective clemencies during the 1970s as an emergency measure to solve the problem of backlog in the execution of prison sentences. At the beginning of 1977, a new bottleneck developed in penal corrections. The *waiting list for assignments* to Dutch correctional facilities increased to a total of 11,500 sentenced persons (cf. Schaffmeister, 1978, p.333). No informative statistical data exist for the early 1980s. One does know, however, that massive efforts are being made to remodel old and build new penal institutions. In the Netherlands, every prisoner is supposed to have a single cell. During the daytime every inmate can take part in community activities. Even those prisoners assigned to collective correctional facilities are to have a single-bed cell at night. In those facilities in which larger sleeping quarters exist, the attempt is being made to provide each prisoner with a separate area for his personal use (ECCP, 1980, p.41).

## 5. Employment and Advanced Training

Every prisoner in the Dutch correctional system has a duty to work (Art.32 Law 1951; §49 DPrR). The prisoner's particular interests and needs are to be considered when jobs are assigned, since the purpose of this employment is to maintain, advance or create the prisoner's vocational skills to the greatest extent possible (Art.38 Law 1951; §51 DPrR). Employment periods are supposed to be the same within the institution as they are in the rest of society. Presently, they include an 8-hour day and a 40-hour week (ECCP, 1980, p.67). Prisoners in open institutions may accept employment in private businesses outside the institution (Fiselier, 1979, p.74; Short, 1979, p.60).

The statutorily determined goals of prison employment, however, are almost impossible to attain. Because of the extremely short prison sentences, it is difficult to provide the prisoner with suitable employment or to train him to perform more advanced vocational skills (ECCP, 1980, pp.67ff.). For this reason, prisoners generally perform simple routine jobs.

Prison wages are determined by the Justice Department (Art.34 Law 1951, and §56 DPrR). Part of these wages may be used by the prisoner for his personal needs and part of them must be saved. The system of wage-fixing and division, however, is seen to be unsatisfactory (ECCP, 1980, p.68).

According to statute and correctional regulations, every inmate must be provided training during his free time. This training should encourage personality development and assist the prisoner in the realization of future social needs. In special cases, this training may be conducted during the work day. Since less than five percent of all prisoners are serving terms of one year or longer, however, this training cannot be balanced effectively nor oriented toward long-range goals.

## 6. Treatment, Release and Aid to Released Prisoners

Fixed elements of Dutch corrections are social assistance and welfare aid. Since the personnel ratio in the correctional system is so high, these goals can be realized in practice. The van-der-Hoeven-Kliniek in Utrecht and the van Mesdag-Kliniek in Groningen also have been considered for some time to be superior examples of socially therapeutic facilities. The *opening and relaxation of penal corrections,* as well as the conditional release programs, are oriented toward the supreme correctional goal of social reentry. The Law of 1951 provided for the establishment of open institutions and the granting of vacation leaves. Art.47 of this law created the basis for §97 of the Dutch Prison Rules. According to this statute, the prison director can grant a prisoner a maximum of three days' vacation within the last eight months of his prison term. Today, prison vacation is considered to be a part of individual treatment, giving the prisoner the opportunity to make contact with the outside world and helping him to realize the importance of this contact (ECCP, 1980, 88). For this reason, the Dutch government, in agreement with Belgium and Luxembourg, has proposed the expansion of the Standard Minimum Rules, in order to attain as intensive use of vacation as possible.

After the prisoner has served at least two-thirds of his sentence, which must amount to at least nine months, he may be conditionally released (Art.15DPC). "Confinement" sentences, however, are not subject to conditional release (Fiselier, 1979, p.55). In practice, the *relevance of conditional release* in the Netherlands is *insignificant* (Pompe, 1976, p.33), since hardly more than 10 percent of all sentences exceed six months. Sentences of one year or more account for only 4.2

percent of all sentences awarded (cf. Table 9). In order to increase and expand upon the function of conditional release, during the 1970s pre-trial detention periods were credited against the minimum prison term required for conditional release.

**Table 9:** Unconditional Prison Terms Awarded between 1965 and 1975 (in percent)

| Year | 1 Month | 1–3 Months | 3–6 Months | 6 Months to | 1 Year | More than 1 Year and less than 3 Years | 3 Years and more | Total |
|---|---|---|---|---|---|---|---|---|
| 1965 | 50,0 | 17,3 | 15,9 | 11,1 | 1,6 | 3,6 | 0,5 | 100 (11,872) |
| 1970 | 57,6 | 16,7 | 15,5 | 7,5 | 1,0 | 1,4 | 0,3 | 100 (12,954) |
| 1975 | 56,7 | 18,8 | 13,7 | 6,6 | 1,1 | 2,3 | 0,8 | 100 (14,797) |

Sources: *Fiselier* 1977, p.36; Criminele statistiek 1973, p.25; 1975, p.25.

## 7. Evaluation and Developmental Tendencies

The Dutch corrections system has occupied a superior position within the international reform movement for some time. No other correctional system can compete with it in regards to personnel, investment, institutional construction, intensity of treatment efforts, and low prison population. The average prison term in the Netherlands is only 1.5 months (CrimJAbstr. 1981, p.243; cf. also Table 9). Even the Scandinavian countries and Switzerland have almost twice as many prisoners, compared to total population as the Netherlands. For this reason, one refers to a ''Dutch model'' which extends back to the end of the sixteenth century, and to its predecessor, the Amsterdam penitentiary.

These short prison sentences, however, are a source of disturbance, since they cause constant changes in the prison population, with corresponding unrest among longer-term prisoners and prison staff. In addition, considerable radical changes in the types of crime generally committed, which have occurred over the last 15 years, have not been insignificant in the Netherlands. The Dutch crime level has reached the level existing in West Germany, England and France. This increase has resulted in altered decision and sentencing patterns in the criminal courts and correctional system. Renewed increases in the prison population reflect the extent and intensity of the problem (cf. Chart 3). Collective clemencies and waiting lists for prisoners offer only temporary solutions. The absence of statistical data for the last three years indicates that the Dutch model has had setbacks in its future-oriented reform policy. The recent conspicuous restraint in the Dutch literature and in official government statements on correctional developments also indicate possible problems. Even if one does not overvalue the importance of a legal foundation for prisoners' rights and judicial review thereof, one still cannot determine to what extent the prisoner's need for legal protection is satisfied in the Netherlands. On the other hand, the formation of advisory boards in every penal institution, the extent of prisoner assistance through trained correctional personnel, and the lack of scandals and revolts in Dutch prisons all attest to the fact that the Dutch correctional system has remained free of the eruptions and extraordinary disturbances common in the other major European countries. Another factor of significance is the low number of female prisoners in the Netherlands.

**Chart 3:** Development of Prison Population in the Netherlands 1960–1977 (1960 = 100)

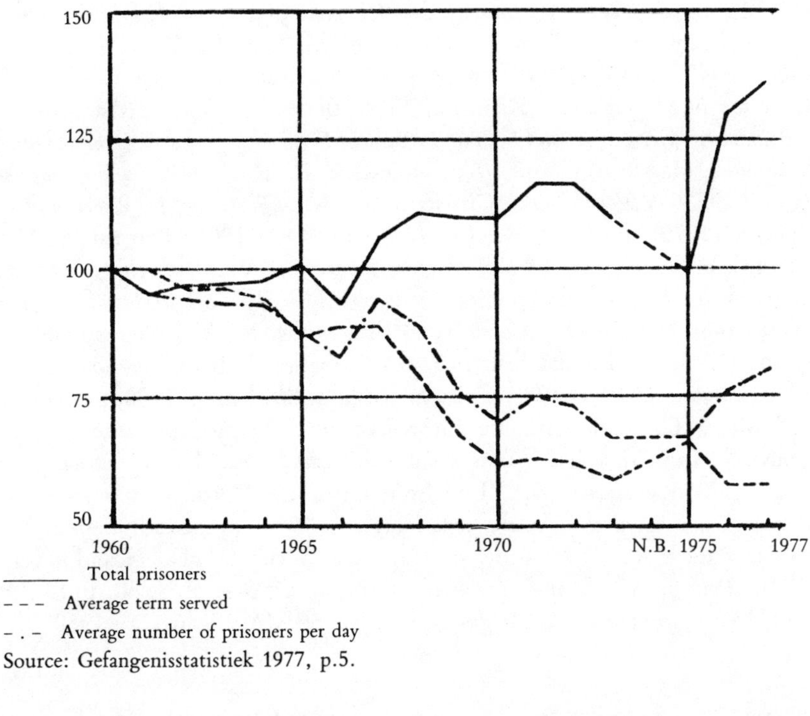


Source: Gefangenisstatistiek 1977, p.5.

# VII. Scandinavia

**Citations:** Simson, G.: *Das nordische Strafvollstreckungsgesetz in Schweden.* ZStW 77(1965), pp.167–187; Sveri, K.: *Die Behandlung der gefährlichen Gewohnheitsverbrecher in den nordischen Ländern.* ZStW 80(1968), pp.176–188; Hilbers, M., Lange, W.: *Abkehr von der Behandlungsideologie. Erfahrungen mit modernen Vollzugsformen in Skandinavien.* KrimJ 1973, pp.52–62; v.Hofer, H.: *Behandlung und Strafe.* ZRP 1974, pp.81–84; Brodersen, K.: *Die neue Strafvollzugsdiskussion in Skandinavien.* KrimsozBibl 9/10(1976), pp.20–33; Sansone, J. (Ed.): *Sentencing Corrections and Special Treatment Services in Sweden, Denmark and the Netherlands.* Hartford, Conn. 1976; Doleschal, E.: *Rate and Length of Imprisonment.* C&D 1977, pp.51–56; Christie, N.: *Neo-Classicism in Penal Policy.* NTfKrim 67(1979), pp.5–20; id.: *Limits to Pain.* Oslo 1981; Thornstedt, H.: "Die Strafrechtsreform der skandinavischen Staaten im Vergleich mit der Strafrechtsreform in der Bundesrepublik Deutschland." In: *Strafrechtsreform und Rechtsvergleichung,* ed.by H. Lüttger. Berlin, New York 1979, pp.66–85; Bondeson, U.: "Conditional Sentence and Probation." In: *Crime and Crime Control in Scandinavia 1976–1980,* ed.by N. Bishop. Stockholm 1980, pp.59–69; Joutsen, M.: "The Indeterminate Incarceration of Dangerous Offenders in Scandinavia." In: *Crime and Crime Control in Scandinavia,* loc.cit. Stockholm 1980, pp.70–73; Kyvsgaard, B.: "Imprisonment in the Nordic Countries." In: *Crime and Crime Control in Scandinavia,* loc.cit. 1980, pp.53–58; Lenke, L.: "Criminal Policy and Repression in Capitalist Societies—The Scandinavian Case." In: *Policing Scandinavia.* ScandStudCrim 7. Oslo et al. 1980, pp.5–30; Umbreit, M.: *Corrections—A Scandinavian Perspective.* Michigan City 1980.

## 1. Similarities in Scandinavian Correctional Forms, Punishment Execution and Criminal Policy

For the last two decades, the Scandinavian countries have been cooperating closely in the fields of criminal policy, criminal justice, and penal corrections. As a result of this cooperation, prison directors and release assistants have been meeting regularly and exchanging personnel. Criminal legislation is parallel and sometimes even identical in the various Scandinavian countries. One of the early products of this cooperation was the northern Punishment Execution Act of 1963. This law was adopted and incorporated into the individual criminal codes of Denmark, Finland, Iceland, Norway, and Sweden. With its adoption, these countries agreed to accept the judgments made in any other Scandinavian country with respect to the levying of fines, execution of prison sentences, and treatment after release (conditional sentence and release). This agreement made it possible to execute all punishments within the sentenced individual's native country (cf. on Sweden, Simson, 1965, pp.167ff.).

The Scandinavian public strongly approved of this governmental cooperation. During the 1960s, organizations were formed which assisted in reforming the correctional systems in all Scandinavian countries. Their members included social workers, psychologists, lawyers, and previous prisoners. The goal of these organizations was to provide treatment of non-incarcerated delinquents and to totally abolish prisons (Hilbers et al., 1973, p.56).

In Sweden, the Reich Association for the Humanization of Corrections (KRUM) was founded in 1966. In Denmark, the Union for Humane Criminal Policy (KRIM) was formed in 1967. In Finland, the so-called November-Movement came to life in 1967, which varied in its goals from the other neighboring organizations. For this reason, the Reich Association of Prisoners (KRIM) was formed in Finland and the Union for Criminal Law Reform (KROM) was founded in Norway in 1968. (See, Brodersen, 1976, p.20.)

The adopted goals of these organizations, as well as of many academic groups and governmental agencies, were to develop alternatives to the prison sentence and to depart from repudiated ideologically treatment attempts within criminal institutions. Alternative forms of sanctioning such as the conditional sentence, monetary fine and intensive supervision were favored (cf. Table 10), and preventive measures were to be strengthened. As a result of this altered punishment philosophy, juvenile prisons were abolished (cf. Thornstedt, 1979, p.83). On the basis of these same considerations, the prison term of unspecified length also is to be eliminated in all Scandinavian countries (cf. Joutsen, 1980, pp.72f.; Kyvsgaard, 1980, p.53; as to the problematic and previous application of these so-called internments, see Sveri, 1968, pp.178ff.).The number of prisoners in the individual Scandinavian countries can be seen in Table 11.

**Table 10:** Judicially Awarded Freedom-Depriving Criminal Sanctions, Conditional and Suspended Sentences in Scandinavia during the Period from 1968 to 1977 in Absolute Numbers and per 100,000 Population

| Year / Country | Freedom-Depriving Criminal Sanctions | | | | Conditional Verdicts and Suspended Sentences | | | |
|---|---|---|---|---|---|---|---|---|
| | 1968 | 1971 | 1974 | 1977 | 1968 | 1971 | 1974 | 1977 |
| Denmark | 5005<br>103 | 5,835<br>117 | 5,954<br>118 | 5,481<br>108 | 3,442<br>71 | 4,706<br>95 | 5,789<br>115 | 5,297<br>104 |
| Finland | 9864<br>210 | 11,363<br>246 | 14,995<br>320 | 14,041<br>296 | 4,767<br>101 | 6,992<br>151 | 10,249<br>218 | 14,379<br>303 |
| Norway | 2055<br>51 | 2,759<br>69 | 3,583<br>90 | 3,573<br>89 | 2,478<br>62 | 3,019<br>76 | 3,639<br>91 | 3,631<br>91 |
| Sweden | 8155<br>103 | 7,539<br>93 | 6,177<br>75 | 6,987<br>84 | 11,583<br>146 | 12,279<br>151 | 10,490<br>128 | 10,405<br>126 |

Source: *Bondeson,* U.: Conditional sentence and probation. In: Crime and Crime Control in Scandinavia, ed. by Scandinavian Research Council for Criminology. Stockholm 1980, p.62.

Regardless of this remarkable unity and the corresponding efforts which have been made, differences in criminal justice and corrections certainly cannot be overlooked among the Scandinavian countries. Divergencies in the level of industrialization, in the density of population, in ethnic mixtures, and in previous patterns of attitudes and decisions are particularly obvious between Denmark, Norway and Sweden on the one hand, and Finland on the other. The principles of the so-called treatment ideology were never adopted and accepted by the Finnish correctional system (Lenke, 1980, p.8), and the important humanizing effect which is based on the idea of resocialization, therefore, is lacking. It is not surprising that the number of prisoners in Finland is at least twice as high as in the remaining Scandinavian countries (cf. Lenke, 1980, pp.7f.; further Bondeson, 1980, p.62 and Kyvsgaard, 1980, p.54).

**Table 11:** Average Daily Number of Prisoners in the Scandinavian Countries (including pre-trial detainees and based on rate per 100,000 general population)

| Year / Country | 1975 | 1976 | 1977 | 1978 |
|---|---|---|---|---|
| Denmark | 67 | 58 | 54 | 58 |
| Finland | 116 | 118 | 117 | 113 |
| Norway | 47 | 45 | 44 | 43 |
| Sweden | 50 | 49 | 51 | 52 |

Source: *Kyvsgaard,* B.: Imprisonment in the Nordic Countries. In: Crime and Crime Control in Scandinavia, ed. by Scandinavian Research Council for Criminology. Stockholm 1980, p.54.

## 2. Sweden

**Citations:** Eriksson, T.: "Die Erfahrungen mit offenen Gefangenenanstalten in Schweden." In: *Erziehung zur Freiheit durch Freiheitsentzug,* ed.by M. Busch et al. Wiesbaden et al. 1969, pp.281–291; Nestius, H.: *Behandling som straff.* Verdandi-Debattenschrift. Oskarshamn 1969; Trube, G.: *Strafvollzug in Schweden.* ZfStrVo 18(1969), pp.322–334; Simson, G.: *Behandlung statt Strafe.* ZRP 1972, pp.262–267; id.: *Das schwedische Kriminalgesetzbuch, übersetzt, erläutert und eingeleitet.* Berlin 1976; id.: "Entwicklungslinien im schwedischen Kriminalrecht." In: *Festschrift für E. Dreher.* Berlin, New York 1977, pp.747–762; Ward, D.A.: "Inmates Rights and Prison Reform in Sweden and Denmark." *Journal of Criminal Law and Criminology 1972,* pp.240–255; id.: "Sweden: The Middle Way to Prison Reform." In: *Prisons: Present and Possible,* ed.by M. Wolfgang. Toronto 1979, pp.89–167; Isola, H.: *Humaner Behandlungsvollzug hinter schwedischen Gardinen.* ZfStrVo 22(1973), pp.139–151; Bishop, N.: "Aspects of European Penal Systems." In: *Progress in Penal Reform,* ed.by L. Bloom-Cooper. Oxford 1974, pp.83–100; id.: "Beware of Treatment." In: *Some Developments in Nordic Criminal Policy and Criminology.* Stockholm 1975, pp.19ff.; id.: *Developments in Criminal Law and Penal Systems 1978;* Sweden. CrimLR 1979, pp.582–584; Bondeson, U.: *Fangen i Gangsamhellet.* Malmö 1974; id.: "Conditional Sentence and Probation." In: *Crime and Crime Control in Scandinavia.* Stockholm 1980, pp.59–69; Gross, E.: *Eindrücke vom dänischen Strafvollzug—Erfahrungen einer Studienreise.* ZfStrVo 23(1974), pp.125–135; v.Hofer, H.: *Behandlung und Strafe.* ZRP 1974, pp.81–84; id.: *Die Entwicklung der Freiheitsstrafe in Schweden.* KrimJ 1975, pp.278–290; Marnell, G.: *Penal Reform: A Swedish Viewpoint.* Howard Journal 19(1974), pp.8–24; id.: "Treatment of Long-Term Prisoners: The Swedish Approach." In: *Confinement in Maximum Custody,* ed.by D.A. Ward et al. Wayzata/Minn. 1981, pp.131–146; Arndt, H.: *Der schwedische Strafvollzug im Umbruch.* ZblJugR 1975, pp.463–472; Agge, I., Thornstedt, H.: "Das schwedische Strafrecht." In: *Das ausländische Strafrecht der Gegenwart,* ed.by E. Mezger et al. Vol.5. Berlin 1976, pp.249–472; Geijer, L.: *Einige Gesichtspunkte zum Freiheitsentzug im Strafrecht.* Festschrift für Chr. Broda. Vienna 1976, pp.49–63; id.: *Strafvollzug in Schweden. Schriftenreihe der Polizei-Führungsakademie.* Hiltrup 1977, pp.81–91; Sansone, J.M. (Ed.): *Sentencing, Corrections, and Special Treatment Services in Sweden, Denmark, and the Netherlands.* Hartford, Conn. 1976; Snortum, J.: *Sweden's "Special" Prisons. Correctional Trends and Cultural Traditions.* Criminal Justice and Behavior 3(1976), pp.151–168; Soblik, K.: *Vergleich eines schwedischen Vorschlags zum Gesetz über den Anstaltsvollzug mit dem deutschen Entwurf eines Strafvollzugsgesetzes unter besonderer Berücksichtigung des schwedischen Strafvollzugs.* Jur.Diss. Göttingen 1976; Siegel, H.: *Criminal Justice—Swedish-Style: A Humane Search for Answers.* Offender Rehabilitation 1(1977), pp.291–298; Brenzikofer, P.: *Gedanken zum Besuch schwedischer Strafanstalten.* StrVoSchw 101(1978), pp.12–26; Jescheck, H.-H.: *Der Einfluss der neueren schwedischen Kriminalpolitik auf die deutsche Strafrechtsreform.* ZStW 90(1978), pp.777–803; The Swedish National Council for Crime Prevention: *A New Penal System. Ideas and Prospects.* Stockholm 1978; Ysander, U.: *Neue Trends der schwedischen Kriminalpolitik.* BewHi 1978, pp.324–333; ECCP: *Report on the Standard Minimum Rules for the Treatment of Prisoners.* Strasbourg 1980; Kühlhorn, E.: *Crime and Measures against Crime in Sweden.* Stockholm 1980; Nelson, A.: *Crime and Responses to Crime.* Stockholm 1980; id.: *Imprisonment and the Criminal Justice System in Sweden.* Information Bulletin of the National Swedish Council for Crime Prevention No.2(1981), pp.1–16; Christie, N.: *Limits to Pain.* Oslo 1981; Cornils, K.: *Die Freiheitsstrafe und ihre Surrogate im schwedischen Recht.* JR 1981, pp.309–315; Sveri, K.: *Recent Changes in Correctional Policies and Practices in Sweden.* UNAFEI-Resource Material Series 19(1981), 97–109.

## *2.1 Legal Foundation for Penal Corrections*

Corrections are governed by the Criminal Justice in Penal Institutions Act of April 19, 1974 (No. 203) and by the publication of April 26, 1974 on the execution of this law: 203 on Criminal Justice in Institutions (No. 248). (See Simson, 1977, pp.757f.)

The legal foundation for freedom-depriving criminal sanctions is contained in the Swedish Penal Code (Brottbalken) of January 1, 1965. (See Agge et al., 1976; Simson, 1976.) The principally applied sanction is the prison sentence (ch.26 §1 Brottsbalken). Internment (ch.30 §§1–8 Brottsbalken), which corresponds to the German security custody, has declined significantly in frequency. Juvenile prisons (ch.26 §1) and protective supervision (ch.26 §3), to the extent that they involved a deprivation of freedom, were abolished at the end of 1979 (cf. Nelson, 1980, p.36). Prison terms must be imposed for at least one month to ten years or for life. Efforts are being made to reduce the minimum penalty to fourteen days (Nelson, 1980, p.34).

Internment is a relatively unspecified period of confinement, which is intended to protect society from particularly dangerous criminals but not to exclude the prisoner's possible social reentry (see Agge, 1976, p.294; Simson, 1976, p.70). As can be seen from the Swedish corrections statistics, the yearly number of internments has dropped by two-thirds since the middle of the 1960s. The 224 cases in 1979 approximately correspond to the number of individuals in security custody in West Germany. A 1979 proposed legislative draft to abolish internment, which was developed by the Justice Department, indicated that the two original motives, viz., the possibility of long-term intensive treatment and the protection of society, no longer could justify maintaining this type of confinement. Treatment efforts have been discontinued because of their ineffectiveness, and protection of society can only be effectuated for a limited period of time (Cornils, 1981, p.313). This proposal, however, leaves the "treatment" of interned prisoners unclear, since the main purpose of internment was the protection of society.

## *2.2 Correctional Goals and Responsibilities*

The Swedish Criminal Justice in Penal Institutions Act of April 19, 1974, specifies the goal of corrections in §§4f.:

> "Treatment within the institution should be organized to further the prisoner's reentry into society and to counteract the damaging effects of freedom deprivation. To the extent possible without endangering society, treatment should be guided by the idea of preparing the prisoner through directed measures for the situations existing outside the institution. Efforts toward preparing the prisoner for his release or conditional release should be made well in advance."

Furthermore, in §9 of this law it is provided:

> "The prisoner should be treated with respect for his human dignity. His treatment also should take the difficulties inherent to institutional confinement into account."

Although the 1974 legislation replaced the previous 1964 legislation, the changes made in formulation and accentuation have resulted in hardly any functional differences in penal corrections. The prisoner's social reentry possibilities and the preparations to be made for his release, however, have been emphasized more clearly than they were previously. The Swedish rule essentially corresponds to the purpose of corrections in West Germany and the principles expressed in §§2f. of the West German StVollzG. Agge and Thornstedt (1976, p.263) also characterize Swedish corrections "by its considerable amount of individualization of treatment and differentiation among prison inmates as well as by the levelled transition to assistance outside the institution and to post-release aid after the actual sentence has been served." Whether Simson (1972, 267) is correct in his assertion that blameworthiness is the criterion for applying general prevention in West Germany and humanity in the Scandinavian countries seems doubtful, especially in light of the difficulties in quantifying humanity and blameworthiness. It is true that the concepts of humanity and blameworthiness arise from different criminal law theories and criminal policy movements and apparently are associated with different effects on the formation of a correctional system.

## *2.3 Prisoners' Legal Rights and Judicial Review of Correctional Measures*

The law and practice of penal corrections and the protection of prisoners' legal rights have corresponded totally to the United Nations Minimum Rules for the Treatment of Prisoners for some time in Sweden. This assumption also was confirmed in the recent report of the ECCP (1980, pp.37–74). Swedish efforts to intensify the prisoner's contact with the outside world and to grant the prisoner vacation leaves as often as possible even exceed the requirements contained in the Minimum Rules. In addition, it has been recommended recently that the strict division of prisoners and prison staff according to sex be relaxed (ECCP, 1980, pp.93ff.).

Although the Criminal Justice Act of 1974 does not specify that the prisoner has a right to a private cell at night, the ECCP report (1980, p.42) indicates that this minimum standard is met in Sweden. Other requirements regarding the prisoner's accommodation, his right to own property, to engage in written correspondence, and to receive information and have contact with the external world all are satisfied in Sweden (cf. §§13, 17, 24ff. of the Law of 1974). Disciplinary violations have increased in Sweden, which probably relates to the general opening of the correctional system (cf. Kriminalvården, 1979, p.41).

The procedure for making a complaint is covered thoroughly in §§55–61 of the Criminal Justice Act. Particular emphasis is placed upon the prisoner's right to protest denials of vacation leave and of special stays outside the institution. Swedish law, however, does not recognize the prisoner's right to make a judicial challenge of court administrative files. The complaining party may call for judicial control through the administrative courts only on direction of the National Administration for Corrections and Release Assistance (Marnell, 1981, p.135).

No information is available, however, on the frequency and importance of this type of judicial decision. Any further provision of legal remedies for violations of prisoners' legal rights, however, does not appear to be under consideration. The prisoner, therefore, essentially can file complaints within the corrections and release assistance administration, which in turn is responsible to the Justice Department. The supervisory committees are each headed by one judge (Kriminalvården, 1978, p.8). Sweden also has the "Justice Ombudsman", who is responsible for questions pertaining to penal corrections. In 1979/80, he processed 760 prisoner complaints (Ward, 1979, p.111; Nelson, 1980, p.19).

## *2.4 System and Organization of Penal Corrections*

The Swedish correctional reform of 1974 led to a reorganization of the correctional system. The previous division of penal institutions into eight different regions was abandoned and replaced by the distinction between local and federal penal facilities (§3 Criminal Justice Act of 1974; further Ysander, 1978, p.356; Nelson, 1980, p.58). The local facilities (54 in 1980) have an average capacity of 20 to 60 prisoners each (cf. Kriminalvården, 1980, pp.66f. with Table 6). In 1980, 90 percent of all individuals sentenced to a prison term were admitted to local institutions (Kriminalvården, 1980, p.8), and only 10 percent were assigned to the 20 available federal prisons. Local prisons are given preference so that the prisoner may serve his term close to his family and previous place of employment (Ysander, 1978, p.326). For this reason, §6 of the Criminal Justice Act provides that only sentences of 12 months or more are to be served in federal prisons. Even in these cases, however, the prisoner is to be relocated to a local prison at the end of his term, in preparation for his release and social reentry.

In 1974, Sweden was divided into thirteen regions, in order to facilitate unity and coordination between the stationary and supervised released correctional systems. Within each of these regions, the organization of correctional institutions (Kriminalvård-anstalterna) and release assistance facilities (frivarden) are united (Jescheck, 1978, p.785; Nelson, 1980, p.16). This union is intended to assist in making release preparations and furthering the prisoner's social reentry at the earliest feasible date.

Swedish law emphasizes the difference between open and closed corrections more exactly than the laws of other nations. Section 3 (2) of the Criminal Justice Act of 1974 provides that every institution or division of a local or federal institution be exactly specified as an open or closed facility, and §7 defines the prerequisites which determine whether a prisoner is to be assigned to one or the other of these correctional facilities. Accordingly, a prisoner is assigned to an open facility when his assignment to any other facility is not necessary because of the danger of his escape or for other security reasons, because of more suitable employment possibilities, or because the application of advanced training or treatment measures is indicated. Contrarily, confinement in a closed institution essentially should occur only when the prison term exceeds two years and no better correctional assignment is possible. This clear statutory preference for open correctional institutions, which extends beyond the comparative German legislation, has resulted in an expansion of these facilities and an increase in the personnel employed therein (cf. Geijer, 1977, p.85). Open institutions, in fact, were introduced in 1945 through the criminal law reform of that time. (Ward, 1972, p.240; Eriksson, 1969, pp.281ff. offers a description of open corrections in the 1960s.) Of the 4,564 prisoners incarcerated in 1980, approximately 1,600, or 35 percent, were in open facilities (Kriminalvården, 1980, pp.21, 69, 79, 81).

## *2.5 Employment and Advanced Training*

According to Swedish correctional law, the prisoner should be offered appropriate employment which also is suitable for the period after his release. Every prisoner requiring further education or vocational training should be provided therewith during the time of his prison employment (§10 of the Act of 1974). To the extent possible, several prisoners should work at a common place of employment (§17 (1)). Prisoners are to receive wages even when they are participating in advanced training courses. These wages, however, are not full employment compensation, but rather a reward for work performed. In 1975, Swedish prisoners were receiving two Kronen per hour (Arndt, 1975, p.465). In 1978, approximately 1,700 prisoners were employed outside the institution (Nelson, 1980, p.59).

## *2.6 Treatment, Conditional Release and Social Reintegration*

Although the type and form of treatment measures applied in Sweden hardly have changed over the past decade, they have gained new relevance. They are intended primarily to minimize the damaging effects of freedom-deprivation and to prepare the prisoner for his release and reentry into society. The mere assignment of a prisoner to a local institution greatly facilitates intensive contact with the outside world, particularly with his family, his employer, and available training facilities. Furthermore, these measures are intended to provide the prisoner with the opportunity of participating in pastime activities outside the institution. The prisoner also has the right to use the social facilities provided by the federal government.

Paragraph 11 of the Act of 1974 permits prisoners to leave the penal institution during normal working hours for purposes of employment, advanced training or other necessary activities. In 1979, 16 percent of all prisoners were taking advantage of such possibilities. In 80 percent of these cases, the prisoner's absence from the institution presented no problems.

Paragraph 14 (2) contains the prerequisites for temporary leave from the institution when the prisoner wants to participate in pastime activities. Sections 32–34 contain provisions for short vacations, leave in preparation for release and long-term leave to facilitate social reentry. In 1979, more than 45,000 leaves were granted. In five percent of these cases, vacation leaves were misused, but only rarely did this misuse result in renewed crime commission. Residence outside the institution under the provisions of §34 was granted in 460 cases in 1979. In the majority of these cases, however, this leave was granted to alcoholics or drug addicts for their special treatment in another correctional institution. These leaves were granted for two months to one year, and no misuse was reported in two-thirds of these cases.

Conditional release, which usually is granted after at least two-thirds of the sentence has been served and after a minimum of three months, also is directed toward the stated goals of corrections. Young prisoners and prisoners with long sentences can be released after one-half of their sentence has been served (Nelson, 1980, p.34). Conditional release is granted in 90 percent of all cases (Gross, 1974, p.128). Normally, this type of release is connected with a one-year parole period and placement under a parole officer (Nelson, 1980, p.75).

The Swedish correctional system also is plagued by prisoners' narcotic consumption. Drug use is so common that a drug-free institution scarcely exists today (Ysander, 1978, p.329). Twenty-nine percent of all inmates either use drugs or are addicted to narcotics (Kriminalvården, 1979, p.38; Nelson, 1980, p.60). Although treatment efforts have been made, they have not had any measurable success. The Swedish correctional system also has facilities for mentally ill and abnormal convicts (see Sansone, 1976, pp. 75ff., 99ff.), although these facilities play a rather insignificant role.

Of particular importance is the fact that in 1979, the 4,407 prisoners were cared for, supervised and under the administration of 4,315 prison staff members (Kriminalvården, 1979, pp.47, 70). Over 9,000 voluntary assistants were available for post-release assistance (cf. Kriminalvården, 1980, p.10), each of whom was assigned to rarely more than one or two cases.

## *2.7 Evaluation and Developmental Tendencies*

The rate of recidivism in Sweden, as in other countries, depends upon whether one considers first offenders or previous recidivists. Even in Sweden, prisoners who have served several prison terms are relatively often recidivists, at a rate of 44 to 73 percent (Kriminalvården, 1979, pp.10f.). The intensity of post-release assistance through the high number of release assistants and their concentrated supervision apparently has not reduced the rate of recidivism. This combined confinement and supervision system, however, has resulted in the fact that the majority of prisoners serve terms of less than four months. The correctional system also could be opened and relaxed to an extent possible only in Scandinavia up until now. The organizational union of prisons and release assistance has proved advantageous in the realization of this program, and the high number of available voluntary release assistants is unheard of in the rest of the world. New variations and alternatives to the prison term also are being considered (The National Swedish Council, 1978, pp.61ff.), such as weekend confinement, night imprisonment, and alternative sentences requiring the prisoner to provide social services or to engage in particular free-time activities (cf. also Cornils, 1981, p.315).

In light of the recent extreme denial of the improvement goal, the question remains open of how to define the basic criminal law or sanctioning philosophy in Sweden. Retribution is certainly not a feasible consideration, and general prevention hardly seems applicable. (See critically Christie, 1981, pp.27ff.; Siegel, 1977, pp.292, 297f., speaks of "humanism . . . directed toward rehabilitation rather than punishment," although in light of the high rate of recidivism, success seems unattained under this theory.) The most plausible explanation of this philosophy seems to lie in the goal of special prevention through individual deterrence. In light of the wide range of correctional relaxations available, however, this explanation also appears to be insufficient. The relevant Swedish literature remains silent on this question. In practice, i.e. in correctional reality, little has changed and any need for change seems to be lacking.

## 3. Denmark

**Citations:** Lauesen, B.: *Spezialprävention als Hauptzweck im dänischen Strafvollzug.* ZfStrVo 22(1973), pp.158–161; Gross, E.: *Eindrücke vom dänischen Strafvollzug—Erfahrungen einer Studienreise.* ZfStrVo 23(1974), pp.125–135; Lønberg, A.: *The Penal System of Denmark.* Copenhagen 1975; Brodersen, K.: *Die neuere Strafvollzugsdiskussion in Skandinavien.* KrimsozBibl 1976, pp.20–33; id.: *Neue Ansätze zum Verhältnis "Kriminalfürsorge—Sozialfürsorge in Dänemark".* KrimsozBibl 4(1977), pp.5–14; Brydensholt, H.: *Crime Policy in Denmark. How we Managed to Reduce the Prison Population.* C&D 26(1980), pp.35–41; Rotthaus, K.P.: *Das dänische Staatsgefängnis in Ringe—ein Gegenmodell zur Sozialtherapeutischen Anstalt?* ZfStrVo sp.iss. 29(1980), pp.99–102; Umbreit, M.: *Danish Views of Prisoners and Community Alternatives.* FedProb 44/2(1980), pp.24–28; Andersen, E.: "Ringe: A New Maximum-Security Prison for Young Men and Women in Denmark." In: *Confinement in Maximum Custody,* ed.by D.A. Ward et al. Lexington, Mass. 1981, pp.159–173; Quack, J.: *Strafvollzug in Dänemark.* Blätter für Strafvollzugskunde 5/2(1981), pp.1–6; /3, pp.5f.

## *3.1 Legal Foundation for Penal Corrections*

The statutory basis for corrections in Denmark is contained in §§31ff. of the Danish Criminal Code in the revised version of July 1, 1973. Publication Nr. 423 of June 21, 1973 on the execution of prison terms contains the individual regulations on the correctional system.

The reform of 1973 abolished criminal sanctions of unspecified length and other special forms of sanctioning, such as juvenile prisons, work houses, security custody, and special treatment of the mentally ill and alcoholics (Lønberg, 1975, p.16; Brydensholt, 1980, p.38). Since this reform, the only freedom-depriving measures still being applied are the light penalty of confinement (haeft), imprisonment (faengsel), and a special form of security custody (forvaring).

Individuals sentenced for seven days to six months are placed in confinement. These sentences usually are imposed for drunken driving, insignificant forceful acts, and other minor criminal offenses (Lønberg, 1975, p.19). Confinees have more rights than individuals sentenced to prison, e.g. the right to wear non-prison clothing or to receive visitors more frequently. Confinement is usually executed in open facilities in local institutions so that the confinee can maintain his contact with the outside world and can take advantage of employment opportunities close to his previous residence. Two days of imprisonment can be equated with three days of confinement (Lønberg, 1975, p.20).

Imprisonment is awarded for life or for a determined period not exceeding 16 years (Lønberg, 1975, p.21). Prison terms are generally served in state prisons, which are either closed or semi-open facilities. Only short prison terms, i.e. 30 days to four months, can be served in local institutions (Lønberg, 1975, p.21).

Security custody in its original form has not existed since 1973. Although previously this type of punishment was reserved for criminals who required special treatment because of mental abnormality, today it is limited to individuals who have been sentenced for the commission of particular crimes, viz., murder, robbery, arson, rape and other serious sexual offenses. In addition, the perpetrator must present such a high risk of danger to general security that this risk cannot be excluded by imprisonment alone. The necessity of receiving psychiatric treatment is no longer a prerequisite for security custody (Lønberg, 1975, p.25). Accordingly, the number of security custody inmates today, viz., 14 to 19 per year, is extremely low and represents less than ten percent of the number of individuals so confined in the 1960s (cf. Danish Corrections Statistics "Beretning om faengselsvaesnet i danmark,'' 1966, p.79, 1970, p.100; Kriminalforsorgen, 1979, p.155).

### *3.2 Correctional Goals and Responsibilities*

The criminal law reform of 1973 not only affected the individual types of criminal sanctions and their application but also redefined the purpose of criminal corrections. Rehabilitation was dropped in favor of specific deterrence as a means of attaining the goal of individual prevention (cf. Lauesen, 1973, pp.158ff.; Lønberg, 1975, pp.33f.). The question of how specific deterrence is to be attained during short prison terms in semi-open or open institutions is not answered. Danish corrections up until now also have been directed toward creating conditions as close to those in the outside world as possible. This effort is reflected in the fact that the majority of prisoners are employed outside the institution and that vocational training within the institution is oriented toward practicality for the post-release period (Lønberg, 1975, p.66).

### *3.3 Prisoners' Legal Rights and Judicial Review of Correctional Measures*

The prisoner's legal rights in the Danish correctional system are determined by the above-referenced correctional goals. This orientation can be seen most clearly in the rules concerning the prisoner's private property, accommodation, freetime activities and contacts with the outside world. Potential limitations on the prisoner's freedom are avoided in an open correctional system in order to simulate conditions in the outside world as much as possible. (See Gross, 1974, pp.125ff.) In general, the prisoner is permitted to wear his own clothing, to possess countless personal possessions, to plan his own free time, to receive money, to make unlimited telephone calls, and to possess his own cell door key. These privileges are expected to give the prisoner a higher sense of responsibility and to allow him considerable personal influence on his daily routine. Although the arguments for this type of correctional system are persuasive, they are not directed toward the goal of specific deterrence.

The rules governing vacation leaves also have become more liberal, particularly through the 1973 reform (Lønberg, 1975, p.85). Hourly leaves and short vacation leaves can be granted relatively early during the prison term. In open institutions, these leaves can be granted after four weeks of the sentence have been served and in closed institutions after ten weeks. Weekend leave can be granted every third week-end. Day leave is permitted for employment or vocational training to the extent that these opportunities are not available in the institution (Brodersen, 1976, p.26). Hourly leaves, day leaves and vacations are rarely misused. In 1973, 14,728 leaves were granted, of which only eight percent were misused, and of this eight percent, only 1.2 per cent resulted in recidivism (Lønberg, 1975, p.86).

## 3.4 System and Organization of Penal Corrections

Like Sweden, Denmark has combined the organization of penal corrections with post-release assistance. The Directory of Prisons and Prison Welfare, which is the highest administrative office for this purpose, heads the two-part organization. This directory is the central office for thirteen federal prisons, fifty smaller local prisons and six criminal welfare offices.

The total prison system can accommodate 4,200 individuals. This capacity, however, is not always filled. In 1973, 1,250 places were occupied in the ten open institutions and approximately 1,650 in the local prisons (Lauesen, 1973, p.159). The remaining individuals were confined in closed state prisons or in special institutions. In 1979, an average of 2,940 individuals were incarcerated on any one day and approximately 30,000 individuals were incarcerated at some time during the entire year (Brydensholt, 1980, p.38). These prisoners were attended to by a staff of 3,000. This one-to-one personnel ratio facilitates significant individualization within the Danish prison system (Brodersen, 1976, p.25).

Capacity varies from institution to institution, although the closed facilities are usually larger than the open ones. The largest prison in Denmark is the Copenhagen State Prison, with a capacity of 700. Most of the inmates in this prison, however, are in pre-trial detention or in the prison hospital (Lønberg, 1975, p.58).

## 3.5 Employment and Advanced Training

With the exception of the Reubeats experimental institution, all Danish penal institutions require the prisoner to work. The prisoner may fulfill this requirement, however, by participating in basic and advanced vocational training courses. Vocational training is designed to be practical for the prisoner after his release (Lønberg, 1975, pp.66ff.).

## 3.6 Conditional Release and Social Reintegration

After a prisoner has served two-thirds of his sentence, the prison director is required to decide on his early release in consultation with the Department of Corrections and Release Assistance. In practice, this decision usually is made by the prison director, with the Department of Corrections and Release Assistance intervening only in particularly difficult cases or in cases of denial (Lønberg, 1975, p.42).

In exceptional cases, conditional release is also possible after at least four months and only one-half of the prison sentence has been served. A case can be considered an exception when particular personal-situation factors are present and justify early release, such as his youth, a favorable prognosis of his future, or the availability of sufficient training and employment offers (Lønberg, 1975, pp.42f.). Today, there is a tendency to grant conditional release after one-half of the sentence has been served (Brydensholt, 1980, p.40). In 1973, more than 91 percent of all prisoners were granted conditional release.

### *3.7 Evaluative Control and Developmental Tendencies*

No particular difficulties appear to exist in this essentially relaxed, open, and generously operated correctional system. Penal institutions are not overcrowded, and crimes of violence are relatively infrequent. Although no empirically verifiable correctional philosophy can be found, the goal of Danish criminal policy can be only to further reduce the prison population to the extent possible (so also Brydensholt, 1980, pp.36ff.). This approach is feasible if the remaining, relatively high, crime rate does not increase significantly and if it continues to be tolerated.

## 4. Norway

**Citations:** Hildebrandt, H.: *Strafvollzug in Norwegen.* ZfStrVo 12(1963), pp.74–86, 136–147; Mathiesen, Th.: *The Defense of the Weak. A Sociological Study of a Norwegian Correctional Institution.* London 1965; id.: *The Future of Control Systems—The Case of Norway.* International Journal of Sociology of Law (1980), pp.149–164; Hansen, U.: *Das norwegische Sanktionensystem.* Entwicklung—geltendes Recht—Reform. Jur.Diss. Freiburg 1979; Kjerschow, A.: *Legal Protection and Legal Control During the Execution of Prison Sentences.* NTfKrim 67(1979/80), pp.45–52.

### *4.1 Legal Foundation for Penal Corrections*

Corrections in Norway are governed by the Prison Law of December 12, 1958.

### *4.2 Correctional Goals and Responsibilities*

According to §14 of this law, prisoners are to be treated firmly and in such manner as to further their social adaptability. The damaging effects of freedom-deprivation should be avoided to the extent possible.

### *4.3 Evaluation and Developmental Tendencies*

In Norway, as in many European and especially Scandinavian countries, the prison term is being limited as much as possible, and the attempt is being made to replace it with more humane and less costly criminal sanctions which can be applied in an environment of freedom (Hansen, 1979, p.132). The so-called "White Paper No.104 on Criminal Policy," which was issued by the Norwegian government on May 26, 1978, further recommends that the age of criminal responsibility be raised from fourteen to fifteen years of age, that the length of pre-trial detention be reduced, that the minimum prison term be lowered from three weeks to seven days, that prison sentences for theft and all life sentences be abolished, that security custody of mentally abnormal criminals be eliminated, and that community service according to the English model be introduced. (See Mathiesen, 1980, pp.149ff., 162). Until the present, however, none of these recommendations have been undertaken and effectuated in legal policy.

## 5. Finland

**Citations:** Lahti, T.: *Criminal Sanctions in Finland: A System in Transition.* ScandStudLaw 1977, pp.121–157; id.: "Deprivation of Liberty and Loss of Civil Rights." Paper presented at the Scandinavian-Polish Workmeeting Denmark 1981, pp.203–220; Anttila, I.: "Corrections in Finland." In: *International Corrections,* ed.by R. Wicks et al. Lexington, Mass. 1979, pp.103–122; Backman, E.: "Über die Entwicklung der Kriminalpolitik und des Strafrechts der finnischen Gesellschaft." In: *Finnish Criminal Policy in Transition,* ed.by E. Backman et al. Helsinki 1979, pp.6–15; Koskinen, P.: "Über die jüngsten Reformen des finnischen Strafrechts—eine Betrachtung ihres Hintergrundes und ihrer Ziele." In: *Finnish Criminal Policy in Transition,* loc.cit.1979, pp.16–19; Lehtimaja, L.: "The Impact of Contemporary Criminal Policy on the Shaping of Penal Sentence in Finland." In: *Finnish Criminal Policy in Transition,* loc.cit. 1979, pp.20–32; Short, R.: *The Care of Long-Term Prisoners.* London 1979; Mäkinen, I.: "The Population of Closed Institutions." In: *Research Report Summaries 1979,* ed.by Research Institute of Legal Policy Helsinki 1980, pp.19–24; Christie, N.: *Limits to Pain.* Oslo 1981.

## 5.1 Legal Foundation for Penal Corrections

Corrections in Finland are governed by the Penal Corrections Act of December 19, 1889, which was published simultaneously with the Criminal Code. Several significant changes, however, have been made since that date. On January 17, 1969, the monetary fine was introduced as the single form of alternative punishment, and on July 1, 1975, the Criminal Code was changed to abolish the penitentiary. Imprisonment, therefore, is the only form of confinement in Finland (Lehtimaja, 1979, p.26). Since juvenile prisons have been abolished and security confinement of dangerous recidivists for an unspecified period of time is also to be discontinued (Anttila, 1979, p.114), the only freedom-depriving measure available as a criminal sanction is the prison term. Imprisonment is permissible as a restriction of freedom for a definite period of time and can be imposed for fourteen days to fifteen years and for life (Anttila, 1979, p.104). Life imprisonment, imposed two to three times a year, is rare in Finland. The average correctional period is only 4.5 months (Short, 1979, p.63), and in 1975 only 10 percent of all prisoners were serving a term of one year or longer (Anttila, 1979, p.104). With the exception of Austria and the socialist countries, however, Finland still has one of the highest prison rates in Europe.

## 5.2 Correctional Goals and Responsibilities

According to Anttila (1979, p.110), the responsibilities of Finnish corrections can be described as follows:

a) To simulate conditions in the outside world as much as possible within the institution;
b) to minimize the prisoner's awareness of loss of freedom;
c) to facilitate, rather than inhibit, the prisoner's reentry into society and to reduce the disadvantages of confinement.

In Finland, as in the other Scandinavian countries, these principles are derived from an abandonment of the treatment ideology (Koskinen 1979, p.16) and adoption of the basic tenet of imposing freedom-deprivation only as a last alternative (Anttila, 1979, p.107; Lehtimaja, 1979, p.25). The concept of imprisonment as an ultimate alternative has been advocated in Europe since the turn of the century but has not resulted in any universal legal policy consequences. In addition, the treatment ideology never was accepted in Finland, and its rejection, therefore, required no extensive persuasion. The prison rate in Finland, however, has remained constantly high with the exception of a few minor variations. (See Mäkinen, 1980, for complete details.)

## 5.3 *System and Organization of Penal Corrections*

The Finnish correctional system consists of forty-two institutions including three security prisons, one of which is for women; eight semi-open institutions; seven so-called classification centers; and eighteen work colonies. These work colonies usually are operated as open institutions.

Prisoners are assigned to open institutions if they are serving alternative prison sentences or prison sentences of less than two years, provided they present no danger to the general public (Anttila, 1979, p.108). In these open institutions, prisoners receive normal wages but may use only 25 percent of this money for their personal needs.

Since 1970, vacation leaves have been granted relatively often (Short, 1979, p.66). At least two months of the prisoner's term must have been served, however, before he is eligible for a vacation. Long-term inmates may be granted vacation leave every four or six months. Life-termers may receive weekend leave only after they have been confined for at least three years (Anttila, 1979, p.111; Short, 1979, p.66). In 1966, 10,768 prisoners were granted vacation leave, of which 37 percent returned to the institution without violating any correctional regulation (Anttila, 1979, p.111).

Conditional release may be granted after at least two-thirds of a prison sentence has been served, if this sentence is for longer than three months (Lehtimaja, 1979, p.27).

## 6. Summary

Although differences in the laws of sanctioning and corrections exist among Finland and the other Scandinavian countries, considerable unity prevails in the reduction and limitation of prison sentences and in the opening of the remaining correctional system. Typical similarities lie in the various attempts to reduce damages resulting from confinement, to simulate life outside the institution within the prison, to facilitate the granting of vacation leaves, and to open the correctional system. Still, humanization, liberalization and correctional relaxation do not answer the question as to which penal and correctional theories are basic to the system involved. Any concept which is totally convincing is not recognizable. Branches of the neoclassical theories certainly are not applicable. (See Christie, 1981 for a criticism hereof.) Pragmatic correctional strategies based on the principles of humanity and social welfare seem to offer the most satisfying explanation of Scandinavian policies. We cannot estimate the extent to which constitutional requirements are being met nor to which efficiency in crime control is being provided, since both of these aspects have not been awarded much attention in the relevant literature.

# VIII. Penal Corrections in Socialist Countries

## 1. East Germany

**Citations:** Szkibik, H.: *Sozialistischer Strafvollzug.* (East) Berlin 1969; Friedrich-Ebert-Stiftung (Ed.): *Kriminalität, Strafvollzug und Resozialisierung in der DDR.* Bonn-Bad Godesberg 1977; Fricke, K.: *Vervollkommnung der "sozialistischen Gesetzlichkeit"? Erneut Revision des Straf- und Strafvollzugsrechts in der DDR.* Deutschland-Archiv 1977, pp.452–457; v.Lindheim, Th.: *Das neue Strafvollzugsrecht der DDR.* ROW 23(1979), pp.12–16; German Democratic Republic: "Experience of the German Democratic Republic in the Application of Penalties with and without Imprisonment and in the Field of Reintegration of Citizens, Released from penal Institutions into Social Life." In: *To Some Aspects of Crime Prevention in the German Democratic Republic.* Articles of the Delegation of the German Democratic Republic to the Sixth United Nations Congress on the Prevention of Crime and the Treatment of Offenders. W/o.pl. 1980; Wittenbeck, S., Schröder, R.: *Die Anwendung der Geldstrafe als Haupt- und Zusatzstrafe.* NJ 34(1980), pp.15–18; Freiburg, A.: *Kriminalität in der DDR.* Opladen 1981; Finn, G., Fricke, K.: *Politischer Strafvollzug in der DDR.* Cologne 1981; Lammich, S.: *Das Strafensystem und die Strafpolitik in der DDR und in anderen sozialistischen Staaten.* ROW 25(1981), pp.141–154.

### *1.1 Legal Foundation for Penal Corrections*

On April 7, 1977, the People's Chamber passed legislation governing the execution of prison sentences (Corrections Act; GB1 I, p.109) and the prisoner's social reentry after release (Rehabilitation Act; GB1 I, p. 98). The First and Second Administrative Specifications on the Corrections Act also were adopted on April 7, 1977. The new statutory regulations went into effect on May 5, 1977. Although it is true that "the definite tendency of the new GDR-corrections laws" is toward simplicity (Fricke, 1977, p.454), significant improvements in this correctional system also were introduced, such as the distinction between first offenders and recidivists (§11 GDRCorrAct) and the provision for prisoner's employment compensation.

The new statutes replaced the old Corrections and Rehabilitation Law of January 12, 1968, which had been modified on December 19, 1974. This law was the first complete, unified regulation of East German corrections.

The new GDRCorrAct contains the principles and practical descriptions of the penal correctional system. It emphasizes training, defines the prisoner's rights and duties, indicates the special nature of juvenile confinement, and provides for the prisoner's accommodation and treatment. It regulates reprieves, interruptions, stays and releases and assigns responsibility for executing prison sentences and for public prosecutorial review thereof. It also contains specifications regarding transition and conclusion of punishment. For the first time, this new statutory code expressly determines not only the prisoner's duties, but also his rights (to the whole Friedrich-Ebert-Stiftung, 1977, pp.19ff.; v. Lindheim 1979, pp.12ff.).

### *1.2 Correctional Goals and Responsibilities*

As is true of the correctional regulations in other socialist countries, the East German corrections laws place extreme emphasis on the *training* one should receive through the penal institution during the correctional period. The prisoner's sense of duty and responsibility, his self-discipline and his active and creative cooperation in the work process'' should be furthered particularly *through "socially useful employment."* Accordingly, all prisoners capable of working must perform the work assigned them by the corrections administration.

### *1.3 Prisoners' Legal Rights and Judicial Review of Correctional Measures*

The new East German Corrections Code provides for both the prisoner's right and his duty to work and for his employment compensation. The prisoner's possibilities of having contact with the outside world were increased, although his right to receive written correspondence and packages still is regimented and limited considerably. In more relaxed correctional facilities, the prisoner may receive visitors only one hour per month and in the normal facilities only one hour every two months. Security measures may not be excessive and must bear a relationship to the purpose for their application. This requirement was given express constitutional formalization for the first time in the new code. Religious participation, which was forbidden initially and later discouraged and burdened with disadvantages for the prisoner, now is permitted expressly under the new regulations.

Judicial control of correctional measures, however, is not possible. Conditional release can be granted by the judiciary only on application of the corrections administration and public prosecutor. The prisoner, however, cannot make such an application (Lammich, 1981, p.148).

## *1.4 System and Organization of Penal Corrections*

In East Germany, the prison sentence is executed in various types and forms of penal institutions. The East German Corrections Act of 1977 reduced the number of different correctional levels from four to two: general and relaxed corrections. Relaxed corrections are applied for first offenders and for individuals convicted for negligent commission of an offense. General corrections are applied particularly for socially dangerous criminals and for recidivists. The differences in these two correctional levels lie primarily in the extent of the prisoner's permissible contact with the outside world, in his freedom of movement within the penal institution, in the type of work he may engage in, in the possible privileges he may be granted, and in the intensity of disciplinary measures which may be applied. Corrections may be carried out more or less strictly depending upon variations in these factors. General corrections may be applied in constantly closed or partially open prison facilities or in non-closed facilities for prisoners exhibiting generally good behavior. The director of penal institutions for relaxed corrections also has various corresponding possibilities which may be carried out in open or semi-open institutions (Lammich, 1981, p.148).

According to West German estimates (Freiburg, 1981, p.57), the number of prisoners in East Germany was 46,000 in 1977, which represents a ratio of 274 prisoners to 100,000 population. Recent information gives reason to assume that 55,000 prisoners are confined in East Germany today, although this figure is denied by the East German government (FAZ Nr.139, June 20, 1981). It is clear, however, that the 1972 and 1979 amnesties, resulting in the release of 25,000 and 22,000 prisoners respectively, only briefly reduced the prison population. These grants of amnesty were not based purely on policy considerations which are subject to modern legal policy principles, but also represented repeated attempts to solve the problem of prison overcrowding.

## *1.5 Evaluation and Developmental Tendencies*

Contrary to international criticism, which also is being expressed within the socialist countries, the prison sentence still has a central position both in the Criminal Code and practices of East Germany. The 1979 expansion and tightening of criminal law on political crimes also indicates that even the number of prison sentences in relation to the total number of sentences imposed probably has increased. Actually executed prison terms occur more often in East Germany than suspended sentences or fines. In 1978, twice as many prison terms were executed per 100,000 population in East Germany than in West Germany (Lammich, 1981, p.143).

Recent legal regulations in the Corrections and Rehabilitation Codes, however, are directed more strongly toward humanizing penal corrections by resocializing the prisoner. One example of this effort is the provision for conditional release, which can be granted for sentences of up to six years. It also can be granted for longer sentences, with the exception of life terms, after at least one-half of the sentence has been served. Both special and general deterrence purposes, however, are considered when conditional release is granted. This consideration usually plays an important role in the release of political delinquents and recidivists, who represent groups with which East German criminal law policy has had only limited success. Whether the United Nations Minimum Rules for the Treatment of Prisoners are followed in East Germany cannot be determined from the evasive position assumed by this country and by the other socialist countries in 1980. Empirical examinations of the actual correctional system in East Germany are either scanty or totally unavailable (cf. German Democratic Republic, 1980, pp.31ff.).

## 2. Poland

**Citations:** Buchała, K.: "Der Beitrag der Gesellschaft zum Strafvollzug in Polen." In: *Strafvollzug und Öffentlichkeit,* ed.by H. Kury. Freiburg 1980, pp.204–213; Wasik, J.: "Zur Effektivität der von polnischen Gerichten verhängten Strafen, gemessen an der Rückfälligkeit." In: *Strafvollzug und Öffentlichkeit,* loc.cit. 1980, pp.214–228; Lammich, S.: "Einführung." In: *Das polnische Strafvollstreckungsgesetzbuch vom 19. April 1969, übersetzt und mit einer Einleitung versehen von S. Lammich.* Berlin, New York 1981, pp.1–50; id.: *Strafvollzug in Polen.* ZfStrVo 30(1981), pp.94–97; Ostrihanska, Z., Szamota, B.: "Zur kriminologischen Problematik des Rückfalls." Text of the lecture given at the German-Polish Colloquy in Zaborow/Warsaw, 1–3 December 1981, pp.1–31.

### *2.1 Legal Foundation for Penal Corrections*

The Polish Penal Execution Code of April 19, 1969 (PolPExecC), regulates the execution of all punishments and penal measures awarded by the courts during a criminal procedure. According to Art.1 (1) of this code, the provisions also apply to the execution of prison terms imposed during a procedure on infractions before the "Council for Infractions" (Lammich, 1981, p.5). The execution of penal measures for juveniles, however, is not subject to the provisions of this code.

The statutes on corrections contained in the Polish Penal Execution Code are detailed further in the provisional Order on Executing Prison Terms of January 25, 1974, in the Regulation on the Classification of Sentenced Persons and in the Regulation on the Organization, Jurisdiction and Procedural Methods of the Corrections Commission of February 19, 1974, to name a few. These orders and regulations were issued by the Justice Department and are contained in the official Justice Department publications but are not published in the law gazette.

The provisional correctional order of January 25, 1974 was altered by a later regulation of the Justice Department on May 19, 1981. This alteration cancelled the existing strict form of penal execution for multi-recidivists and the requirement that prisoners in stricter correctional facilities perform heavy manual labor. This regulation also expanded upon the prisoner's possibility of engaging in written correspondence, of receiving visitors and of making purchases. It abolished head shavings and food rationings as possible disciplinary measures and created the possibility that sentences for negligence might be served in semi-open institutions (FAZ Nr.119, May 23, 1981).

## 2.2 Correctional Goals and Responsibilities

According to Art.37 PolPExecC, resocialization, in relation to the prisoner's personal attitude and behavior, is of central importance. During the execution of the prison term, the prisoner should be taught to conform his attitudes to those of the general society, to perform useful work, and to follow the legal order so that he will not become a recidivist. These goals are to be attained through resocializing the prisoner by placing him under institutional discipline and order, by requiring him to work and receive educational training, and by providing him with culturally oriented activity. Resocialization efforts also should be oriented toward making the prisoner aware of the social damage inherent in the crime he has committed and toward developing and solidifying his sense of responsibility, social discipline, community awareness, respect for others, and general correct behavior in normal day-to-day life.

## 2.3 Prisoners' Legal Rights and Judicial Review of Correctional Measures

According to Art.7 (2) PolPExecC, the limitations imposed on the prisoner's legal rights may not exceed those which are necessary for correct execution of a punishment imposed or disciplinary measure applied. Punishment is to be "executed in a humane manner in recognition of the prisoner's human dignity" (par.3). The prisoner's legal rights were specified more exactly in the provisional Corrections Order of 1974 in its altered form of May 19, 1981. One of these rights involves participation in religious activities. The prisoner may participate in religious activities "in a manner not disturbing the peace and determined order," may possess the objects necessary for participating in these activities, and may request religious counsel. Some of the prisoner's rights are dependent upon the type of correctional facility in which he is confined. He is given duties and "granted privileges which affect his freedom of movement within the institution, the percentage of wages he may actually use, his contact with persons outside the institution and his right to purchase certain items used in everyday life" (Art.40). Although the term "privileges" is used in the statutory language, these specifications actually involve reviewable legal rights (cf. Lammich, 1981, p.32). The prisoner's legal rights, as specified in the provisional order on corrections, can be summarized as follows:

a) the right to keep at least 20 percent of his wages if he is confined in general correctional facilities and to keep five to ten percent more in the relaxed correctional facilities;
b) the right to send and receive two private letters a month—in relaxed corrections more, in strict corrections less;
c) the right to receive visitors, provided they are close family relatives (also other visitors with the director's permission) once a month in the general correctional facilities for up to thirty minutes under supervision;
d) the right to make purchases twice a month in general corrections;
e) the right to participate in social activities within the penal institution;
f) the right to receive up to three food packages per year.

These rights can be restricted in general correctional facilities and liberalized in relaxed correctional facilities. They can be expanded upon for juveniles and female prisoners and relaxed to a certain extent for inmates who are sick.

According to Art.8 PolPExecC, the prisoner may file petitions and complaints against decisions which have been issued in a correctional procedure and as specified in the code. According to Art.9, the prisoner generally can engage the services of a defense attorney if he requests assistance for the correctional proceeding. Polish attorneys, however, critically have pointed out that the prisoner's realization of this legal right is problematic, particularly since the prisoner has difficulties in making contact with an attorney. The defense attorney's intervention in the levying of disciplinary measures by the prison director is not permitted. (See, Lammich, 1981, p.36) The prisoner also is left without recourse to disciplinary measures imposed by the institution director. Only the correctional court judge, in his supervisory capacity, can change or cancel the order to impose such measures (cf. Art.58 PolPExecC). The correctional court judge also can change or cancel decisions of the Correctional Commission which violate the law or the principles of correctional policy (Art.42,2).

Under Art.27, the correctional court judge and the public prosecutor are to exercise control over the legality and actual execution of the prison sentence, military arrest, pre-trial detention and confinement in a resocialization center. According to Art.28, the correctional court judge's control is to be exercised primarily over the correct execution of the punishment sentenced or disciplinary measure employed and over the application of methods and measures of resocialization during penal corrections. The public prosecutor's control, under Art.29, is to be directed toward the legality of execution of the punishment sentenced or disciplinary measure employed in recognition of the rights and duties of the individual whose freedom has been withdrawn. It is also to be directed toward correct confinement and accommodation in penal institutions, pre-trial detention centers or resocialization centers and toward the observance of safety standards in these institutions. Under these provisions the public prosecutor is more responsible for the formal observance of legal requirements regarding the correctional system, and the correctional court judge for the correct content of resocialization measures applied in the correctional system. The standards of execution, as referenced in Art.30, still have not been enacted (Lammich, 1981, p.37). The approximately 80 correctional court judges exercise their control according to guidelines and orders issued by the Justice Department. They do not enjoy judicial independence, however, in exercising their control functions (Lammich, 1981, p.38). In the Polish literature on the practical relevance of controls exercised by the correctional court judge and the public prosecutor, it has been emphasized that these controls do not fulfill their statutorily defined function and that they have lost relevance over the past few years for the correctional system (Lammich, 1981, p.38). Only internal administrative controls, therefore, appear to exist, which act more in the interest of the supervisory officials than of the prisoners.

## *2.4 System and Organization of Penal Corrections*

The Polish correctional system is divided into general, relaxed and strict correctional facilities. This differentiation is seen in all aspects of the correctional system including the actual construction of the institutions and the assignment of prisoners to one of these institutions. The level of discipline exercised and the extent of duties and privileges granted also vary according to this division. These three types of correctional facilities not only form the structure of the entire Polish correctional system but also affect the regime in each of the individual institutions, in which various types of correctional measures are carried out. After a certain period of time, the prisoner may be transferred to a more relaxed or stricter correctional facility depending on evaluations of his resocialization progress. In 1979, 42.2 percent of all prisoners were in general correctional facilities, 10.8 percent in relaxed facilities, 38.6 percent in strict facilities and 8.4 percent in extremely strict facilities (Lammich, 1981, p.95).

The effects of this system on the prisoner's resocialization, however, increasingly have been criticized in the Polish literature. Particularly attacked is the fact that the possibilities for resocialization decrease as the correctional facility becomes stricter. This decrease is seen to result from the prisoner's lack of contact with his family and the outside world and from his reduced opportunity to participate in educational programs within the institution. Criticism also has been directed toward the strictest form of corrections, which is used for recidivists, since, according to the specifications of the correctional order of 1974, the purpose therein is no longer resocialization but rather specific deterrence from renewed recidivism. This specification, however, was cancelled by the May 1981 legislative changes of this order.

Polish correctional facilities are either semi-open or closed, depending upon the degree of security required. One estimates that 60 to 70 percent of all prisoners are in closed and 30 to 40 percent in open correctional facilities. Although the construction of open facilities as so-called transition institutions has been planned since 1966 (cf. Art.39 [1] No.3), these facilities still do not exist in Poland (Lammich, 1981, p.94). According to Art.39, the following types of institutions are to be provided: work centers, regular prisons, transition institutions, and institutions for juveniles, recidivists, individuals requiring special treatment or training, and for military detention. The Justice Department also can provide for the construction of additional institutions. The specified facilities, however, are provided for the serving of prison terms only. In addition, so-called centers for resocialization or centers for social adaptation (cf. Buchała, 1980, p.211) have been established (Art. 95f. PolPExecC). Whereas negligent criminal actors, for example, are confined in open work centers, dangerous criminals or recidivists can be confined in either particularly strict correctional facilities or in resocialization centers. Assignment to these centers, as to security custody facilities, can be made only for recidivists as defined in Art.60 of the Polish Penal Code (PolPC). Repeated recidivists, in the meaning of Art.60 (2) PolPC, are assigned to these centers automatically in the criminal court verdict regarding their offense. The period of confinement is not specified, but may not exceed five years nor be less than two years (Art.65 PolPC). The correctional court may order release from a resocialization center after at least two years of confinement and on favorable prognosis of the prisoner. The director of the resocialization center may apply for this release. Three types of resocialization centers exist in Poland, viz., those with normal conditions of resocialization, those with stricter conditions and those in which necessary therapeutic or social training measures can be applied. According to statute, the primary goal of these centers is resocialization. The Polish literature, however, criticizes the fact that, in practice, security interests are dominant and these centers are more like prisons or detention centers. Between 1970 and 1978, 13,917 recidivists were assigned to resocialization centers, which roughly correspond to the West German security custody facilities. (Lammich, 1981, p.44; Also see Ostrihanska et al., 1981, pp.20ff., emphasizing the difficulty of influencing recidivists' high alcohol consumption.)

In 1980, 107,000 individuals were confined in the Polish correctional system (Lammich, 1981, p.37). These prisoners are classified according to particular criteria, such as type of crime committed, prison term received, previous sentences served, and "level of demoralization." A correctional commission, which consists of three correctional officials headed by the prison warden as chairman, makes this classification and the resulting assignment to a correctional facility. This decision, of course, is not challengeable by the prisoner. Prisoners are confined in group cells. Although the effectiveness of this solution is debatable, it is the only one possible in light of the overcrowded Polish penal institutions. Prisoners are divided according to their classification group. Prisoners from different groups are mixed only during work or training periods and only if this mixture is not contradictory to resocialization interests.

## 2.5 Employment and Advanced Training

According to Art.47, the prisoner has the duty to work, to participate in training programs, to follow institutional rules, to conform to institutional discipline, and to have a conscientious attitude toward his work. The duty to work and receive training, therefore, exists in Poland. This employment can be with or without compensation. General institutional chores and commonly useful work activities are not compensated. In 1979, almost all prisoners capable of working were employed. Eighty-five percent of those employed were receiving wages, and 15 percent were not. Almost 40 percent of all prisoners, and usually those individuals assigned to work centers, were employed outside the institution in non-prison-operated companies (Lammich, 1981, p.33).

Employment compensation is based on generally applicable wage rates. The prisoner receives only 20 to 30 percent of his wages for his own personal use, however, depending upon the type of correctional facility in which he is confined. The state receives the remaining 70 to 80 percent, of which five percent is used for general crime prevention and post-release assistance. Prisoners are covered by the State Accident Insurance but not by the Social Retirement Program. The Polish literature criticizes the fact that prison work seldom is oriented toward resocialization and that it mainly serves economic interests. Heavy manual labor required in stricter correctional facilities also is criticized as being a means of repression, and it was abolished by the May 1981 alteration of the Penal Execution Code.

In addition to the prisoner's duty to work, he also has the duty to participate in educational and vocational training programs if he does not have a grade school education or trained vocation and if he is not too old or his prison sentence so short as to make such training useless. Over the past three years, approximately 10,000 prisoners received vocational training annually, of which one-third were trained in vocational schools and two-thirds in special training courses (Lammich, 1981, pp.34f.).

## *2.6 Treatment, Aid to Released Prisoners and Conditional Release*

The principles of differentiation and classification applied throughout the entire Polish correctional system indicate that it is influenced by the concept of finely levelled correctional progression. The system of granting privileges and awarding disciplinary measures also is adapted to this concept. Any rehabilitative influence resulting from this system essentially is the result of the prisoner's employment.

Conditional release can be granted after two-thirds of the sentence has been served in normal cases, after one-half in cases involving juveniles, and after three-fourths in cases involving recidivists, if the correctional court is convinced that the prisoner has a good prognosis. In 1976, about one-half of all individuals released from penal institutions were released conditionally. Most of them were placed under the supervision of a probation officer. These post-release assistants are usually voluntary workers. In 1978, over 15,000 voluntary and 600 professional release officers existed. More than 100,000 individuals were under their supervision (Lammich, 1981, pp.96f.).

Post-release assistance is available when justified in light of the released prisoner's financial or family situation. This assistance is cancelled, however, if the released person refuses to accept employment or breaches one of his post-release duties. Post-release assistance consists primarily of supporting the former prisoner in his search for employment, in providing him vocational training, in finding him a temporary place of residence, in supplying him with medical treatment, and some financial assistance. As mentioned above, the costs of this assistance and of crime prevention measures in general are covered in part by the deduction of five percent of the prisoner's salary during his prison employment (Lammich, 1981, p.97).

## *2.7 Evaluation and Developmental Tendencies*

Although Poland has a similarly high number of prisoners and many structural similarities to the other socialist countries, the situation here is nevertheless distinctive. The Polish academics during the 1970s were able to review correctional problems much more openly than were their East German counterparts, or academics in any of the other socialist countries. For this reason, at least a small critical public developed and to some extent have influenced changes in correctional law and practices. The structural elements in the Polish correctional system, however, are still far removed from those of a Western correctional system. The prison penalty, in number imposed and manner executed, is too central in the entire correctional system in Poland and in the other socialistic countries for this structural similarity to exist. In addition, the high number of assignments to so-called resocialization centers, which are comparable to West German security custody facilities, also underlines this structural dissimilarity. The question arises as to whether the purpose and meaning of resocialization is not in fact contradicted in these centers.

## 3. Soviet Union

**Citations:** Schmidt, H.Th.: *Das neue Strafvollzugsrecht der Sowjetunion.* Jahrbuch für Ostrecht 11/2(1970), pp.7ff.; Geilke, G.: *Der sowjetische Strafvollzug der Besserungsarbeit.* WGO 13(1971), pp.169–171; Aleksejev, N.: *Die Geldstrafe im sowjetischen Strafrecht.* ZStW 86(1974), pp.614–620; Karpez, I.: *Die Strafe. Soziale, juristische und kriminologische Probleme* (translation from Russian into German). (East) Berlin 1975; Juliver, P.: *Revolutionary Law and Order: Politics and Social Change in the USSR.* New York 1976; Shtromas, A.: *Crime, Law, and Penal Practice in the USSR.* Review of Socialist Law 1977, pp.298ff.; Kovalev, M.: *Die neue Strafgesetzgebung der UdSSR vom Jahr 1977.* Osteuroparecht 25 (1979), pp.73–83; Amnesty International: *Politische Gefangene in der UdSSR. Ihre Behandlung und ihre Haftbedingungen.* Frankfurt/M. 1980; Stručkov, N.: *Kriminalpolitik und Strafvollzug.* Translation of the Russian lecture of December 2, 1980 at the First German-Soviet Penal Colloquy. Freiburg i.Br. 1980; Christie, N.: *Limits to Pain.* Oslo 1981.

## *3.1 Legal Foundation for Penal Corrections*

Since 1969, the Soviet Union has had a general correctional code, viz., "Basic Principles of Penal Corrections in the U.S.S.R. and the Union Republics." The prison penalty is called "improvement work" (Geilke, 1971, pp.169ff., including the text of the Improvement Work Law of the Russian Socialist Federate

Soviet Republics). According to Art.7 of the "Basic Principles," the punishment meted out and the correctional measures applied should serve to improve and resocialize the criminal actor (Stručkov, 1980, p.16).

The individual union republics also issued correctional statutes in 1970 and 1971. In 1979, these statutes and the "Basic Principles" were altered and expanded upon through decisions of the higher echelons of the Soviet Union government. This reform was directed essentially toward reducing the use of the prison penalty, and toward opening and generally humanizing criminal corrections (Stručkov, 1980, 14f.).

### 3.2 Correctional Goals and Responsibilities

According to the 1961 program of the Communist Party of the Soviet Union, criminal punishment should be replaced by measures directed toward social influence and rehabilitation as criminality disappears. As long as "forms of criminality exist, however, it is necessary to apply strict penal measures to individuals who commit socially dangerous crimes, who violate the rules of socialist community life and who refuse to participate in honest employment." Strict penal measures, one of which is the deprivation of freedom, therefore, are reserved programatically for more serious, socially dangerous criminals. The entire U.S.S.R. penal system, however, is devoted to *preventing crime.* Correctional goals also are oriented toward this purpose (cf. Art.20 of the "Basic Principles of Crime Legislation" and Art.1 of the "Basic Principles of Penal Corrections"). Accordingly, penal corrections have the following *purposes:*

a) Improvement and rehabilitation of the sentenced individual;
b) prevention of renewed crime commission by the sentenced person (individual prevention);
c) prevention of crime commission by other individuals (general prevention).

In addition, the correctional system "should assist in the general abolition of criminality." The prison penalty as a form of retribution or general deterrence is rejected absolutely since the *goal of improvement and rehabilitation has top priority* (Stručkov, 1981, pp.24f.). The prisoner's participation in socially useful work is supplemented by his political rehabilitation and by vocational and general educational training. Political rehabilitation includes ideological, explanatory, cultural and physical exercise measures, which are directed toward teaching the prisoner to develop an honest attitude toward work, to strive toward an exact fulfillment of the laws and to recognize the rules of socialist community work. This rehabilitation also is supposed to stimulate the prisoner's effective attitude toward socialist property, to raise his awareness and cultural standard, and to develop his useful initiatives (Art.30 of the ''Basic Principles of Penal Corrections''; hereto Stručkov, 1980, pp.19f.).

### *3.3 Prisoners' Legal Rights and Judicial Review of Correctional Measures*

Article 8 of the ''Basic Principles of Penal Corrections'' defines the legal position of individuals sentenced to prison, to exile, to residency restrictions, and to forced labor without deprivation of freedom. These determinations apply to both citizens of the Soviet Union and to foreigners and individuals who are stateless. An individual sentenced in the Soviet Union is also subject to those limitations on his rights as defined in statute, in the court's decision or in the correctional regulations (Stručkov, 1980, p.22). The criminal and penal correctional statutes emphasize ''that neither the punishment nor the execution thereof should cause physical suffering or violate the individual's human dignity.''

The prisoner's legal rights are to be secured through a system of controls among which are the following:

a) Public control over the legality of correctional measures;
b) Supervision by the public prosecutor over the observance of statutory requirements for correctional institutions;
c) Internal administrative control and review by the supervisory officials of the corrections administration over the implementation of normative documents which regulate order and the conditions for executing the prison sentence;
d) Judicial control over ''the execution of an entire series'' of legally relevant correctional measures;
e) Control through the prisoner's right to file a complaint against an action taken by the judicial administration which violates his rights;
f) Control through the prisoner's right to employ the legal assistance of an attorney (Stručkov, 1980, p.23).

The Soviets see this system of controls as sufficient to secure the prisoner's legal rights and to guarantee that ''the real prerequisites for a strict and persevering maintenance of the principles of socialist legality'' are provided. In practice, controls exercised by the public prosecutor and judicial administrative agencies probably have precedence. Individual data, not to mention empirical investigations, are not available.

### 3.4 *System and Organization of Penal Corrections*

According to the Soviets, their correctional system is organized according to general principles of differentiation which correspond to the prisoner's relevant classification characteristics. Prisoners are assigned to a particular institution depending on legally fixed criteria. This differentiation is determined essentially by the degree of social danger and criminal contagion presented by the individual prisoner. The undesirable influence on young prisoners that could result from mixing them with career criminals particularly should be avoided. The severity of the punishment imposed and the level of rehabilitative influence required also play a role in the prisoner's classification and resulting assignment.

"Negligent criminal actors with sentences of up to five years, or in exceptional cases of up to ten years, serve their prison terms in improvement work colonies, first offenders who committed less serious or serious crimes with sentences of up to three years serve their prison terms in improvement work colonies of the general correctional system; first offenders who committed more serious crimes with sentences of more than three years serve their sentences in improvement work colonies of the strict correctional system. Recidivists serve their sentences in improvement work colonies of the severe correctional system and recidivists who are particularly dangerous are confined in special correctional facilities. Particularly dangerous recidivists who have committed severe crimes can be confined in prisons" (Stručkov, 1980, pp.17f.).

In the Soviet Union, therefore, the prison penalty is served in *different types of correctional facilities* (improvement work centers and traditional prisons) in which various forms of correctional measures are applied (regimes). This differentiation affects the prisoner's freedom of movement, type of work, number of privileges and the severity of punishment execution in general. Unlike East Germany with its two types of correctional forms, the Soviet Union and the other socialist countries recognize four forms of corrections, viz., relaxed, general, strict and severe. Soviet correctional law uses the concept "regime" to designate these various correctional forms, and the Soviets believe that this differentiation most adequately can guarantee the attainment of correctional goals and discipline.

The assignment of prisoners to one particular institution is not irreversible. The special system of positive and negative sanctions within any one regime, in fact, is intended to encourage the prisoner's "improvement." This improvement also should be furthered by the three-phase division of the correctional period according to the progressive concept:

a) In the first phase, the prisoner is placed "under conditions of isolation." These conditions can be strengthened or relaxed depending on the prisoner's behavior.

b) During the second phase, the prisoner can be transferred to a colony or can be conditionally released with the requirement that he work. Conditional release is possible if the further improvement and rehabilitation of the prisoner can be carried out without isolating him from society and if general controls on his actions are adequate. Transfer to a colony is made for prisoners who are "on their way toward improving" but who need to be confined in a penal institution. Accordingly, controls on a prisoner in a colony are more intensive than on an individual conditionally released.
c) In the third phase the prisoner is conditionally released when he has "demonstrated his improvement through model behavior and a conscientious attitude toward work or training."

According to the Soviet viewpoint, this levelled system provides the possibility for individualized decisions (Stručkov, 1980, pp.21f.).

The Soviet literature provides no additional information on the structure of their correctional system and, in particular, on individual penal institutions, correctional staff, and number of prisoners. According to Western estimates the *population in Soviet correctional facilities* was between 900,000 (Shtromas, 1977, p.298) and 1.5 million (Juliver, 1976, p.106) in the period between 1972 and 1978, or 360 to 660 prisoners per 100,000 general population. (See Umbreit, FedProb 44(1980), pp.2, 24 with an estimate of 391, and Christie, 1981, p.32 with an estimate of 660.) In these estimates, the number of sentenced individuals released conditionally and performing obligatory jobs under supervision is not included. As in the other socialist countries, the U.S.S.R. granted four amnesties during the 1970s. These amnesties certainly were granted in an effort to solve the problem of overcrowding in penal institutions. (See, Lammich ROW, 1981, p.147.)

## *3.5 Employment and Advanced Training*

In the Soviet correctional system, prisoners have the duty to work. Statutory support for this duty not only is found in correctional legislation, but primarily can be deduced from the "main legal premise" that all U.S.S.R. citizens have a general constitutional duty to work. The type of work and the conditions of production in the penal institutions correspond to general requirements for employees of industrial concerns. Correctional officials are required to provide the prisoners with socially useful work and to consider the prisoner's employment capabilities and vocational training in making work assignments. Prisoners receive wages for their work, which are calculated according to the general norms of employment compensation.

### 3.6 Conditional Release

In relatively few situations, a prisoner can be released conditionally before serving his entire prison term if he is serving a sentence of more than three years, has served at least two-thirds of this sentence and has demonstrated improvement. Prisoners serving long prison terms, recidivists, murderers and other criminals who have committed particular offenses against the state cannot be conditionally released. After serving at least two-thirds of their sentence, however, they may be transferred from an ''improvement colony'' to a so-called colony settlement, in which milder correctional measures are applied in semi-open facilities. According to Art.46 of the ''Basic Principles of Penal Corrections'' other grounds for early release are: amnesty and pardon, judicial changes in the prisoner's verdict, and dismissal of the criminal procedure. Pre-term release which is granted because of the prisoner's improvement is seen to be an essential element of the Soviet correctional system (Stručkov, 1980, p.21).

### 3.7 Evaluation and Developmental Tendencies

An evaluation of the Soviet correctional system is almost impossible because of the lack of statistical data and empirical information. The high number of prisoners in the Soviet Union, as estimated in the Western literature, exceeds even that in Poland and East Germany. The extreme efforts which have been made toward providing more effective social control, toward making careful differentiations in the types of penal institutions and the classification of prisoners as well as the use of relatively long prison terms, therefore, do not seem to have resulted in significant criminal policy success. This lack of success also could be the reason for the non-publication or secrecy of empirical information on the correctional system. Although the U.N. Minimum Rules for the Treatment of Prisoners, their application, and the five-year duty to report to the General Secretary of the U.N. are hailed in the Soviet Union, information as to the actual situation in the Soviet system is scanty. Supervision of the correctional system and ''socialist legality'' is assigned to the ''higher'' government echelons. The possibility of initiating review seems rarely available. Nevertheless, revisions based on Western law, such as the granting of prison vacations for prisoners in the relaxed correctional regime or in juvenile institutions, are not unheard of (cf. Kovalev, 1979, p.77). Through judicial control the Soviets have attempted to bind judicial and correctional administration to statutory requirements, thus limiting the possibility of individual determination. Particularly the maintenance of a severe correctional regime, which recently was abolished in Poland because of such wide criticism, however, seems to indicate that deterrence is of primary importance regardless of the contrary legislative intent. Although Karpez (1975, p.22) maintains that freedom-deprivation ''must be continually reduced under the conditions of a socialist society'' this attitude is supported only minimally in the practices of the U.S.S.R. and of most of the other socialist countries.

## 4. Hungary

**Citations:** Földvári, J.: *Über die kriminalpolitischen Konzeptionen des neuen ungarischen Strafgesetzbuches.* Osteuroparecht 1980, pp.36ff.; id.: ''Criminal Law.'' In: *New Traits of the Development of State and Legal Life in Hungary,* ed.by Hungarian Lawyers Association. Szeged 1981, pp.105–127; Rácz, G.: *Probleme des Strafvollzuges mit Berücksichtigung des neuen ungarischen Strafvollzugsgesetzes.* DRiZ 1980, pp.414–420; Vigh, J.: ''Crime and its Prevention in Hungary.'' In: *Cahiers de défense sociale* 1(1982), pp.37–50.

### *4.1 Legal Foundation for Penal Corrections*

The order of the Presidential Committee No.11/1979 on the execution of punishments and penal measures became law with the adoption of the new Hungarian Penal Code on July 1, 1979 (Rácz, 1980, p.415). The new legal regulations replaced the 1960 correctional statutes. One hundred twenty-seven statutes now regulate the execution of all punishments and penal measures which are recognized in Hungarian criminal law. The new law replaced the previous inflexible and somewhat militaristic regimentation of the correctional system and adopted a milder, more pragmatic and humanistic form of penal corrections. ''The previous orientation toward custody was intentionally abolished.'' The prisoner should be seen more as an ''independent personality'' within the given statutory limitations.

Hungarian law recognizes the death penalty, life imprisonment, general prison sentences, monetary fines, and improvement and rehabilitative employment. Improvement employment in Hungary is only a freedom-limiting punishment and not, as in the U.S.S.R., a freedom-depriving penalty.

### *4.2 Correctional Goals and Responsibilities*

''In the interest of social protection, the purpose of punishment is to prevent the actor or any other person from committing criminal acts'' (§37 HngPC). The correctional regulations limit this clearly prevention-oriented goal to special prevention, which is to be accomplished primarily through the actor's rehabilitation. Accordingly, the *main goal* of correction is to prepare the prisoner for his social reentry and to discourage him from the commission of further criminal acts. Other correctional regulations provide that the prisoner be treated humanely and with respect for his sense of human dignity. These and other similar regulations insure that the atmosphere in the penal institutions is more humane and liberal than it has been in the past (Rácz, 1980, p.416). According to new law, the entire correctional system and "the common activities of its active organs are to be directed toward rehabilitating the imprisoned individual." Central emphasis is placed on the prisoner's rehabilitation and his employment, which is seen as a rehabilitative measure. Rehabilitation is correctly seen as resocialization, since it should "reform the individual's antisocial character into a responsible personality." Through correctional and rehabilitative measures the prisoner should acquire the internal conviction not to commit crimes after his release. The intention is not to produce well-behaved prisoners but rather to create good citizens who do not commit crimes. Resocialization is particularly emphasized for juveniles and prisoners serving long prison terms. The possibility of a prisoner's resocialization, however, may not be excluded for any prisoner regardless of how many times he has been a recidivist (Rácz, 1980, p.418).

## *4.3 Prisoners' Legal Rights and Judicial Review of Correctional Measures*

The prisoner loses his personal freedom through the legally recognized criminal verdict and upon his entrance into the correctional system. His other rights, however, can be limited or temporarily suspended only in accordance with statutory provision. The prisoner's rights and duties are determined according to the three different types of criminal corrections practiced in Hungary. In principle, however, any deviations within the correctional system from life within a free society should be permitted only to the extent absolutely necessary for execution of the penalty imposed.

The revised law of corrections strengthens the prisoner's legal position in that it recognizes his subjective rights rather than granting him privileges for good behavior. Its encouragement of the prisoner's contact with the outside world is one example of this new orientation. Written correspondence with one's relatives, and with other individuals when permitted by the prison director, is unlimited. The number of visitors a prisoner may receive is limited, but the prisoner may receive more visitors now than previously. Short prison vacations, which were permitted only in the most relaxed of the three types of correctional facilities, now are granted even for prisoners in the stricter correctional facilities. According to available data, these leaves are misused very infrequently in Hungary (Rácz, 1980, p.417).

Relatively broad judicial responsibility for correctional matters is seen to insure that statutory requirements are met and that the prisoner's personal rights are guaranteed. For this reason, Hungarian law also recognizes the so-called correctional judge. This type of judge is employed in a one-judge courtroom in every District Court and in the courts of every major city. The correctional judge is not seen as having "merely administrative responsibilities but rather as having a real judicial purpose in relation to the correctional system, which he exercises independently from the decisions of the other correctional agencies" (Rácz, 1980, p.416). This judge may select sanctions and determine the appropriate correctional facility for a prisoner on the basis of his individual needs even during the period of confinement. The main function of the correctional judge, however, appears to be the granting or cancelling of conditional releases. He apparently does not engage in judicial review of the so-called judicial administrative files for the correctional system. The position of the Hungarian correctional judge, however, greatly exceeds that awarded the same office under Polish law and is most similar to the comparable West German or French institutions.

## *4.4 System and Organization of Penal Corrections*

Hungarian correctional law recognizes three types of correctional institutions, which differ according to the strictness of the correctional regime practised, viz., work houses, penitentiaries and prisons. These three correctional facilities roughly correspond to the Polish or Russian strict, general and relaxed correctional institutions.

Life prison terms; all prison terms exceeding three years imposed for crimes against the state, killings, terrorism, rape or robbery; and prison terms of at least two years imposed upon multiple recidivists are served in work houses. Prison terms for other crimes are served in penitentiaries and those for infractions in prisons. Recidivists receiving prison terms for infractions, however, are also confined in the penitentiaries.

Considerable differences exist within these three types of correctional facilities, which vastly exceed what one would expect from the labels assigned them. Distinctions are made in the degree of the prisoner's isolation from the outside world, in the level of security exercised, in the amount of supervision and custody practiced, in the prisoner's freedom of movement within the institution, in the granting of privileges and the imposition of disciplinary measures, and in the prisoner's possibility of participating in pastime activities. In the work houses, the prisoner's life style is determined in every detail. He is supervised constantly and confined in a locked cell. Most prison terms, however, are executed in the penitentiaries. These confinees can move about more freely and, in some exceptional cases, can be employed outside the institution or granted short vacation leaves. These correctional relaxations are no longer the exception in the prison facilities. Here the prisoners can use their free time according to their own discretion and can move about freely within the institution. Most of these prisoners are serving terms for the negligent commission of a criminal act. In all three types of correctional institutions, however, the prisoners initially are confined in common rooms. Solitary confinement is a disciplinary measure. The danger of criminal contagion and of other disadvantages associated with common confinement are not ignored but rather are to be avoided through directed differentiation in the grouping of inmates. Past ideological objections against classifying and differentiating prisoners have been abandoned and the grouping of prisoners within one type of correctional facility now is not only possible but also recommended. Since the prison population is extremely heterogeneous, numerous homogeneous groups of prisoners are formed to facilitate the resocialization of these inmates. Differentiation also is based on considerably more factors than on the typical criteria of the prisoner's sex, age, the severity of crime he committed and the frequency with which he has committed criminal acts (recidivism). Prisoner groups can be formed according to pedagogic and criminological factors. The prisoner's personality characteristics and the degree of social danger he presents are to be considered to the extent possible under the reliable methods derived from the existing empirical research (cf. Rácz, 1980, p.418).

Very little reliable information on the exact structure of the Hungarian penal institutions, correctional staff and prisoners confined is available, as is the case in all of the socialist countries with the exception of Poland. Statistics on the prison population and its composition are completely lacking. It has been reported, however, that the number of executable prison terms has dropped by more than 30 percent since 1970, and the proportion of fines as alternatives to imprisonment presently has fallen by about 22 percent (cf. Rácz, 1980, p.416; Lammich ROW, 1981, p.143). In Hungary, with 138 prisoners per 100,000 population in 1978, fewer prison terms appear to be executed than in the other socialist countries. Accordingly, one can estimate that a prison rate of approximately 200 prisoners to 100,000 population exists today.

## *4.5 Employment and Advanced Training*

Since employment and resocialization are given central importance in the Hungarian correctional system, it is not surprising that employment during the correctional period is regarded as "a major factor in the prisoner's resocialization." Recently, the rehabilitative effect of prison work has been emphasized more than its pure economic utility. According to new correctional law, the purpose of employment is "to rehabilitate the prisoner, to accustom him to a working life style, to develop his vocational abilities and skills and thereby to prepare him for his later reintegration into society." Regular employment in mainly industrial or agricultural enterprises is seen to be essential. The prisoner is not only required to perform the jobs assigned him but also has an inherent right to work. The general norms contained in the labor legislation, including those relating to working hours, place of employment and employment compensation, also are applicable to prison work. Although it is unclear whether the prisoner receives full wages or only a small reward for his work, that which he does receive must be used to pay for the costs of his own accommodation and for the support of his family. He may use only a minimal part of this money for his own pleasure. After his release the prisoner is given any money that could be saved from his wages for his transitionary period.

All inmates under forty years of age are required to finish an eighth-grade elementary school education. Older inmates are provided with this possibility. Since a considerable proportion of the prisoners never have received any vocational training, the correctional system provides such training to assist the prisoner in preparing for employment after his release. The rate of recidivism for trained releasees is apparently lower than for non-trained releasees.

## 4.6 Assistance, Treatment and Conditional Release

An attempt is being made to permit groups of prisoners to direct their own pastime activities, but this attempt has been only partially successful. The Hungarian correctional system also is directed toward allowing a certain amount of self-administration by prisoners in the future. Discipline and regulations on disciplinary measures in the correctional system have been changed to facilitate the prisoner's resocialization before his release. The military regimentation of prison life and the strict "barrack style" of accommodations finally are being abolished. Modern law has abolished strict solitary confinement and confinement in total darkness as disciplinary measures, since their damaging side-effects were contradictory to the principle of humane treatment. General solitary confinement, however, has been maintained as a disciplinary penalty. Its length varies, depending on the type of correctional facility in which the prisoner is confined.

The *progressive system* was abolished in the Hungarian correctional system in 1950, but was partially reintroduced with the new Penal Code in 1979. Accordingly, prisoners sentenced to penitentiaries or workhouses must be transferred to so-called transitionary groups shortly before, and in preparation for their release. Similar measures are also applicable to prisoners confined in security custody facilities to prepare them for transition to a life of freedom.

After at least four-fifths of a workhouse sentence, three-fourths of a penitentiary term or two-thirds of a prison term have been served, the court can conditionally release the prisoner if he has a good social prognosis. Only certain categories of recidivists are excluded from *conditional release*. Life-termers also can be conditionally released after they have been confined at least twenty years in a correctional facility (Rácz, 1980, p.415). The prisoner who has been conditionally released may be required to receive release assistance. This assistance is mandatory for all prisoners released from security custody. The execution and supervision of release assistance are under the auspices of the judiciary.

### *4.7 Evaluation and Developmental Tendencies*

Correctional regulations in Hungary have more similarities to Western law than have the correctional laws of any of the other socialist countries. Although the application of the prison penalty has been limited considerably, it is still used twice as often in Hungary than in either Austria or West Germany. The maintenance of security custody and the exact differentiation of correctional levels in a progressive system based on prisoner classification indicate that recidivism is still an important factor in criminal policy making. Its importance is not diminished by the fact that security custody has been used only for multiple recidivists and excluded when feasible for offenders against less significant criminal statutes since 1979 (Rácz, 1980, p.420; Lammich ROW, 1981, p.152). Perhaps because of its rising rate of recidivism, Hungary strongly maintains the institution of security custody even though it is seen to be contradictory to the basic principles of socialist criminal law in all of the other socialist countries with the exception of Poland (Rácz, 1980, p.420; ROW, 1981, p.113). Although the correctional judge, who has more authority in Hungary than in Poland, occupies a position similar to the comparable judicial position in Western correctional systems, he still is unable to review prisoners' complaints of correctional violations and thereby gain influence on the correctional system and practices.

## 5. Conclusion

**Citations:** Roggemann, H.: *Langfristige Freiheitsstrafen in den sozialistischen Staaten.* Osteuroparecht 1977, pp.233–250; Nowack, M.: *Die Durchsetzung des Internationalen Paktes über bürgerliche und politische Rechte.* EuGRZ 7(1980), pp.532–544; Schultze-Willebrand, B.: *Das Strafrecht der europäischen sozialistischen Staaten. Gemeinsamkeiten und Unterschiede.* Tübingen 1980; Franke, E., Kolferts, P.: *Der gegenwärtige Stand des Strafvollzugswesens in der VR China.* Osteuroparecht 1981, pp.265ff.; Lammich, S.: *Das Strafensystem und die Strafpolitik in der DDR und den anderen sozialistischen Staaten.* ROW 25(1981), pp.141–154; id.: *Einige Probleme des Strafrechts und der Strafpraxis der sozialistischen Länder im Lichte der polnischen Reformdiskussion.* ROW 26(1982), pp.61–70.

The basic principles of socialist corrections are contained in statutes and regulations. Correctional law has been revised or modified in almost all of these countries over the past ten years and now is more oriented than before toward international standards such as the United Nations Minimum Rules for the Treatment of Prisoners.

The socialist correctional systems are oriented toward the goal of resocialization primarily through the prisoner's employment, education, training, moral influence and levelled discipline. This goal is so influential in socialist ideology that the individual prisoner, as is the case with the normal free citizen, has little possibility for self-realization. Although the execution of punishment is supposed to follow statutory law, control in fact is exercised through correctional administrative regulations and supervision and through public prosecutorial review. In cases in which the prisoner does have the right to file a complaint, his complaint has only internal administrative relevance, since judicial review thereof, with few exceptions, is not possible. Even the institution of correctional judges in Hungary and Poland has not led to judicial review of correctional measures.

Socialist correctional systems and structures are determined without exception by principles of differentiation, classification and stratification. General and relaxed correctional facilities exist in all of these countries and in most of them corrections also are differentiated into strict and more severe correctional facilities. The majority of prisoners, however, appear to be confined in general correctional facilities. Since in socialist criminal law and practice the prison penalty is still of central importance, it is not astonishing that this penalty is imposed relatively frequently and for longer periods than in Western European countries. As a result, the prison population is more than twice as high in the socialist countries as in Western nations. Repeated grants of amnesty also indicate that the socialist nations have a problem with overcrowding in prisons.

Correctional relaxations and attempts to open the correctional system are scarce and actually affect only a very small percentage of prisoners. When made, these relaxations usually are structured exactly according to the principles of the progressive system, as is the case with conditional release and the various correctional levels. Efforts toward therapeutic treatment seem almost non-existent, even in facilities such as the Polish Center for Resocialization (or social adaptation) in which one would assume them to exist. In fact, practices in this facility are far removed from any real form of resocialization treatment, perhaps because of the lack of qualified personnel.

Little is actually known, apart from some impressions and descriptions, about the number of political prisoners and their situation in socialist prisons. One can assume that general prevention is emphasized more strongly in the ordering and execution of punishment for this type of prisoner than normally is the case.

In an evaluation and assessment of socialist correctional systems, one may not point only to the repressive nature of penal correctional practices, to the aberrations in the concept of resocialization and to the high number of imprisoned individuals, but rather also must consider the efforts and undoubtable success achieved in the area of crime control. Terrorism and narcotic problems within the correctional institutions are essentially unknown in these countries. Certainly, the now greater transparency in the correctional systems of the socialist nations and the institutionalization of independent judicial control thereover should appease some of the concerns expressed in Western European countries. The allowance of individual complaints, according to the facultative protocol of the International Pact on Civil and Political Rights, which all of the East-block countries ratified (cf. Nowak, 1980, p.534), and thereby the appeal to the U.N. Committee for Human Rights and Improvement of Conditions, particularly assisted in providing transparency and possible control over socialist corrections as was possible in Western Europe after the European Human Rights Convention. Actual recognition of individual complaints should be facilitated by the fact that the East-block members of the U.N. Committee for Human Rights "participate so constructively in discussions on the process of individual complaints" (Nowak, 1980, p. 543), even though this type of instrument to enforce human rights is seen to be a violation of the state's sovereignty by these experts and by the ruling theory in these countries.

# PART THREE

## Significant Correctional Systems Outside Europe

A comparative analysis of European corrections cannot completely ignore the correctional systems in countries in other parts of the world. Particularly important in light of the wide divergent situations and tendencies are the correctional systems in Japan and the United States.

Our historical review of corrections indicated that European correctional systems have been influenced significantly by the U.S.A. Even though this influence is not as strong with respect to legal policy solutions today as it was at one time, American changes in criminal policy and penal corrections still affect discussions in Europe. This influence was most recently seen in the so-called abandonment of the treatment ideology or in the renaissance of the idea of punishment.

Japanese corrections also deserve recognition. Although the Japanese were traditionally influenced by the Europeans, they have been able to demonstrate how a highly industrialized nation can produce one of the lowest prison rates in the world. The demands of crime and the treatment of criminals apparently is handled in a completely different manner in Japan with varying degrees of success. This difference in treatment is reason to give the Japanese system its deserved recognition.

# I. Japan

**Citations:** Hirano, R.: *Kritik des Reformentwurfs zum StGB in Japan.* ZStW 85(1973, pp.503ff.; Miyazawa, K.: *Die Entwicklung des japanischen Strafrechts- und Vollzugswesens.* KrimGegfr 11(1974), pp.161–164; Saito, S.: "Die Reformrichtung des japanischen Strafvollzugsgesetzes." In: *Strafrecht und Strafrechtsreform,* ed.by K. Madlener et al. Cologne et al. 1974, pp.185–189; Bindzus, D., Ishii, A.: *Strafvollzug in Japan.* Schriftenreihe Japanisches Recht 2, Cologne 1977; Suzuki, Y.: "Corrections in Japan." In: *International Corrections,* ed.by R. Wicks et al. Lexington, Mass.1979, pp.141–161; Asakura, K., Sato, T., Sato, H., Yagi, K., Morichita, T. (Eds.): "Improvement and Welfare Law in Japan." Vol. 1 "Penal Corrections" (only Japanese: Nihon no gyosei to hogo, Gyokei-hen). Tokyo 1981; Ministry of Justice, Research and Training Institute: Summary of the White Paper on Crime 1980. Tokyo 1981, pp.37–43, 67–77; Ohtsuka, H., Hiramatsu, Y. (Eds.): "The Modern Viewpoint in Penal Corrections" (Japanese). Tokyo 1981.

## 1. Legal Foundation for Penal Corrections

The statutory basis for Japanese corrections is the Corrections Code (CorrC) of March 28, 1908. This code was adopted simultaneously with the Japanese Penal Code of 1907, which was influenced essentially by the German Penal Code of 1871. The Japanese Justice Department also issued Regulation Nr. 18 CorrC to expand upon this code. This regulation, in contrast to the almost unaltered actual code, has been modified and expanded upon often since its promulgation (reprint of the Japanese statutory material on corrections by Bindzus et al., 1977, pp.91ff.). The ideas of v.Seebach, who was the theoretical expert on corrections in Japan before the turn of the century, and his student Ogawa were incorporated into the Japanese law of corrections (Miyazawa, 1974, p.162).

Through the initiative of the Japanese penologist Akira Masaki, levelled penal corrections were introduced in Japan through Regulation No.35, which was promulgated by the Justice Department in 1933. Although this regulation has been modified frequently, it is still effective and will be anchored in its modified form in the new Corrections Code (Bindzus et al., 1977, p.32). Statutes No.142 (1949) on the rehabilitation of criminal actors, No.203 (1950) on post-release assistance and, in limited form, also No.169 (1948) on juvenile institutions and No.17 (1958) on improvement homes for prostitutes also are a part of the broader legal basis for Japanese corrections (see Bindzus et al., 1977, pp.32f.).

As historical development reveals, Japanese corrections have been strongly influenced by the legal and correctional systems of Europe and the United States. This influence is so predominant that hardly any relevant variations in legal structure can be found between the Japanese and Western correctional systems. A look at correctional practices, however, reveals that significant differences in fact do exist. For this reason it is not easy to adequately present and compare Japanese corrections with Western concepts and ideas (Suzuki, 1979, p.143). The importance of this comparison can be seen immediately from the goals set for penal corrections.

## 2. Correctional Goals and Responsibilities

Although over the past decades an interest in special prevention has made its way into Japanese criminal law, deterrence through just retribution is seen to be the unchanged goal and purpose of punishment. Contrarily, since the introduction of the levelled correctional system in 1933 the statutory goal of corrections is principally improvement and resocialization. The lacking or only partially existing unity between the purpose of punishment and the goal of penal corrections is not seen to be disturbing or contradictory, but rather is explained through the different functions and according to different levels of penal legislation, punishment allocation and penal corrections (Bindzus et al., 1977, pp.44f.). Japanese corrections, therefore, are oriented toward resocializing the prisoner to be a good and responsible citizen, as are most Western correctional systems. This goal is understood differently in different parts of the world, however, because of existing divergencies in value judgments and social structures. Western correctional systems are directed principally toward assisting the prisoner to lead an independent and responsible life in a free society. The Japanese system, on the other hand, attempts to motivate the prisoner voluntarily to integrate into the recognized and rigid hierarchically structured social order. Perhaps for this reason, Japan steadfastedly has maintained the principle of levelled corrections. This system is supposed to assist the prisoner in adapting to life in free society by increasing his feeling of regret and his desire to improve and simultaneously granting him gradually levelled correctional relaxations. Although correctional goals with regard to the prisoner's future lawful behavior are essentially the same in Japan as in Western systems, their anchoring in a totally different cultural system and the use of different treatment methods to attain these goals make comparisons between the Japanese and Western correctional systems possible only within certain limitations (Bindzus et al., 1977, p.45).

## 3. Prisoners' Legal Rights and Judicial Review of Correctional Measures

The referenced differences in correctional goals and responsibilities affect the prisoner's legal position and particularly the formulation and recognition of his rights. Typical of the Japanese mentality is that legal rights usually are not enforced through the judiciary. For this reason, the courts have been engaged infrequently in clarifying the prisoner's legal position. During the period from 1954 to 1966, only 131 administrative court procedures involved this problem. In 1975 less than 100 cases were pending on the issue of prisoners' rights. (For documentation hereof see Bindzus et al., 1977, p.46.) Common to both administrative correctional practices and judicial decisions is the assumption that a particular power relationship exists between the state and the prisoner. Accordingly, all interferences with the prisoner's rights are permissible to the extent that they are necessary to attain the correctional goal. This practice has been maintained regardless of decade-long academic criticism that this type of power relationship raises serious constitutional questions. In particular, the influential Japanese correctional scholar Akira Masaki, who was influenced by Freudenthal (cf. Miyazawa, 1974, p.162), demanded that prisoners' rights be statutorily determined even as early as the pre-war period. According to Masaki, the Corrections Code should be considered to be the prisoners' "magna charta." Present Japanese law, in its weak formulation of prisoners' rights, however, is still far removed from this demand.

Japanese prisoners are guaranteed only the constitutional rights of life and bodily integrity. These two rights logically and statutorily include the right to sufficient nourishment (Art.34), to outdoor physical exercise (Art.38), and to medical care (Art.49). In addition, the prisoner has the right of petition (Art.7). In practice, however, this right has been exercised infrequently in the past, although it is being exercised more frequently today. This right allows the prisoner to file a complaint with the Minister of Justice regarding any correctional measure, but not to demand a decision thereon. The granting of correctional relaxations, as provided in the Corrections Code, lies totally within the discretion of the correctional administration. The denial of any of these relaxations or the ordering of stricter correctional measures such as disciplinary punishment is subject to only limited, and to some extent debatable, administrative judicial control (cf. Bindzus et al., 1977, p.77, with references; further, Suzuki, 1979, pp.152f.). A prisoner nonetheless may file a complaint against the prison administration with the prison director, the Minister of Justice or the visiting correctional inspector. Judicial review, however, can be employed only for legal violations. It is not surprising, therefore, that the official yearly reports of the Japanese Justice Department almost never contain information on corrections, the treatment of prisoners, the prisoner's legal position or the complaints filed by prisoners (cf. Ministry of Justice, 1981, pp.37ff., 67ff.). The planned reform of the correctional system is intended to define the prisoner's rights and duties and essentially to expand upon his rights. Because of security interests, strong limitations presently are placed on the prisoner's possibility of having contact with the outside world. Order and security are seen to be the prerequisites for the effective implementation of resocialization programs and for the efficient administration of the correctional system (Suzuki, 1979, p.153). Prison rebellions have not occurred since the period directly following World War II.

## 4. System and Organization of Penal Corrections

In accordance with the hierarchically divided Japanese state structure, the correctional administration is centrally organized and placed under the direction of the Ministry of Justice. The Justice Minister has a permanent committee for consultation on questions concerning corrections and rehabilitation. The correctional administration has access to information provided by an academy on penal corrections. Correctional administration is divided into eight regions with individual head offices, which have the power of central decision making and control (Bindzus et al., 1977, pp.33f.).

The Corrections Code divides penal institutions according to the type of punishment or disciplinary measures to be applied within the facility. Prison terms can be imposed with and without an obligation to work. They usually are executed within the same penal institution under the same confinement conditions, but the prisoners are separated into different divisions, depending upon this obligation. In addition to the normal prisons, confinement institutions exist in which penalties of one to thirty days are served. Prisoners on pre-trial detention are confined in separate facilities. Prison facilities generally are divided according to sex and age. The organization of all prisons and pre-trial detention centers is structured identically (Bindzus et al., 1977, pp.35ff.).

**Chart 4:** Development of the Average Daily Prison Population in Japanese Correctional Institutions (1973–1979)

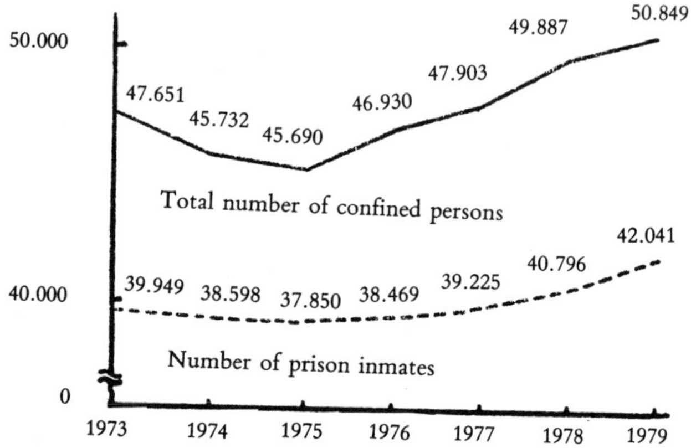


Source: *Ministry of Justice,* Research and Training Institute: Summary of the White Paper on Crime 1980. Tokyo 1981, p.38.

In 1980, the Japanese correctional system included sixty-five main prisons and confinement institutions, to which 115 sub-facilities were connected, and nine juvenile institutions (Ministry of Justice, 1981, p.37). Some of the larger institutions have capacities of 1,000 to 2,700 confinees (Bindzus et al., 1977, p.39).

Although the number of prisoners dropped between the post-World War II period and the middle of the 1970s to approximately 46,000, it since has increased to almost 51,000 (cf. Chart 4). Only three percent of these prisoners are females. One-half of all prisoners are serving terms of one year or more. Approximately 25 percent of all prisoners admitted in 1979 were connected with the organized underworld. This percentage has increased since 1975 (Ministry of Justice, 1981, pp.38ff.).

The strict organization of the Japanese correctional system, of course, also is reflected in its personnel structure. Prison staff wear uniforms with rank insignia and exhibit military-like behavior patterns. In the 1970s, 17,000 individuals were employed in the Japanese correctional system (Bindzus et al., 1977, p.42; Suzuki, 1979, p.149) resulting in a personnel-prisoner ratio of 1:3. This ratio is not better than that existing in the West German correctional system (hereagainst Bindzus et al., 1977, p.42). Social workers are not employed in the Japanese correctional facilities. Prisoner mobility from one penal facility to another is almost two-thirds less than it is in Germany. Since Japan is an island, only an extremely low number of foreigners are incarcerated here, viz., less than one percent. The vast majority of the imprisoned foreigners in Japan are members of the American military forces. The Japanese statistics, however, do not include the number of Korean minority residents who are confined in Japan. Although this minority consists of only about 0.6 percent of the Japanese population, it still accounts for over three percent of all new admissions to the correctional system and, therefore, is over-represented (Bindzus et al., 1977, p.50). One-third of all individuals who were newly admitted to the Japanese correctional system had no regular employment before their prison term began. This proportion is astonishingly high considering the general discipline and work-oriented Japanese mentality. In addition, the level of intelligence and completed education of newly admitted prisoners is far below the Japanese average.

Although the accommodation of prisoners varies according to the principles of levelled corrections, confinement usually occurs in multi-inmate cell. The cells are Spartanic in their furnishings, and food is limited to the absolute minimum required. State expenditures per prisoner are extremely low, at one-third the amount spent for the aged or for members of the military forces (Bindzus et al., 1977, pp.52ff.).

## 5. Employment and Advanced Training

Work is the central activity in the Japanese correctional system. It is seen as a means of both resocialization and punishment (here critically, see Hirano, 1973, p.508). Japanese correctional authorities steadfastly maintain the maxim of English correctional reformist John Howard: "Make men diligent and they will be honest." The prisoner is persuaded, therefore, to increase his diligence, abilities, perseverance and achievement to the extent possible. The Japanese correctional authorities have relative freedom in making work assignments. The estimated level of prison production, however, is not particularly high (Bindzus et al., 1977, pp.69f.), although it did double during the 1970s. Accordingly, prisoner productivity is given great emphasis in the official report of the Ministry of Justice (1981, p.42). The prisoner's income, however, has been sufficient to cover only one-fourth of the costs incurred from corrections, compared to the one-third coverage in West Germany, even though the average Japanese prisoner only receives the equivalent of 10 German Marks per month (Bindzus et al., 1977, pp.70f.) and no social security coverage is paid for him during and after his prison term.

The goal of increasing the prisoner's vocational ability and achievement is central in the planning of educational, vocational and even pastime activities. Vocational training courses and seminars are offered only to juveniles and first offenders. A very low percentage of the prison inmates, therefore, can take advantage of such offers. Only juvenile inmates have the opportunity of repeating unsuccessfully completed schooling. In addition, an empirical investigation conducted in one correctional facility revealed that only 60 percent of the prisoners who completed vocational training during confinement actually were employed in this vocation after their release. According to another study, only one-fifth of all prison-trained inmates use any of the vocational qualifications acquired in prison for corresponding employment after release (to the whole Bindzus et al., 1977, pp.72ff.; Ministry of Justice, 1981, pp.42f.).

## 6. Assistance, Treatment and Aid to Released Prisoners

The Japanese prisoner's daily routine is much more rigorous than that of a prisoner in the western hemisphere. In an atmosphere of generally poor living conditions he also is subjected to strict discipline and order as well as to severity and loneliness. During working hours, not only alcohol, but also cigarettes and conversation are forbidden. After working hours, all prisoners must participate in pastime activities directed toward their resocialization. Cell lights are turned off at 9:00 p.m. (Bindzus et al., 1977, pp.50ff.). Male prisoners are forced to have extremely short hair. The prisoner is not permitted to purchase extra food with his own money or with money received from his family. It is not surprising that disciplinary violations occur often in such a Spartanic setting, regardless of the obedient Japanese mentality. On an average, almost 50 percent of all prisoners have been prosecuted for disciplinary violations (Bindzus et al, 1977, p.60). The types of disciplinary violations and the procedures used for their violation, therefore, are criticized in Japan (Bindzus et al., 1977, p.62).

All measures are included under the concept "treatment," which in the broadest sense of the word could be of assistance in the prisoner's resocialization. Even cosmetic operations, such as the removal of tatoos, are included under treatment if thought to facilitate the prisoner's social reentry. Since the success or failure of the correctional system, however, is judged on its maintenance of security and order, and the main function of penal corrections still is considered to be retribution for the crime committed, psychotherapeutic treatment methods geared toward the Eastern mentality or goal-oriented treatment concepts, with the exception of the so-called "Naikan-Therapy," have not been developed (Bindzus et al., 1977, pp.75ff.). The Naikan-Therapy has been applied in Japanese correctional facilities with success in respect to rates of recidivism.

Although administrative preparations for the prisoner's release are begun at the time of his admission, full-time social workers are not employed in the Japanese prisons (Bindzus et al., 1977, p.79). The prisoner, after receiving his personal possessions and prison employment compensation, leaves the institution unprepared for freedom, regardless of these administrative release preparations. Funds available for the prisoner's transitionary period also are very low, at less than an average of 100 DM. Post-release assistance measures are limited to providing the prisoner with money for travel, food, and necessary clothing. Released prisoners are assigned to private post-release assistance organizations, which seldom provide them with housing or any form of general assistance and support during their search for employment. One must remember, however, that more than 20 percent of the prisoners belong to a Japanese underworld organization and that approximately 50 percent are recidivists. For this reason, post-release rehabilitation measures appear to be limited in their chances of success.

The decision on a prisoner's conditional or pre-term supervised release is not made by the courts but rather by special administrative agencies. Although according to statute, conditional release may be granted after one-third of the prison penalty has been served and after 10 years of a life term, in practice the regional boards are very restrictive. This restrictiveness is seen to result from the fact that the prisoner may not make a petition for his own pre-term release. Since the prison director is concerned primarily with the possible failures of pre-term releases, he is relatively conservative in applying for them (Bindzus et al., 1977, pp.80f.).

According to the newly adopted administrative rules on prisoner classification of April 1972, prisoners in each of the eight regions are placed in classification or admission centers and assigned to penal facilities according to newly formulated classification criteria (Ministry of Justice, 1981, pp.39ff.). Special treatment categories also exist according to which individual treatment plans are formulated and assignments to relaxed correctional facilities are undertaken. In practice, however, the number of prisoners who are treated in open facilities is very low, at not more than 1,000 in 1979 (Suzuki, 1979, p.150). Usually only first offenders and traffic violators are assigned to these facilities. A few penal institutions grant inmates with good diagnoses and prognoses day leaves for employment outside the institution under relaxed security circumstances (critical of the Japanese classification system, Bindzus et al., 1977, pp.64f.).

## 7. Evaluation and Developmental Tendencies

One positive aspect of the Japanese correctional system is its relatively low number of prisoners, even though this number tends to be increasing. Although Japan's general population is twice as high as West Germany's, its prison population is the same. Even the rate of recidivism, at approximately 50 percent since the middle of the 1960s, is not exceptionally high. Initial examination of the Japanese correctional system, therefore, leads Europeans to the opinion that it is successful and not burdened with many problems.

Several aspects leading to tension and difficulties in the Japanese system, however, cannot be overlooked. Numerous disciplinary penalties, i.e. over 30,000 per year, and the Japanese criticism thereof (see Bindzus et al., 1977, pp.60, 62). are indicators of these problems. One must realize, of course, that a strictly regimented correctional system is consonant with a levelled correctional regime oriented toward discipline. The question remains, however, as to how much assistance this discipline is for the prisoner's post-release phase. A further striking aspect of the Japanese correctional system is that the number of personnel is far lower than the number employed in the systems of West Germany or England and Wales, and that social workers are completely lacking. The fact that only 2 percent of all prison inmates are in open correctional facilities is also particularly relevant. Relatively little or no information is provided in the official reports of the Ministry of Justice concerning penal corrections, on the opening of correctional facilities, on the intensification of the prisoner's contact with the outside world, on the granting of vacation leaves, on the provisions for employment compensation and on the security of the Japanese prisoner's legal position. The fact that Japanese prisoners are becoming more aware of their fundamental rights and are filling an increased number of complaints in the form of petitions to the Minister of Justice (Ministry of Justice, 1981, p.70) is clear, but also merely abbreviated, information. One would expect that judicial reviews of the relevant correctional measures would result in the bringing of more complaints and the maintaining of more legal procedures in light of the severe disciplinary measures employed. The questions of prisoner employment compensation and social security also have not been solved satisfactorily. The Korean minority and gangster nuisance present problems for the judiciary and correctional system, as is revealed in the over-representation of members of these two groups in the Japanese prisons.

Regardless of legislation and verbal testimony, it remains doubtful whether resocialization actually is attempted or attainable in Japan, or whether individual deterrence is not emphasized primarily.

Steps toward reform have been taken by the Japanese Ministry of Justice for some time, and commissions have been set up to advise it on the new correctional statutes (cf. Ministry of Justice, 1981, p.67; on the development of the most recent reform phase, see, Miyazawa, 1974, pp.162ff). This reform, however, has taken place until now under exclusion of the public. The content and goal of the new Criminal Code and the revision of the Correctional Code also appear to be the subjects of intensive debate.

# II. United States of America

**Citations:** Lipton, D., Martinson, R., Wilks, J.: *The Effectiveness of Correctional Treatment: A Survey of Treatment Evaluation Studies.* New York 1975; Alpert, G. (Ed.): *Legal Rights of Prisoners.* Beverly Hills 1978; Blumstein, A. et al.: *Deterrence and Incapacitation: Estimating the Effects of Criminal Sanctions on Crime Rates.* Washington/D.C. 1978; Burns, H.: "Prison Reform: To Minimize the Damage." In: *Penology,* ed.by G. Killinger et al. St.Paul 1979, pp.203–214; Cahalan, M.: *Trends in Incarceration in the United States since 1880.* C&D 25(1979), pp.9–41; Killinger, G. et al. (Eds.): *Penology: The Evolution of Corrections in America.* 2nd ed. St.Paul 1979; Sechrest, L. et al.: *The Rehabilitation of Criminal Offenders: Problems and Prospects.* Washington/D.C. 1979; Simon, R. et al.: "Women in Prison and on Parole." In: *The Criminology of Deviant Women,* ed.by R. Simon and F. Adler. Boston 1979, pp.308–312; U.S. Dept. of Justice: Profile of Prison Inmates. Washington/D.C. 1979; id.: Profile of Jail Inmates. Washington/D.C. 1980; id.: *Prisoners in 1980.* Washington, D.C. Bulletin May 1981; Williams, V.: *Dictionary of American Penology.* Westport, London 1979; Wolfgang, M. (Ed.): *Prisons: Present and Possible.* Lexington, Mass. 1979; Carlsson, N.: *Der Strafvollzug in den Vereinigten Staaten heute: eine Bilanz.* ZfStrVo 34(1980), pp.221–227; Christianson, S., Dehaes, R.: *The Black Incarceration Rate in the United States: A Nationwide Problem.* Albany, N.Y. 1980; Clute, P.: *The Legal Aspect of Prisons and Jails.* Springfield, Ill. 1980; Dillingham, D. et al.: *Complaint Procedures in Prisons and Jails—An Examination of Recent Experience.* Rockville, Md. 1980; Moynahan, J. et al: *The American Jail. Its Development and Growth.* Chicago 1980; National Institute of Justice (Ed.): *American Prisons and Jails.* Vol. 1. Summary Findings and Policy Implications of a National Survey. Washington, D.C. 1980; Newton, A.: *The Effects of Imprisonment.* CrimJAbstr 12(1980), pp.134–151; Platt, T. et al. (Eds.): *Punishment and Penal Discipline. Essays on the Prison and the Prisoners' Movement.* Berkeley, Ca. 1980; Schwartz, M., Clear, T., Travis, L.: *Corrections. An Issues Approach.* W/o.pl. 1980; Allen, F.: *The Decline of the Rehabilitative Ideal. Penal Policy and Social Purpose.* New Haven et al. 1981; Austin, J. et al.: *Wider, Stronger, and Different Nets: The Dialectics of Criminal Justice Reform.* JResCrim 18(1981), pp. 165–196; Bronstein, A.: "Offender Rights Litigation." In: *Justice as Fairness,* ed.by D. Fogel et al. Anderson

Publ.Co. USA 1981, pp.270–291; id.: "Need for Policy Informed Strategies for Correctional Reform." In: *Special National Workshop: State Legislative Strategies for Correctional Reform.* U.S. Dept. of Justice. Washington, D.C. 1981, pp.15–20; Christianson, S.: *Our Black Prisons.* C&D 27(1981), pp.364–375; Fedo, M.: *Free Enterprise goes to Prison.* Corrections Magazine 7(1981), pp.5–13; Fogel, D. et al. (Eds.): *Justice as Fairness,* loc.cit. 1981; Reid, S.T.: *The Correctional System. An Introduction.* New York et al. 1981; Ward, D. et al.: *Confinement in Maximum Custody.* Lexington, Mass. 1981.

## 1. Legal Foundation for Penal Corrections

U.S. penal corrections are regulated by the *laws of the individual states,* which also have legislative jurisdiction in this field. The differences existing among the 52 sanctioning systems, however, make any form of unified approach to U.S. corrections almost impossible, especially when one realizes that corrections are regulated regionally in some states (Burns, 1979, p.213; Schwartz et al., 1980, p.23). The minimum on unity existing in correctional law is secured by the Constitution, federal laws, and controlling court decisions.

Another reason for possible unity lies in the fact that state law on penal corrections is usually oriented toward organizational problems. The *statutes,* sometimes contained in a separate code, *"Correction Laws,"* or included within the applicable *"Penal Codes,"* are directed toward the structure and organization of the correctional administration, the competence of individual agencies, the procedure through which parole is granted and the responsibilities of the individual penal institutions, and usually are not directed toward the actual rights of prisoners.

The Correction Law of New York, for example, contains only generally formulated minimum requirements regarding the prisoner's clothing, accommodation and treatment (§§136ff.). The type of work to be undertaken by prisoners is assigned to the jurisdiction of the state executive office through a few basic statutes on the issuance of legal orders (§§171ff.). Particular attention also is given in the state code to guaranteeing the prisoner's right to free and undisturbed religious participation (§610).

Although the relevant sections of the Penal Code of California (§§199 to 10 005) contain mostly organizational rules, they do include a counter-example of the formulation of a prisoner's rights. Expressly provided is that prisoners may be subjected only to those limitations on their rights which are unavoidable for institutional security or protection of the general public (§2600). In particular, the right to own and administer property, the right to receive printed material of any kind (to the extent not conflicting with basic institutional interests), the right to receive visitors, the right to maintain civil suits, the right to marry, etc. all are guaranteed statutorily (§2601). The permissibility of any particular disciplinary measure is basically subject to recognition of the prisoner's rights

(§2652). The minimum wage laws are even applicable to work performed during the penal term (§2700).

The secondary importance of individual state correctional law is also seen from the fact that the literature on corrections seldom gives attention to state law (cf. Alpert, 1978 and Clute, 1980). The most important national *control* over corrections exists in the *federal courts'* power to review the compatibility of individual state law with the Constitution and the few applicable federal laws (Schwartz et al., 1980, pp.23f.). These decisions usually do not concern special regulations contained in the various correction codes. They most often consider the question of whether the prisoner's claimed constitutional right is incompatible with his status as a prisoner and with the correct goals of penal corrections and, therefore, whether it properly is being limited (Alpert, 1978, p.3; Carlsson, 1980, p.224).

This practice by the courts resulted from a basic shift in legal decision-making which began in the middle of the 1960s. Until this time, prisoners' complaints were rejected on the ground that their constitutional rights were rescinded during the confinement period (Carlsson, 1980, p.224). Interferences in the jurisdiction of executive administration were to be avoided completely. (So-called hands-off-doctrine; see Alpert, 1978, p.2; Bronstein, 1981, p.274.) As a result, the penal institutions were subject to almost no external controls.

Paragraph 1983 of the Civil Rights Act of 1871 provided the courts with a starting point for this change in decision-making capacity. This section guaranteed legal review of actions taken by state employees which violated constitutional rights. In a major decision in 1974, the Supreme Court finally determined that particularly the rights secured by the First Amendment could be limited only to the extent that they interfered with a justified correctional interest. This decision followed over 1,000 cases which had been brought on this issue since 1965 (Carlsson, 1980, p.224). Initially the courts found it sufficient to consider the individual aspects of confinement when determining whether conditions were unconstitutional. In light of the considerable differences in correctional practices among the individual states, however, the principle evolved that only the totality of confinement conditions was relevant in making this determination. In particular, one must consider whether such severe interferences were balanced by other existing correctional advantages (National Institute of Justice, 1980, p.34). On the basis of this decision, practically all of the large penal institutions and over one hundred jails were declared to have unconstitutional confinement practices (Newton, 1980, pp.135,144). A national code of the minimum standards for penal corrections now also is being drafted (Bronstein, 1981, p.17).

Two more recent Supreme Court decisions, however, give reason to question whether a return to the "hands-off-doctrine" is to be expected. In *Bell v. Wolfish* (cf. National Institute of Justice, 1980, p.37), the Court determined that the lower court incorrectly had decided over interests that were under the competency of the corrections administration. In *Rhodes v. Chapman,* on June 15, 1981, it maintained essentially the following position (No.80332; Criminal Law Reporter 29(1981), pp.3061–3072):

> The grounds determinative for the lower court (exceeding total prison capacity, insufficient room in doubly occupied one-man cells, excessive length of confinement within common cells, and deviations in the periods of confinement) could not support its determinations on constitutionality. The aspects considered are considered correctly by the legislature and state corrections administration rather than by the courts. When exercising the court's control function, it should not be assumed that the individual state legislature and corrections authorities devote no attention to the Constitution or to social problems in finding the best possible effectuation of punishment goals within the confines of the criminal law.

Corrections are being affected *indirectly by* a series of more recent *federal laws,* which primarily concern the length of confinement. Since 1977, "mandatory sentencing statutes" were passed in 37 states, and "determinate sentencing laws" in 15 states (U.S. Dept. of Justice, 1981, p.1). Common to all of these laws is the fact that the punishment term determined therein cannot be shortened by parole grants. The "mandatory sentencing" laws also exclude the possibility of pre-term release and release on probation.

These laws generally are applicable only to certain types of offenders, e.g. recidivists, or offences, e.g. crimes of violence, crimes committed using a firearm, or narcotic offenses (U.S. Dept. of Justice, 1981, p.3). Only four states have completely abolished parole. These laws, however, lead to longer prison terms and to a resulting increase in the number of prisoners. When parole grants cannot be made, the possibility of shortening sentences for good behavior ("good time;" cf. Williams, 1979, p.86), which has been practiced in almost all of the United States and more recently used only as a disciplinary measure, also is limited considerably.

## 2. Correctional Goals and Responsiblities

Corrections in the United States today are hindered by a whole line of difficulties which arise from the increasing number of prisoners and the overcrowding of penal institutions at a time when available financial means are low and stronger limitations on public spending are encouraged. Increasing public and professional *uncertainty as to the goal of corrections* adds to this problem. In light of the problem of crime control, rapidly changing conceptions of correctional responsibilities have increased the disagreement on the purpose of penal corrections: punishment versus treatment. Modern empirical research has placed in doubt all of the opposing attitudes toward the purpose of penal corrections which have been experienced over the past century and has come to the conclusion that "nothing" works.

For the above reasons, one cannot give an exactly determined goal of U.S. corrections. Agreement, not to mention a unified legal definition of correctional responsibilities, hardly can be expected in the near future.

§136 of the Correction Law of New York, for example, provides that a program of individually oriented rehabilitation should be available in the interest of resocializing every prisoner. On the goal of corrections it is stated:

> "The objective of this program shall be the return of these inmates to society with a more wholesome attitude toward living, with a desire to conduct themselves as good citizens and with the skill and knowledge which will give them a reasonable chance to maintain themselves and their dependents through honest labor."

Contrarily, more modern legislation is tending toward the direction taken by §1170 1a of the Penal Code of California in its 1976 form:

> "The legislature finds and declares that the purpose of imprisonment for crime is punishment."

Seen totally, arguments of general deterrence and crime prevention, as well as the "justice model," more recently are playing a decisive role in U.S. corrections.

To many, the concept of resocialization appears to have failed (cf. Allen, 1981) in light of the further increase in the number of prisoners in 1980, the continuously increasing number of recidivists (Carlsson 1980, p.223; critically, Williams, 1979, pp.217ff.), the essentially exhausted possibility of granting paroles, and the generally poor prison climate characterized by fear, intolerance and violence. Even if one does believe in the possibility of resocializing prisoners, indeterminate sentencing, which is designed for this type of individual treatment, is lacking as an alternative. To the extent that a return to the concepts of deterrence and incapacitation is demanded, criticism is made that the average penal term is too short as a result of parole grants. This latter position is being adopted more often in public opinion, and longer punishment terms are being demanded (Bronstein, 1981, p.16).

The "justice model" (see Fogel et al., 1981), developed during the 1970s, called for prison terms of fixed duration. It was not intended to result in generally longer prison terms, but rather to eliminate crass differences in the penalties awarded different offenders for the same offence and to bring fairness to the state's reaction toward an offender. This model regards resocialization through treatment as completely impossible only if it is attempted against the prisoner's will. The prisoner must be able to decide freely, i.e. in the absence of a threat of increased punishment, whether he wants to participate in treatment programs (Williams, 1979, p.119; Carlsson, 1980, p.223). This movement toward requiring judges to award more non-prison sanctions in the form of parole grants or assignments to semi-open penal institutions through exactly defined statutes has not been adopted in the more modern U.S. legislation.

## 3. Prisoners' Legal Rights and Judicial Review of Correctional Measures

The above-referenced changes in case law have confronted penal institutions with considerable problems. According to §1983 of the Civil Rights Act of 1871, correctional officers are personally liable for their acts which disrespect a prisoner's rights. On the other hand, in light of the overwhelming number of new cases on this issue, most of these officers are not sufficiently trained and do not receive the legal advice required to know the state of the law at any one time (Carlsson, 1980, p.226). For this reason, disagreement exists regarding the *development of the prisoner's legal rights.* On the one hand, demands are made that the prisoner have increased opportunities to maintain his rights. It is argued that at least one reason why he is in prison is that he failed to understand how to use the law to his advantage. On the other hand, it is maintained that open access to the courts is one main reason for the bad atmosphere within the penal institutions.

According to a written questionnaire conducted in 1977, legislation covering prison grievance procedures exists in almost every state and the possibility of appealing to an "ombudsman" is available in approximately one-half of the states (Sourcebook, 1979, p.183). This "ombudsman," however, is similar to that of the Scandinavian model and actually recognized by the legislature in only one state. In the other states, this institution appears to be merely a special form of organization in the correctional system.

The prisoners' rights which have been recognized in major case decisions over the past 15 years can be summarized as follows (see listing by Carlsson, 1980, pp.224f. f.n. 40–53):

*Right to court access and the assistance of an attorney*

Uninhibited access to the courts occupies a special position within the totality of rights guaranteed prisoners. Since this right is absolute, unlike the other rights of prisoners, it must not be balanced against justified correctional interests. (See, Bronstein, 1981, pp.278ff.) The opening and censoring of the prisoner's written correspondence with his attorney has been forbidden, since smuggled weapons now can be controlled in a less infringing manner. The unconstitutionality of punishing a prisoner for corresponding with his attorney or with the courts still has not been determined judicially.

The prisoner's right to the assistance of an attorney presents particular problems, since most prisoners do not have the financial means necessary to hire their own legal advisor. According to a Supreme Court decision, a prisoner must have the right to receive assistance from so-called writ-writers or jailhouse lawyers at least to the extent he is not guaranteed free access to the courts for a particular grievance (Alpert, 1978, p.4). Although over 70 percent of all adult penal institutions have programs of legal assistance for their prisoners, the quality of these programs varies significantly. The practice of allowing representation by coprisoners also has proved to be dangerous (Alpert, 1978, pp.7f.). The advisor is usually paid within the structure of an internal "wage system," which includes everything from servitude to prostitution. In addition, an increased possibility exists that this advice is false and that the prisoner will be led to unfounded hopes. Proposed alternative solutions to this problem are the employment of law students, of full-time prison attorneys or the expanded use of the public defender's office (Alpert, 1978, p.8).

In October 1974, a new procedural system was introduced in the federal prisons which provided for administrative legal assistance in deciding upon complaints filed by prisoners against the conditions of confinement (Carlsson, 1980, p.226).

*Prohibition against cruel and unusual punishment*

The courts often saw extreme overcrowding, inadequate sanitary conditions, poor lighting, low-quality nourishment and insufficient medical care as violations of the constitutional prohibition of cruel and unusual punishment (8th Amendment). Racial segregation and the confinement of pre-trial detainees within the normal prisons also have been held unconstitutional.

*Rights involving individual freedom*

Judgments involving the treatment of members of various religious sects have played a leading role in the recognition of constitutional rights involving the prisoner's individual freedom. Almost all of the unorthodox groups now have the right to equal treatment. Liberalized rules on written correspondence and receiving visitors have been adopted for nearly all prisoners. Finally, it was recognized that prisoners have a right to receive information from the press when this information concerns grievances within the institution or the treatment of an individual prisoner (cf. Alpert, 1978, p.2). The prisoner's right to protection of life and health still must be decided upon by the judiciary.

**Controls over correctional and disciplinary measures**

The courts review *classification* measures only if discrimination or arbitrariness is involved. In general, controls over these decisions are limited to determining whether procedural regulations are being followed (*Clute* 1980, p.143).

*Solitary confinement* orders are judicially reviewed only to the extent that prohibitions against cruel or unusual punishment are being violated (Clute, 1980, pp.144f.).

*Disciplinary measures* also fall under the constitutional requirement of judicial review. The courts, however, do not review the circumstances leading to the application of these measures but rather only the type of measures applied (Clute, 1980, pp.109ff., 115).

**Chart 5:** Number of Federal and State Prisoners Sentenced between the End of 1925 to the Middle of 1981* (in thousands)

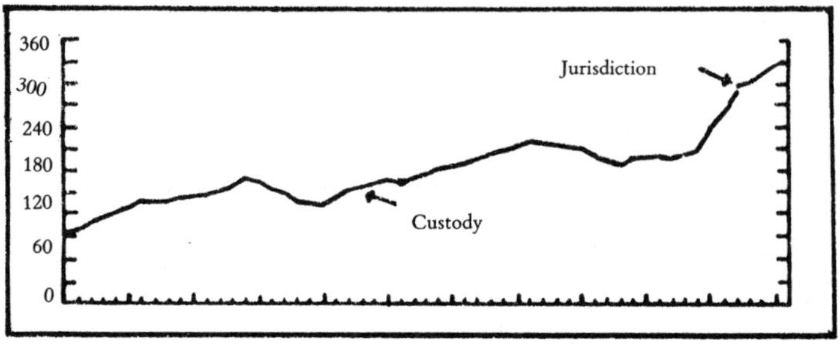


*Before 1979 according to custody, after 1978 according to jurisdiction

Source: U.S. Dept. of Justice: Bureau of Justice Statistics Bulletin, September 1981, p.1.

Of particular relevance for U.S. corrections are the continually increasing number of judgments condemning *overcrowding in penal institutions.* Twenty-eight states have been directed by the courts to correct this situation. According to a representative study conducted in 1978, 43 percent of all prisoners are confined in overcrowded facilities (U.S. Dept. of Justice, 1981, p.1). Relevant legal decisions have defined the minimum standards more exactly regarding room size for double cells, official maximum institutional capacity and floor space required per bed. A national review of these judgments, however, reveals that they vary considerably (National Institute of Justice, 1980, p.34). The above-referenced decision in *Rhodes v. Chapman,* which provided that double occupation of a single cell is permissible only in cells of at least medium size, should be of basic importance to this problem.

## 4. System and Organization of Penal Corrections

U.S. penal correctional institutions are organized on three levels:

— *federal prisons,*
— *state prisons,* and
— *local jails.*

In general, one can say that the federal and state prisons house prisoners serving terms of more than one year and that the local jails contain pretrial detainees and prisoners serving terms of one year or less. According to a 1970 survey, approximately 40 percent of all individuals confined in local jails were on pretrial detention (U.S. Dept. of Justice, 1980, pp.2f.).

**Chart 6:** Profile of the Prison Population in 1971 and 1978

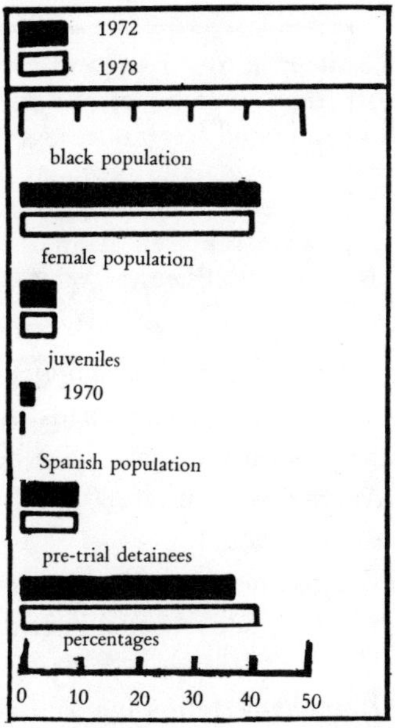


Source: *U.S. Department of Justice:* National Prisoner Statistics Report. Washington D.C. 1980, p.3.

On the other hand, according to a survey conducted in 1974, only two percent of the state prison inmates had been confined without a judically determined verdict having been made, viz., drug addicts, pretrial detainees and individuals confined for observation (U.S. Dept. of Justice, 1979, p.1). The number and distribution of U.S. prisoners are contained in Table 12 and Chart 6. In the 1970s two to three percent of the state prisoners were confined in local jails because of overcrowding in the state institutions.

According to present information, approximately *4,200 penal institutions* existed in the United States in 1980, of which 3,500 were local jails (cf. U.S. Dept. of Justice, 1980 p.1, on local jails in February 1978). A total of *553,523 individuals were confined* within these prisons, of which 27,298 were in federal institutions. The prisoner-to-population ratio was 244.3 to 100,000 (Jericho 6(1981), 24/7). Approximately 299,000 individuals were confined in state prisons and 153,000 in local jails. In addition, about 74,000 children were in custody. According to these figures, the United States presently has more individuals confined in relation to total population than any other Western country with the exception of South Africa.

Since these figures represent averages for the entire United States, one must also note that in some of the individual states such as Connecticut, Hawaii, North Dakota and Vermont, less than 100 individuals per 100,000 are confined, whereas in Georgia and Nevada, more than 400 per 100,000, and in Washington, D.C., over 692 per 100,000 are confined. One explanation for these variations is the over-representation of blacks in these latter states, who account for 6 times as many confinees as whites. (See Christianson et al., 1981, pp.364ff.)

More than one million convicted persons are confined during the course of any one year in American penal institutions (cf. Schwartz et al., 1980, p.31). The statistics on local jails have been estimated based on surveys conducted in 1970 (Moynahan et al., 1980, p.83; National Institute of Justice, 1980, pp.20ff.; see also Chart 5).

Similar to the three-level organizational structure of U.S. corrections into federal, state and local penal institutions, the federal prisons, administered by the U.S. Bureau of Prisons as a division of the U.S. Department of Justice, also are divided into the following different types of facilities (cf. Williams, 1979, pp.65ff.):

- *U.S. penitentiaries,* which contain only male prisoners serving a term of more than five years who have been classified as dangerous. The six existing penitentiaries have a total capacity of almost 8,000 persons.
- *Federal institutions,* which house both males and females serving terms of two to five years. In addition, pretrial detainees and prisoners requiring a particular type of medical attention also are confined in these institutions. The total capacity of the 21 federal institutions is about 9,300 with almost 1,000 female inmates.
- *Federal Youth Centers,* which contain male and female confinees between the ages of 15 and 25 who are serving terms of less than two years. The five existing centers have a capacity of about 1,500, of which 60 are females.
- *Federal Prison Camps,* which are filled with individuals serving short prison terms. Four of these camps exist, in which approximately 1,400 individuals can be confined.
- *Community Treatment Centers,* which are semi-open and strongly oriented toward treatment. The 12 centers all are located in large cities and each have room for 20 to 80 sentenced persons.
- *Federal Correction Institutions,* which, after 20 years of planning, were opened in March 1976, the first of which was a special institution for suicidal or for psychologically abnormal prisoners.

The U.S. Bureau of Prisons inmate population sank by 14 percent in 1980 to 21,449 inmates. This decline could have resulted partially from the fact that correctional authorities were concentrating on white collar criminals instead of ''traditional'' criminals.

**Table 12:** Inmates of Federal Prisons, State Prisons and Local Jails according to Sex—1972 and 1978

| Type of Institution and Sex of Inmates | 1972 N | 1972 % | 1978 N | 1978 % | Increase % |
|---|---|---|---|---|---|
| Federal prisons | 21,713 | 100 | 28,650 | 100 | 32 |
| Male | 20,919 | 96 | 26,956 | 94 | 29 |
| Female | 794 | 4 | 1,694 | 6 | 113 |
| State prisons | 174,470 | 100 | 249,491 | 100 | 43 |
| Male | 168,992 | 97 | 240,141 | 96 | 42 |
| Female | 5,478 | 3 | 9,350 | 4 | 71 |
| Local jails | 141,605 | 100 | 158,394 | 100 | 12 |
| Male | 133,274 | 94 | 148,839 | 94 | 12 |
| Female | 8,331 | 6 | 9,555 | 6 | 15 |

Source: *U.S. Department of Justice:* National Prisoner Statistics Report. Washington D.C. 1980, p.3.

In addition to these federal prisons, a total of 592 *state prisons* exist within the individual states (cf. Sourcebook, 1979, p.177).

Many of these state institutions are large, accommodating more than 1,000 inmates. The prison buildings are almost all more than 50 years old (Schwartz et al., 1980, p.29). The largest of all state prisons is in Jackson, Michigan. It has a capacity of 4,900 (Williams, 1979, p.114) and presently contains more than 6,000 prisoners (Bronstein, 1981, p.18). One advantage in such large institutions is that costs per prisoner are lower than in small institutions. Prisons with a capacity of 750, for example, require almost twice as much money per prisoner as required in the larger institutions (Williams, 1979, p.114).

Three types of state institutions can be distinguished, depending upon the level of security measures utilized: *"Minimum, medium* and *maximum security prisons."* The percentage of prisoners confined in maximum security facilities varies among the individual states from 32 to 59 percent. An interstate average of 44 percent of all prisoners are confined in maximum security prisons (Schwartz et al., 1980, p.9), or approximately 83,000 persons. Only about six percent of all prisoners are confined in minimum security units, viz., in so-called halfway-houses and work-release units.

In the 1970s between 3,500 and 3,900 local jails existed (Sourcebook, 1979, p.975; U.S. Dept. of Justice, 1980, p.1). The number of inmates confined herein varied between 158,000 and 188,000. These figures do not include the confinement possibilities existing at the individual police stations (cf. Schwartz et al., 1980, p.27f.).

Most jails cannot house more than 21 inmates (Sourcebook, 1979, p.175). Essentially they are used to confine pretrial detainees, individuals arrested for other judicial procedures, or individuals being transferred from one institution to the other. Adults serving prison terms of less than one year also are confined in local jails (Moynahan et al., 1980, p.4). Today, the local jails are presented with two major difficulties. Influence, not to mention treatment, is almost impossible because of the continually changing jail population due to the high percentage of confined pretrial detainees. Secondly, financial means are inadequate for almost all of the local facilities (cf. Schwartz et al., 1980, pp.28f.). Although considerably divergent statutory correctional regulations for these jails exist in every state of the United States, they are seldom adhered to since the necessary control agencies are lacking (Moynahan et al., 1980, pp.69,108).

North American penal institutions are administered by more than *100,000 civil service employees* (cf. Sourcebook, 1979, pp.176,178). The ratio of prison-staff-to-prisoners for the total United States was 1 : 3.6 during the first half of the 1970s. Extreme differences exist among both the state prisons and the local jails. These differences result not only from the type of institution involved, but also from regional and local influences. Institutions with agricultural and forest programs usually have a less favorable staff-inmate relationship than do closed institutions. In addition, this ratio varies extremely: among states with at least 15,000 confined persons, from 1:3 in New York to 1:7 in California and 1:10 in Texas; among states with 2,000 to 3,000 prisoners, from 1:2 in Massachusetts to 1:8 in Arkansas and 1:15 in Colorado. Custodial employees responsible for supervision are the largest single group of prison employees and account for 60 percent of total prison staff.

In 1980, correctional employees in the 4,000 penal institutions were responsible for the administration, supervision and treatment of more than 550,000 confined persons (cf. Jericho 6 (1981), 24/7). More than 50 percent of all prisoners were under 30 years of age (Schwartz et al., 1980, p.30). The average prison term being served was 21 months (Newton, 1980, p.134). Approximately 12,000 female prisoners were confined yearly, accounting for about four percent of the total prison population (U.S. Dept. of Justice, 1981, p.1). Almost 50 percent of all prisoners are black, whereby this percentage is even higher for female prisoners. (See also Chart 6.)

## 5. Employment and Advanced Training

Although educational and vocational training programs are provided in both the state and federal prisons, only a very small number of prisoners actually take part in these programs. According to a survey conducted in 1977, only 10 to 12 percent of all prisoners participate in one or the other of these programs, whereas 19 percent of the prisoners participate in vocational training programs (Sourcebook, 1979, p.184). This low level of participation could result from the unattractiveness of these programs or from differently oriented prisoner desires. Financial and personnel deficiencies also lead to considerable limitations on training programs within the penal institutions. It is not unusual to find these courses taught, or partially taught, by the inmates themselves (cf. Burns, 1979, p.210). A large part of the programs offered, therefore, are limited to work within the correctional institution and vocational training for this type of employment.

In the United States, statutory law controls the organizational structure of prison employment and provides that products produced within the prison may be sold only to other state-operated institutions. This law, and the overcrowded prison situation, lead to the result that only one-third of all prisoners actually can be employed. Of this one-third, two-thirds are employed to care for other prisoners and to do odd jobs within the institution, and the remaining are involved in simple administrative tasks and in conducting religious services (Burns, 1979, p.210).

The majority of prisoners who can work at all are employed full-time by the "Federal Prison Industries, Inc." The profits of this federally owned company are distributed completely to other federally owned institutions. Production is limited mainly to electronic devices, shoes and clothing, and wood and metal products. Depending upon the type of work and the prisoner's productivity, he receives an average salary of less than one dollar per hour (Williams, 1979, p.69).

Prisoners who are engaged in "work-release-programs" outside the institution receive salaries in accordance with the free market. They must pay, however, for the costs of their confinement (Williams, 1979, p.256).

The type of work and level of salary vary considerably from state to state. The main goal of the "Texas model," which has been adopted by many states in the United States, is production-oriented toward total self-support of the penal institution. The prisoners here earn between 30 cents and 1 dollar per hour.

A new trend, however, has been developing in states such as Minnesota and Kansas. Since the prison employers in these states are usually private industries, the wages range between three and seven dollars per hour. Of particular importance is the fact that this type of employment provides the prisoner with vocational training and skills he usually can use after release. The number of positions open to the institutions is still relatively low but an increase is planned. Prisoners so employed also are required to contribute to the costs of the penal institution. Emphasis is placed, however, on the prisoner's possibility of paying back personal debts accumulated before his confinement (Fedo, 1981, p.11).

## 6. Assistance, Treatment and Aid to Released Prisoners

Individual treatment programs are rare in the U.S. correctional system. Generally, prisoners are confined in special admission units for the first four to eight weeks of their term and then are assigned to a particular prison. Treatment within the prison usually is oriented toward large groups, which are assumed to have internal similarity (Williams, 1979, pp.39ff.).

The actual extent and intensity of treatment is difficult to determine. Although some studies indicate that less than 100 dollars per inmate per year is expended on social programs such that only five percent of all prisoners could take part in treatment, other studies have come to the conclusion that approximately 40 percent of all inmates take advantage of treatment offers. Although 23 percent of all prison inmates require narcotics therapy, 22 percent alcoholic therapy, 31 percent vocational training, and 68 percent advanced vocational training, less than one-fourth of those even participating in treatment programs take part in programs designed to meet their individual needs.

The success of these various treatment programs cannot be judged reliably. One can say, however, that the programs oriented more toward assisting the prisoner with day-to-day problems have been more successful than the programs using psychodynamic techniques. Prisoners who are classified as endangered benefit more from treatment than do other prisoners. Prisoners confined in top security units usually suffer more personality changes through corrections than those confined in more relaxed correctional facilities (Lipton et al., 1975, pp.522ff., 548).

Increased attention also is being paid to providing legal assistance in solving family problems or problems arising from confinement both during treatment and in preparation for release. These problems are considered in various projects designed to expand upon the prisoner's right to assistance because of poverty. (See, Alpert, 1978, pp.29ff., 47.)

Another important instrument for social reentry is the halfway-house, which exists in almost all of the states. (See, Williams, 1979, pp.93f.) Four different inmate groups are to be distinguished:

— Probationers who require a certain amount of control,
— prisoners who are taking part in a levelled release program,
— prisoners who are to be released on probation,
— prisoners who are to be prepared for social re-entry after having served a complete term.

## 7. Evaluation and Developmental Tendencies

In recent discussions, the U.S. correctional system generally has been evaluated negatively. The fact that more individuals are confined in relation to total population than in any other Western country except South Africa, as can be seen from the data available, is being emphasized constantly. A review of the period between 1880 and the present also reveals that prison sentences have increased in frequency almost continuously in the United States. The proportion of black prisoners, which always has been disproportionately high, has increased even further over the past twenty years (Cahalan, 1979, pp.37ff.).

Resignation has set in with regard to the correctional goal of resocialization, however in the fact that previous treatment attempts were too minimal and lacking in the required intensity has been disregarded. Many of the treatment programs were carried out in the absence of adequate scientific preparation and supporting research. Only one percent of the expenditures allocated to such programs were used for research purposes (Lipton et al., 1975, p.3). On the other hand, one should not overlook the extreme efforts made in the United States toward the reform of juvenile corrections.

One of the most radical changes in penal corrections occurred in Massachusetts. In the spring of 1972, all juvenile training schools were closed. This decision was supported by new criminological findings, continually increasing recidivism rates, rising costs, and the development of new treatment strategies. The goal of this reform, i.e. replacing closed institutions with a community-oriented, decentralized system directed toward ambulant and social-pedagogic assistance, was to avoid confining and isolating juvenile delinquents in closed institutions to the extent possible. Instead, individually differentiated assistance was to be provided according to socially accepted patterns of conflict-solving in the real world. Contact with society and the community structure was to be encouraged, and formal condemnation through a sanctioning system was to be avoided. The difficulties with the Massachusetts-Experiment, even in light of a few "reported successes," of course cannot be overlooked, particularly since the recidivism rate has increased slightly. The main points of criticism are directed toward inadequate administration, the absence of any security facility, the lack of sufficient training of private assistants, and the general lack of success. The general public criticizes the unavailability of a closed institution for particularly difficult juveniles, the lack of sufficient financial means for this program, and the high number of runaways. Although all of the previously existing institutions were closed, the problem remained that some juveniles required stationary confinement. A counter-reform gathered momentum in 1976 and resulted in the construction of many small, closed institutions. Thereafter, the original reform movement was continued. The experiences in Massachusetts over the past decade show that treatment in freedom is presented with extreme practical difficulties. In addition, the superiority of a community-oriented treatment model with emphasis on ambulatory assistance, as opposed to other strategies directed toward crime prevention, has never been proved empirically. The idea of treatment in freedom, however, did gain certain directives through this experiment, such as the principles of decentralization, educational orientation, differentiation, democratization and normalization.

One may not overlook the fact that criminal policy in the United States has been subjected to increasing public pressure. Tax increases and decreases in buying power have led to the taxpayer's increased scrutiny of the use of public funds. The demand for amplified use of less expensive ambulatory sanctioning forms could not be met in light of the rising fear of crime. This fear exists even though the statistical information available does not indicate any development of a "dangerous offender" (Cahalan, 1979, p.38; National Institute of Justice, 1980, p.18). The trend toward more frequent and longer prison terms has been contradicted directly in case decisions over the past ten years. In nineteen states, the courts have declared certain correctional practices, particularly because of prison overcrowding, to be unconstitutional, and cases are pending on this issue in twelve further states. It remains open whether the state courts will be more reserved in their future decisions in light of the recent verdicts of the Supreme Court *(Bell v. Wolfish* and *Rhodes v. Chapman).* The executive and legislative governmental branches are being criticized because they are engaging in short-term crisis management rather than enacting sensibly directed correctional measures (Bronstein, 1981, p.16). Individual state justice departments also have demanded more exact correctional legislation. The goal of this initiative, however, is a return to the so-called hands-off-doctrine and its statutory basis. Appropriate legislation is intended to avoid giving the courts an opportunity to determine what is cruel and unusual punishment (Bronstein, 1981, pp.19f.). A convincing solution to the difficult correctional problems in the United States, however, is not in sight.

# PART FOUR
## Comparative Analysis of Penal Corrections

**Citations:** Conrad, J.: *Crime and its Correction.* An International Survey of Attitude and Practices. Berkeley et al. 1965; Jescheck, H.-H.: *Die Krise der Kriminalpolitik.* ZStW 91(1979), pp.1037–1064; Müller-Dietz, H.: "Der deutsche Strafvollzug im westeuropäischen Vergleich." In: *Grundfragen des strafrechtlichen Sanktionensystems.* Heidelberg et al. 1979, pp.246–266; Wicks, R. et al.: *International Corrections.* Lexington, Mass. 1979; ECCP: *Report of the Standard Minimum Rules for the Treatment of Prisoners.* Strasbourg 1980; Kury, H. (Ed.): *Strafvollzug und Öffentlichkeit.* Freiburg 1980; Lenke, L.: "Criminal Policy and Repression in Capitalist Societies—The Scandinavian Case." In: *Policing Scandinavia.* ScandStudCrim 7, Oslo et al. 1980, pp.5–30; United Nations: The Implementation of the United Nations Standard Minimum Rules for the Treatment of Offenders. Working Paper. New York 1980; Sliwowski, J.: *Kara poszbawienia wolnósci we wspótczesnym swiecíe* (Custodial Sentence in the Present World). Warsaw 1981, pp.103–170; Kaiser, G., Kerner, H.-J., Schöch, H.: *Strafvollzug.* 3rd ed. Heidelberg 1982; Steenhuis, D. et al.: *The Penal Climate in the Netherlands: Sunny or Cloudy?* The Hague 1982.

Now that we have reviewed each of the individual correctional systems, we shall compare the rules, institutions, and structures of criminal corrections in the European nations. Legal requirements for correctional programs and the solutions thereto, i.e. correctional law and reality, provide important criteria for this comparison. Since corrections are legally normed and organized, i.e. based on statutes, legal orders, and administrative regulations, everywhere in Europe, it seems appropriate to analyze correctional law comparatively in light of the degree to which the correctional system is regulated statutorily and to which legal protection is provided prisoners.

# I. Legal Regulations of Penal Corrections, Minimum Rules of the United Nations and Prisoners' Legal Rights

**Citations:** Sekretariat der Europäischen Kommission für Menschenrechte (Ed.): Menschenrechte im Gefängnis. No.1 of the Series "Schwerpunkte der Rechtsprechung." Strasbourg 1971; Ganter, H.: *Die Spruchpraxis der Europäischen Kommission für Menschenrechte auf dem Gebiet des Strafvollzugs.* Bonn 1974; Council of Europe (Ed.): *Yearbook of the European Convention of Human Rights on the Admissibility of Applications from Individuals and States.* Alphen aan den Rijn-Germantown, Md. 1980; Trechsel, S.: *Die Garantie der persönlichen Freiheit (Art.5 EMRK) in der Strassburger Rechtsprechung.* EuGRZ 7(1980), pp.514–532; Gonsa, H.: *Europarat und Strafvollzug.* ÖJZ 36(1981), pp.286–292.

Penal corrections are based on statutory law in almost all European countries. Although more recently, the development of special correctional codes has become prevalent (e.g. in West Germany, East Germany, the Netherlands, Austria and Hungary), individual regulations on criminal procedure and corrections are predominant (e.g. in France, Scandinavia and in the socialist countries). The regulation of the basic problems in penal corrections within the substantive criminal law code is also not unusual (e.g. in Switzerland). The formal organization of corrections within a particular legal branch is unimportant, however, in comparison to the actual process of *providing a legal basis for criminal corrections.*

The European Convention on the Protection of Human Rights and Basic Freedoms adopted in Rome on November 4, 1950 had obvious effects on the actions of the various European countries with respect to penal corrections. West Germany ratified the findings of the convention statutorily on August 7, 1952, with the publication of its effectiveness appearing on December 15, 1953. The Human Rights Convention (HRC) thereby was incorporated into West German federal law. It controls the relationship between national power and the individual, and, within the field of penal corrections, it provides effective limitations on state interferences with the personal rights of prisoners. Of particular importance are Art.3 HRC, which contains the principle of human dignity and the prohibition against torture and inhuman or base punishments; Art.5 HRC, which provides for the prisoner's right to have contact with the outside world; and Art.13 and 25 HRC, which provide for the prisoner's right to file a complaint.

The right of an individual to file a complaint under the jurisdiction of the Human Rights Convention, however, only hesitantly and gradually was recognized by European nations. (See Mikaelsen, 1980, pp.20f.) During the first fifteen years of its existence, the European Human Rights Convention recognized only four of approximately 2,000 individual complaints, 40 percent of which were filed by prisoners. The manner in which these complaints were rejected was disappointing, and a position on factual questions was seldom taken. For this reason, one cannot maintain that the essential impulses for the reform of German criminal corrections came from the decisions of the HRC (cf. Ganter, 1974, pp.184, 188). This situation did not change during the 1970s, although the majority of individual prisoner complaints then were directed against Great Britain and no longer against West Germany. Extremely few complaints are filed by Scandinavians and relatively many by the Swiss. In 1979, only 24 percent of all individually filed complaints were filed by imprisoned persons (cf. Table 13); 10 percent of these complaints were recognized (Council of Europe: Yearbook, 1979, pp.394,397f.; further EuGRZ, 1979, pp.242,383,451,603,670; 1980, p.24).

Essentially independent of the HRC decisions, the laws on penal corrections *in almost all of the European nations* either conform to or have been altered in conformance therewith *over the past ten years,* or entirely new laws have been adopted. In those countries in which a legal foundation for penal corrections was available, as that of the Netherlands which has been in effect for more than 30 years, new needs were satisfied mainly by administrative orders, such as the so-called waiting list of sentenced persons for entrance into the Netherlands' correctional system.

**Table 13:** Development in the Number of Individual Complaints Filed with the Human Rights Convention since its Adoption

| Year | Total Number of Complaints | Individual Complaints filed by Prisoners | |
|---|---|---|---|
| | | Number | Percent |
| 1955 | 138 | 24 | 17 |
| 1956 | 104 | 20 | 20 |
| 1957 | 101 | 25 | 25 |
| 1958 | 96 | 22 | 24 |
| 1959 | 233 | 71 | 30 |
| 1960 | 291 | 67 | 23 |
| 1961 | 344 | 114 | 33 |
| 1962 | 442 | 235 | 53 |
| 1963 | 346 | 175 | 50 |
| 1964 | 293 | 137 | 47 |
| 1965 | 310 | 164 | 53 |
| 1966 | 303 | 143 | 47 |
| 1967 | 445 | 219 | 49 |
| 1968 | 449 | 253 | 56 |
| 1969 | 439 | 206 | 47 |
| 1970 | 379 | 133 | 35 |
| 1971 | 603 | 194 | 32 |
| 1972 | 644 | 237 | 37 |
| 1973 | 442 | 202 | 46 |
| 1974 | 445 | 125 | 28 |
| 1975 | 466 | 227 | 49 |
| 1976 | 427 | 197 | 46 |
| 1977 | 373 | 134 | 36 |
| 1978 | 335 | 117 | 35 |
| 1979 | 378 | 90 | 24 |

Source: *Council of Europe:* Yearbook of the European Convention on Human Rights—1979. The Hague et al., 1980, p.398.

According to more recent reports of the European Council and the United Nations, the *recognized Minimum Rules for the Treatment of Prisoners have been adopted by almost all European nations.* In the official reports of the individual nations, including Eastern Europe, it is maintained that these standards are being followed. In some countries (e.g. the Netherlands), the national regulations and correctional practices even are said to exceed the European minimum standards. In these countries, therefore, not only has the less problematic differentiation of corrections been made, but also the prisoners rights have been defined, and his ability to enforce these rights at least has been intimated. No less clearly revealed in the questionable 1980 reports of the European Council and United Nations, however, is the fact that the maintenance of these minimum standards is still *not* totally *without problem.* Protection of the prisoner's legal rights, particularly through judicial control, is even somewhat more difficult. Although most European nations have adopted similar regulations and corresponding principles of organization, vast differences still exist.

These differences can be seen, for example, in the permissibility and actual granting of relaxations in the correctional system. Some countries have extremely open correctional systems (e.g. Scandinavian countries) as opposed to other nations which are very restrictive in their allowance of any correctional relaxations (e.g. the socialist countries). The actual accommodation of prisoners also varies. Although the socialist countries and Japan prefer collective accommodation, the Western European nations attempt to provide for individual confinement. The recent overcrowding within the correctional systems, with the exception of the Swiss system, however, has thwarted the effectuation of this goal.

The continuous process of codifying criminal corrections also results in *limitations on criminal-pedagogic and therapeutic intervention as well as experimentation, and "imaginative, creative phantasy."* Twenty years ago, this type of ability and effort, however, was valued highly as an advantage and standard for progressive corrections, at least with respect to the background of generally determined controls in the European correctional systems (cf. the criticism of German corrections made by Conrad, 1965, pp.146ff.,169ff.). At that time prisoners' rights and corresponding judicial control hardly were recognized as a problem, much less discussed widely in the literature.

Today, *various models and solutions attempt to guarantee the protection of prisoners' legal rights.* Internal administrative controls (e.g. in England and France), reviews undertaken by independent supervisory commissions (e.g. in the Netherlands), controls exercised by the so-called ombudsman (e.g. in Sweden), and judicial controls (e.g. in W. Germany) are permitted. As mentioned above, one also can appeal to the Human Rights Commission, although these appeals have become less frequent over the past years. The West German correctional system undoubtedly is advanced with respect to the codification of criminal corrections and the provision of judicial controls, as are German social systems in general, e.g. the public school system. (See Gonsa, 1981, p.292, who maintains that the Austrian system is the leader in this field.) This orientation, however, has both its strengths and weaknesses, as can be seen from the age-old controversy between Freudenthal and v.Liszt (1914) on constitutionality and resocialization. (See Kaiser/Kerner/Schöch 1982, pp.14f.) This controversy still remains unsolved today, as revealed in more recent debates on the goals and responsibilities of penal corrections.

# II. Correctional Goals and the Philosophy of Punishment

**Citations:** Eser, A.: "Resozialisierung in der Krise? Gedanken zum Sozialisationsziel des Strafvollzugs." In: *Einheit und Vielfalt des Strafrechts. Festschrift für K. Peters,* ed.by J. Baumann et al. Tübingen 1974, pp.505–518; Kaiser, G.: "Resozialisierung und Zeitgeist." In: *Festschrift für Th. Würtenberger,* ed.by H. Müller-Dietz et al. Berlin 1977, pp.359–372; Müller-Dietz, H.: *Grundfragen des strafrechtlichen Sanktionensystems.* Heidelberg et al. 1979; Roxin, C.: *Wandlungen der Strafrechtswissenschaft.* JA 12(1980), pp.221–227; Zipf, H.: *Kriminalpolitik.* Heidelberg et al. 1980, pp.79ff.; Christie, N.: *Limits to Pain.* Oslo 1981; Gassin, R.: *La criminologie et les tendences modernes de la politique répressive.* RSCrim 1981, pp.265–279; Fogel, D. et al. (Eds.): *Justice as Fairness. Perspectives on the Justice Model.* Anderson Publ. Co. U.S.A. 1981.

Until most recently, the goal of corrections was seen to be *resocialization.* This orientation was influenced by the U.N. minimum standards and the modern concept of social defense (défense sociale nouvelle), and it was supported by psychotherapeutic and behavioral science advancements. The Netherlands, Denmark, and Sweden were the leaders in this movement. It then spread to the correctional laws of Austria, Switzerland, West Germany, England, France, and the socialist countries.

More recently, an *abandonment of this treatment ideology* has been recommended in Finland, but this recommendation has remained essentially verbal and has had little actual affect on correctional practices. In Denmark and Sweden, on the other hand, the treatment-oriented correctional vocabulary (e.g. Kriminalvård and Kriminalforsorgen; see critically Christie, 1981, p.14.) indicates that this ideology has not even been abandoned verbally (see critically Kaiser, 1977, pp.359ff.), although treatment as a strategy for crime control ("treatment against crime") has lost its significance. Agreement still exists that a maximum of treatment should be provided, in order to improve the general situation of an individual who is confined in prison serving a sentence (Christie, 1981, p.48).

The decade-long discussions of penal corrections, which were mainly influenced by the treatment ideology, had an effective and lasting influence on the European correctional systems with respect to approach, humanization, relaxation, and availability of potential assistance.

*Presently, avoidance of the damaging effects of confinement* and *preparation for release* are being advanced as the *main responsibilities of penal corrections* (cf. too ECCP, 1980, p.63). This pragmatic determination of the function of corrections already has been incorporated in many correctional codes and regulations. The recognition of this principle in the formation of the correctional system is undeniably important. (See also §3 W.German Corrections Code.) As the main goal of corrections, however, this principle does not appear realistic, but instead *questionable.* If it were the main purpose of the correctional system, it would be easier, more economical and more humane to avoid stationary confinement completely. Any denial of freedom with the purpose of avoiding the damages resulting from confinement and preparing the prisoner for release seems to be a total contradiction.

On the other hand, if this goal is not primary, one must *ask what the superior purpose* of corrections should be. In more recent theoretical discussions, the neoclassical goals, particularly general prevention and retribution, have been mentioned more frequently. This type of fallback, and the support offered therefor, is unsatisfactory. The "renaissance of punishment," i.e. the postulate that the prison term should be an undesirable experience, is not a persuasive and noncontradictory goal of penal corrections.

The theory of *general prevention* provides no support for why short prison terms executed with a high degree of correctional relaxations and a low number of prisoners should deter or motivate the prisoner to correspond to the law. According to historical experience, one would more likely assume the opposite.

*Retribution* also cannot be the purpose behind the type of corrections practiced in Europe (low number of prisoners, short prison terms, relaxations in corrections). An exactly levelled system of punishments and privileges within the correctional system would correspond much more to the various degrees of wrong committed. Exactly this type of logical consequence, however, apparently is rejected.

*Security* or *incapacitation* is being advanced more recently, mainly in the English literature, as the supreme goal of corrections. Regardless of extensive criticism, this orientation also is being adopted and practiced. The comparatively high number of prisoners in the socialist countries and the increase in longer prison terms in Western Europe are examples of this orientation, even though actual expressions of this theory are relatively rare.

Neither the practices in Scandinavia, with the exception of Finland, nor those in the Netherlands are oriented toward one of the above-mentioned goals. In these countries, penal corrections today as well as during the 1950s and 1960s, *essentially* are *oriented pragmatically* according to the ideas expressed in the U.N. minimum standards or toward what one in West Germany calls "resocialization" or "treatment." Even correctional differentiations do not correspond to the concepts of retribution, general prevention or incapacitation, but rather more to the prisoner's assumed danger, undesirable social influence, and potential treatment needs. In contrast to the Netherlands' flexible pragmatism in correctional policies, dogmatism and the tendency toward perfect solutions, even in correctional regulations and forms, are dominant in the German system. The resulting inflexibility inhibits the expansion of open correctional facilities and the introduction of a compound system which includes post-release assistance (Müller-Dietz, 1979, p.266).

The *determination of a superior correctional goal* remains *problematic.* Even though extensive efforts and improvements were made during the post-war period, penal corrections have fallen into an *identity crisis.* This crisis can be seen clearly in the report of the European Council in 1980. More recent, appealing criticisms demand *more honesty in determining the purposes of punishment and their realization in the correctional system.* (See Fogel et al., 1981, p.v.) Both the treatment ideology and progressive corrections, which are used primarily as an instrument of discipline, have been confronted with convincing criticism. On the other hand, "conventional untruths" are found not only in resocialization but also in the goals of general prevention and retribution. No criminal policy directive or punishment goal is free of false rhetoric. Only an insistence on exact observation, careful analysis, and scientific criticism can be of assistance in solving this problem.

# III. System, Structure and Organization of Penal Corrections

**Citations:** Blau, G.: "Der offene Vollzug im Ausland. Folgerungen für den deutschen Strafvollzug." In: *Tagungsberichte der Strafvollzugskommission* (Bonn) 7(1969), pp.53–88; Council of Europe (Ed.): "European Prison Systems: Broad Comparisons." In: *Prison Management.* Strasbourg 1983, pp.27–34.

Although many of the principles of correctional organization, such as differentiation, classification, and avoidance of confinement damages, have been incorporated into the correctional systems of Europe and have resulted in some unity in actual practices, *considerable differences* still exist among the various *penal correctional models.* In part, these divergencies result from nationally influenced criminal sanctioning systems, from differing usages of the prison penalty, and from difficulties in influencing the infra-structure of penal corrections. Even the number, size and types of penal institutions vary considerably. Vast differences also exist in the relationship between the absolute prison-personnel-to-prisoners ratios (cf. Table 14 and Chart 7), even when the number of incarcerated individuals are adjusted in relation to their number per 100,000 general population (cf. Table 16). Personnel ratios in Western Europe are approximately 1:3, and they are probably considerably more advantageous in the socialist countries. Large differences can be found even between such countries as the Netherlands and Switzerland. Both of these nations have approximately the same number of prisoners, but the Netherlands has almost twice as many correctional employees as Switzerland.

Furthermore, the opening and relaxation of corrections, e.g. by establishing open institutions, granting day leaves and permitting vacations, is regulated completely differently within Europe. In general, Denmark and Sweden appear to have the most open penal correctional facilities. In comparison, the open corrections practiced in France, Austria, the Netherlands, and in the socialist countries appear inferior, although the differences partially result from totally different conditions and basic premises. Experience shows, however, that relaxed and open corrections can be practiced to a great degree without considerably risking the interest in security and general prevention.

On the contrary, insufficient attention is given to the treatment of older prisoners, foreigners, the mentally ill or prisoners with abnormal personalities. Mentally ill prisoners are treated within the correctional systems of some countries. In others, treatment is legally organized and carried out separately from this system. Actual knowledge as to which approach is preferable, however, is lacking. Penal corrections of female prisoners, who rarely account for more than three to five percent of the total prison population in any country, also has become a field for consideration and reform.

**Table 14:** Comparison of Prisoners and Correctional Personnel

| End of the 1950's | England | Netherlands | Sweden | Nordrhein-Westfalen (W. Germ.) |
|---|---|---|---|---|
| 1. Number of Prisoners | 25,000 | 4,500 | 4,500 | 19,000 |
| 2. Number of Prison Personnel | 7,000 | 3,100 | 1,400 | 3,300 |
| 3. Ratio of 2. to 1. | 1 : 3,5 | 1 : 1,5 | 1 : 3 | 1 : 5,9 |

| End of the 1970's | England | Netherlands | Sweden | Nordrhein-Westfalen (W. Germ.) |
|---|---|---|---|---|
| 1. Number of Prisoners | 41,700 | 3,000 | 4,400 | 15,300 |
| 2. Number of Prison Personnel | 22,100 | 4,000 | 4,300 | 6,900 |
| 3. Ratio of Nr.2 to Nr.1 | 1 : 1,9 | 1 : 0,8 | 1 : 0,9 | 1 : 2,2 |

**Chart 7:** Comparison of Prisoners and Correctional Personnel

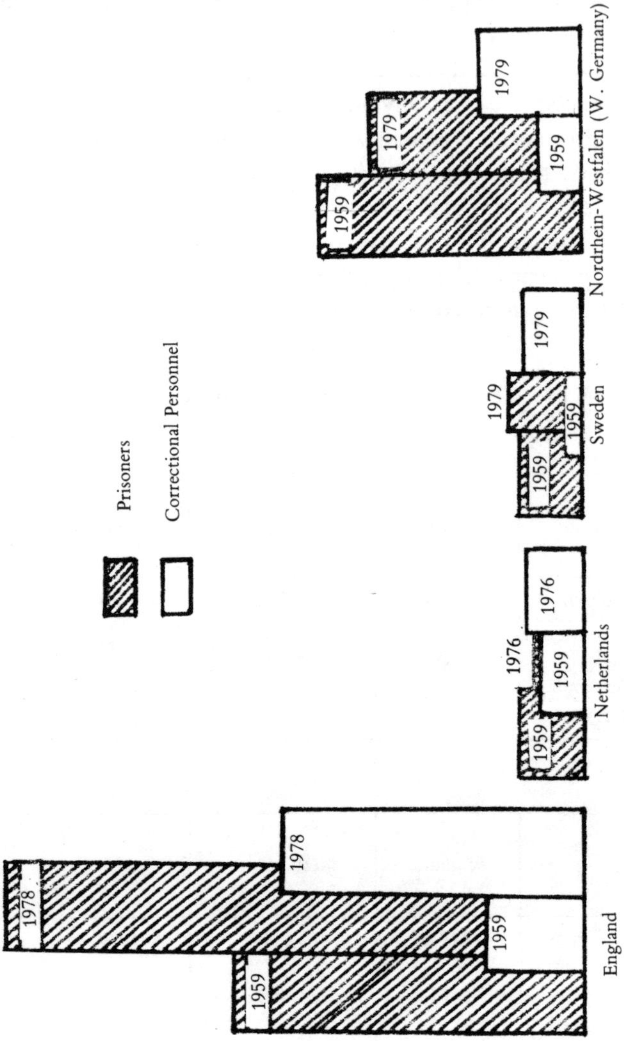


Sources: *Home Office,* 1979, pp.11, 81, 83; Gevangenistatistiek, 1977, pp.14, 24; Kriminalvården, 1979, pp.21, 47; Strafvollzug in Nordrhein-Westfalen 1980, pp.11, 95; *Grunau,* T.: Die Organisation des Vollzugs und der Vollzugsanstalten in einigen ausländischen Staaten, Freiburg 1959, p.193.

# IV. Employment and Advanced Training

**Citations:** Petersilia, J.: "Which Inmates Participate in Prison Treatment Programs?" *Journal of Offender Counseling Services and Rehabilitation* 4(1979), pp.121–135; Supe, E.: *Strafgefangene und Schule. Sekundäre Sozialisationsinstanzen in der rückblickenden und gegenwärtigen Beurteilung von jungen Inhaftierten und ihren Erziehern.* Munich 1980; Dünkel, F.: *Schulbildung im Strafvollzug. Zur Interpretation schulpädagogischer und sozialtherapeutischer Massnahmen.* Recht der Jugend und des Bildungswesens 33(1982), pp.142–155.

*Employment is the central activity in the correctional systems* of Europe and the rest of the world, even in countries in which no statutory provision for a work program exists. Employment within the correctional system, however, does not represent merely an economic factor in a cost-benefit analysis. It also cannot be characterized as a decisive factor in the process of resocialization. Employment is, however, the main activity within all correctional systems, and it is also useful as a daily pastime. The importance of employment is particularly noticeable when prisoners are unemployed or without some form of possible activity. Outdoor activities and day work-leaves are especially beneficial and recognized in Eastern and Western nations alike. Practices with respect to these leaves, however, vary considerably.

Although employment is seen to be important, *monetary compensation* for this employment presents *difficulties in almost every country.* This problem has not been solved satisfactorily even in the Netherlands. One must note, however, that employment compensation is not considered to be as important in other nations as one would assume from the internal discussions in West Germany.

Instead, state assistance, aid, supervision and educational and vocational training programs seem to be emphasized. One reason for this concern is that only a very small number of prisoners seem to be willing or able to undertake and successfully complete such training programs (cf. Petersilia, 1971). The excessive demands on prisoners and their disappointments are immediately noticeable (cf. Supe, 1980, p.113). Although considerable training and educational deficiencies exist, and unwavering efforts are being made to fill these deficiencies, the possibilities for improvement seem to be limited.

## V. Assistance, Treatment, Release and Aid to Released Prisoners

**Citations:** Kaufmann, H.: *Kriminologie III. Strafvollzug und Sozialtherapie.* Stuttgart 1977; Sechrest, L. et al. (Eds.): *The Rehabilitation of Criminal Offenders: Problems and Prospects.* Washington, D.C. 1979; Kaiser, G.: "Differenzierte Behandlungsmethoden im Vollzug." In: *Gibt es ein Recht auf Strafe? Zum neueren Streit, zur Begründung und Ausgestaltung der Strafe.* Loccumer Protokolle 20(1980), pp.79–102; Dolde, G. et al.: "Zusammenfassende Thesen zur Evaluation sozialtherapeutischer Behandlung bei Rückfalltätern und den Tätergruppen des §65 StGB." In: *Bundeszusammenschluss für Straffälligenhilfe: Sozialtherapie als kriminalpolitische Aufgabe.* Empfehlungen zur zukünftigen rechtlichen und tatsächlichen Ausgestaltung der Sozialtherapie im Justizvollzug. Bonn 1981, pp.120–122; Schneider, H.-J.: "Behandlung des Rechtsbrechers in der Strafanstalt und in Freiheit." In: *Die Psychologie des zwanzigsten Jahrhunderts.* Vol.XIV. Zürich 1981, pp.899–935.

Prisoner support and post-release assistance are regarded to be important everywhere. Actual *efforts* to provide this assistance, however, *usually are limited.* The most far-reaching social support is offered by Scandinavia and the Netherlands. Prisoners and released prisoners in these countries are ranked equally with individuals requiring social welfare assistance. On the contrary, Japan has absolutely no social welfare system, and individuals here must rely on the support of informal private groups. The low crime rate and number of prisoners in Japan, however, indicates that in this situation such an approach can be applied sensibly and feasibly, whereas in Western societies, social initiatives and voluntary workers must be employed.

*Treatment in the sense of using therapeutic techniques* is *rare* even in those countries in which it sometimes is applied. This situation is as true of the past as of the present. Even in the Netherlands, only a very low percentage of prisoners are included in therapy programs, and in West Germany this percentage is even lower. During the treatment ideology epoch, to the extent that this theory actually had any effect on correctional practices, treatment in this sense was equally rare. One of the few correctional institutions using this type of treatment was the previous therapeutic facility at Herstedvester in Denmark. One must keep in mind, however, that today, as well as previously, more warnings are given than actual treatment performed, even to those prisoners confined in psychiatric hospitals and resocialization institutions. The situation in correctional institutions is unsatisfactory from both a constitutional and therapeutic point of view. Even if one eliminated all treatment efforts, little would change to improve the situation.

The concept of treatment is not clear. The United Nations Minimum Standards of 1955 and its European edition of 1983 use the *treatment concept in its broadest sense* and include all efforts made to assist prisoners and even the organizational conditions required for this assistance. This broad meaning is incorporated *not only in the West German Corrections Code, but also in the majority of other national corrections laws.* Even the fine differentiations made in correctional institutions according to prisoner characteristics, the adoption of a treatment and corrections plan, the assignment to special treatment groups, and the availability of open and relaxed correctional facilities all are included in this broad definition of treatment. Only superior security interests and, temporarily, the level of crime committed by long-term prisoners logically could be excluded from this definition.

The *relaxation and opening of corrections* and the provision for *conditional release* are considered *to be important instruments for an effective correctional policy* in every nation. The goals of this policy vary from a continuation of the disciplined progressive system to an intentional although risky attempt to reintroduce the prisoner into normal society. In practice, these goals may overlap, since the prisoner's formal, external legal behavior usually is considered to be of primary importance. The reasons for successful or unsuccessful social integration often are not discovered. For this reason, the problem of the prisoner's debts and its solution before his release seldom is considered to be of particular importance in other countries, e.g. in Switzerland.

# VI. Summary

**Citations:** Hennings, E.: *The Prisoner Population of the World.* MschrKrim 28(1937), pp.296–300; Conrad, J.: *Crime and its Correction. An International Survey of Attitude and Practices.* Berkeley et al. 1965; Sekretariat der Europäischen Kommission für Menschenrechte (Ed.): *Menschenrechte im Gefängnis.* Strasbourg 1971; Ganter, H.: *Die Spruchpraxis der Europäischen Kommission für Menschenrechte auf dem Gebiet des Strafvollzuges.* Bonn 1974; Jasiński, J.: *The Punitiveness of Criminal Justice Systems* (A Cross-National Perspective). The Polish Sociological Bulletin 1(1976), pp.43–51; Jescheck, H.-H.: *Die Krise der Kriminalpolitik.* ZStW 91(1979), pp.1037–1064; Grabosky, P.: *The Comparative Study of Penal Severity: Some Methodological Considerations.* International Annals of Criminology 1980, pp.209–222; Ichikava, T. et al.: "Recidivism Viewed from the International Perspective." In: *Bulletin of the Criminological Research Department.* Ministry of Justice. Tokyo 1980, pp.1–8; Kaiser, G.: *Perspektiven vergleichender Pönologie.* MschrKrim 63(1980), pp.366–378; Kury, H. (Ed.): *Strafvollzug und Öffentlichkeit.* Freiburg 1980; Lenke, L.: "Criminal Policy and Repression in Capitalist Societies—The Scandinavian Case." In: *Policing Scandinavia.* ScandStudCrim 7, Oslo et al. 1980, pp.5–30; Mikaelsen, L.: *European Protection of Human Rights.* Alphen aan den Rijn—Germantown, Md. 1980; Austin, J., Krisberg, B.: *Wider, Stronger, and Different Nets: The Dialectics of Criminal Justice Reform.* JResCrim 18(1981), pp.165–196; Bronstein, A.: "Need for Policy Informed Strategies for Correctional Reform." In: *Special National Workshop: State Legislative Strategies for Correctional Reform.* Washington, D.C. 1981, pp.15–20; Christie, N.: *Limits to Pain.* Oslo 1981; Cole, G. et al. (Eds.): *Major Criminal Justice Systems.* Beverly Hills, London 1981; van Dijk, J.: *Public Attitudes towards Crime Policy in Holland.* The Hague 1981; Marnell, G.: "Treatment of Long-Term Prisoners: The Swedish Approach." In: *Confinement in Maximum Custody,* ed.by D. Ward et al. Lexington, Mass. 1981, pp.131–146; Kaiser, G., Kerner, H.-J., Schöch, H.: *Strafvollzug.* 3rd ed. Heidelberg 1982; Steenhuis, D. et al.: *The Penal Climate in the Netherlands: Sunny or Cloudy?* The Hague 1982.

A comparative analysis of European correctional systems reveals both *great similarities and vast differences.* Similarities in the treatment of prisoners, structure of prison staffs, and organization and administration of the correctional system have resulted from both tradition and the efforts made to correspond to the so-called minimum standards and the European Human Rights Convention. In addition, almost every national system has its strengths and weaknesses. *Various correctional models* exist which differ according to the criteria used and factors emphasized.

A low number of prisoners cannot be considered to be the major criterion of a successful correctional system, since countries such as Greece, Iceland or Cyprus accordingly would be ranked higher than the Netherlands. If one considered the number of prison terms imposed to be the most important factor, then Japan would be the highest rated nation. If one considered the degree to which corrections were regulated statutorily, then West Germany would have good chances of taking first place.

A one-sided accumulation of negative or positive characteristics for any particular nation, therefore, cannot be made. *Correctional profiles* which do emerge, however, tend in one direction or the other. The degree to which a correctional system receives international recognition, appears to be favorable, and makes actual progress does not necessarily indicate that those factors all emerge positively when combined in one system.

*On what level, however, is European corrections today, and how does the West German correctional system average in comparison?*

Even if one takes the standard minimum rules as the criterion for situation analysis and evaluation, the methodological *problems of comparing* the *European correctional systems* still is not solved. Although many European nations have made exceptional achievements and have provided beneficial correctional models according to which the West German system could be evaluated, individual descriptions of corrections in each of these nations is insufficient, regardless of how informative the review may be (see, also ECCP, 1980, p.14) and how interesting the survey appears. Only a comparative *horizontal and longitudinal sectional analysis, which incorporates as many dimensions* as possible, can offer additional information. For this reason, the typical listings of prison statistics, regardless of their importance, are not adequate. The general comparisons of prison populations appear to be too isolated. These figures must be analyzed in light of more complex criteria, such as the level of punishments imposed. In addition, one must consider constitutionality, protection of legal rights, socialization potential, and degree of humanization as evaluation criteria (cf. Chart 8).

**Chart 8:**

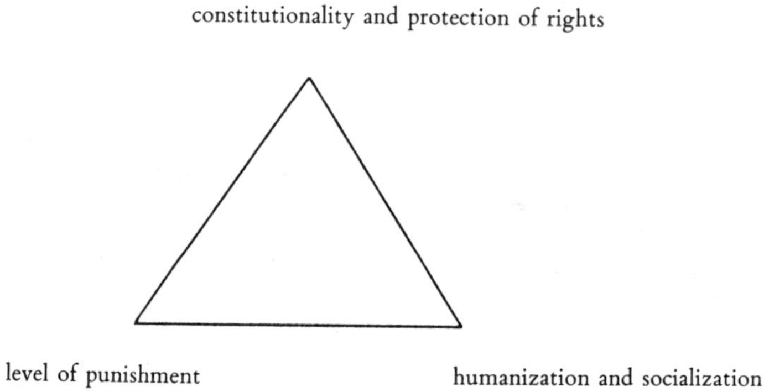


The following attempt to make a horizontal sectional analysis of European correctional systems must follow this model.

## 1. Cross-Section Analysis

Accordingly, level of punishment, constitutionality, and legal protection, as well as humanization and socialization, shall be used as the criteria for our comparison and evaluation.

### *1.1 Punishment* (level and intensity)

Indicators of the level of punishment imposed in any particular country can be taken from the comparative sanctioning statistics and ratios of prisoners to total population. To measure the level of punishment, it is necessary to differentiate between at least two aspects:

1) the frequency with which particular criminal sanctions are imposed and
2) the actual form of their execution (cf. Jasinski, 1976, p.44; Grabosky, 1980, p.215).

A frequently used standard for the level of punishment has been the average number of months a prisoner is confined. According to this standard, Scandinavia (with the exception of Finland) and the Netherlands would be evaluated the most favorably. This standard, however, reveals nothing about the size of the population which is subject to, or repeatedly subject to, the execution of prison sentences. For this same reason, standards, such as the number of prisoners, are insufficient criteria for expressing intensity of punishment.

In order to illustrate our point, it is helpful to compare two countries, one of which imposes relatively short prison terms for a relatively large part of the population (such as Sweden), and one of which imposes longer prison terms for a smaller part of the population (such as West Germany).

Which of these two solutions is preferable is difficult to determine because of the value judgments involved. Of importance, however, is that the standard for determining actual level of punishment be sensitive enough to include both aspects. This standard, therefore, must *include* both the *frequency of punishments imposed* and the *number of prisoners in relation to general population.* In addition, the *entire span of crime control* must be considered, in order to determine how much of the entire population is being supervised by the criminal law. The breadth of the network of criminal controls, therefore, has become increasingly important for scientific observation and criminal policy decisions.

In 1976, approximately 1,981,000 or 921 persons per 100,000 general population were under the administration of the U.S. correctional system (in institutions, on probation, in community treatment, etc.). Since 1965, this ratio had increased by almost 40 percent (cf. Austin, et al., 1981, p.183; Bronstein, 1981, p.15).

For the above reasons, all aspects of the correctional system such as intensive supervision through probation and parole officers, relaxations in corrections, the granting of suspended sentences, and other formal control strategies such as sanctions imposed by the public prosecutor, fines, conflict commission procedures, and pretrial detention must be considered and seen in relation to the protection provided to the minimum standards (cf. ECCP, 1980, p.10). The greatest advances in knowledge generally are attained through the largest possible inclusion of various measurements and methods. This method, of course, is also applicable to the measuring of criminality.

Lenke (1980, pp.11,16ff.), who employed a theoretical conflict approach, maintained that the prisoner-to-population ratio could be used as an indicator of repressive criminal policy, since unfulfilled political demands necessarily would be released through strikes and public protests. Accordingly, this type of protest would result in more repressive control measures. Since the general level of prison terms imposed is related more closely to the actual reality of crime commission and thereby conflict, Lenke not only comes to an overly favorable interpretation of Sweden's sanctioning system, but also to certain ethnocentric results. Sweden in fact does more frequently make use of prison terms, but these terms are for relatively short periods. In addition, this constructed explanation model could give accurate information on the various strategies for crime control only if it included indicators of social conflict, e.g. strikes, protest movements, and legal violations, and also indicators of conflict solutions, e.g. breadth and intensity of judgments and prison terms, and compared these indicators. If Lenke had used this type of analysis in explaining the West German system of crime control, he would not have had to look to the supposed remains of earlier fascist influences to illustrate why a high prisoner population exists in a country with a relatively low number of strikes.

If one compares the number of *prison terms imposed* to the number of individuals affected by these prison terms, one finds that in the Netherlands and in Sweden, considerably more persons per 100,000 population are sentenced to prison terms than in West Germany, England and Wales, and even Japan (cf. Table 15). Other European countries, such as France, Italy, Austria, and Switzerland, however, also dispense prison terms more frequently, when one compares the number of prison terms to the relative group of the country's population. The fact that these countries, with the exception of Austria, still have lower prisoner-to-total population ratios raises the question of how they manage to attain these comparatively low rates. Apparently these countries have adopted a mixed strategy of imposing relatively short prison terms and granting frequent conditional releases, pre-term releases, pardons, and other types of punishment reductions. Otherwise, those countries which are comparable to West Germany in the percentage of long-term sentences imposed, such as Switzerland and France, would necessarily have to have higher prisoner-to-population ratios.

A worldwide *comparison of the number of prisoners* reveals that the lowest prisoner-to-population ratio exists in the Netherlands, with only 22 prisoners per 100,000 total population at the beginning of the 1970s. The position of the Netherlands did not change during the 1970s, although this ratio increased to 27:100,000 (cf. KrimB, 1977, p.68).

Although it appears that Spain, with only 28 prisoners per 100,000 population, also has a relatively low ratio, this statistic includes only those individuals who actually have been sentenced. Since three-fifths of all confinees in Spain, however, are in pretrial detention (cf. FAZ No.224, 28 September 1981), the real ratio is more than twice what it appears to be. In addition, according to a memorandum of the general director for penal institutions, the number of confinees in 1980 increased by 34 percent in relation to 1979.

In comparison, the prisoner-to-population ratio in Japan is 43, in Sweden 51, in Switzerland 55, in France 62, in Great Britain 81, and in West Germany 83 to 100,000 general population (cf. Table 16). In 1978, this ratio was 247 in the United States, 274 in East Germany, 305 in Poland (1980), and 350 to 660 in the U.S.S.R. per 100,000 population. (See Christie, 1981, p.32; Kaiser/Kerner/Schöch, 1982, p.41.)

## **Table 15:** International Comparison of Sentences to Fines, Prison Terms and Probation

| Country/Year | | Total Population | Total abs. | Total rel.* | Fines abs. | Fines rel.* | Suspended Sentences/ Probation abs. | Suspended Sentences/ Probation rel.* | Prison term (not suspended/ w/o probation) abs. | rel.* | abs. | rel.* |
|---|---|---|---|---|---|---|---|---|---|---|---|---|
| D | 1960 | 53,756,000 | 485,661 | 903,5 | 335,978 | 625,0 | 57,225 | 106,5 | 92,458 | 172,0 | 10,117 | 18,8 |
| | | % | (100) | | (69,2) | | (11,8) | | (19,0) | | (2,1) | |
| | 1978 | 61,310,000 | 614,252 | 1001,9 | 507,627 | 828,0 | 67,889 | 110,7 | 37,617 | 61,4 | 12,300 | 20,1 |
| | | % | (100) | | (82,6) | | (11,1) | | (6,1) | | (2,0) | |
| A | 1960 | 7,048,000 | 109,097 | 1547,9 | 60,758 | 862,1 | 17,910 | 254,1 | 27,590 | 391,5 | 1,371 | 19,5 |
| | | % | (100) | | (55,7) | | (16,4) | | (25,3) | | (1,3) | |
| | 1974 | 7,545,000 | 82,093 | 1088,1 | 52,439 | 695,0 | 14,248 | 188,8 | 14,009 | 185,7 | 1,362 | 18,1 |
| | | % | (100) | | (63,9) | | (17,4) | | (17,1) | | (1.7) | |
| CH | 1960 | 5,298,000 | 42,295 | 798,3 | 24,324 | 459,1 | 10,649 | 201,0 | 6,910 | 130,4 | 1,272 | 24,0 |
| | | % | (100) | | (57,5) | | (25,2) | | (16,3) | | (3.0) | |
| | 1978 | 6,337,000 | 50,050 | 789,8 | 20,225 | 319,2 | 20,640 | 325,7 | 9,120 | 143,9 | 1,409 | 22,2 |
| | | % | (100) | | (40,4) | | (41,2) | | (18,2) | | (2,8) | |
| GB* | 1960 | 45,755,000 | 928,212 | 2028,7 | 836,409 | 1828,0 | 18,285 | 40,0 | 31,330 | 68,5 | 5,965 | 13,0 |
| | | % | (100) | | (90,1) | | (2,0) | | (3,4) | | (0,6) | |
| | 1978 | 49,119,000 | 1,775,021 | 3613,7 | 1,568,174 | 3192,6 | 61,637 | 125,5 | 43,992 | 89,6 | 10,761 | 21,9 |
| | | % | (100) | | (88,4) | | (3,5) | | (2,5) | | (0,6) | |
| F | 1960 | 45,730,000 | 213,509 | 466,9 | 107,736 | 235,6 | 48,993 | 107,1 | 56,693 | 124,0 | 9,170 | 20,1 |
| | | % | (100) | | (50,5) | | (5,2) | | (26,6) | | (4,3) | |
| | | *** | 956,769 | 2092,2 | 859,616 | 1879,8 | 49,885 | 109,1 | 64,187 | 140,4 | 9,170 | 20,1 |
| | | % | (100) | | (89,9) | | (5,2) | | (6,7) | | (1,0) | |
| | 1974 | 52,577,000 | 237,478 | 451,7 | 97,305 | 185,1 | 72,056 | 137.1 | 66,821 | 127,1 | 11,774 | 22,3 |
| | | % | (100) | | (41,0) | | (30,3) | | (28,1) | | (5,0) | |
| | | *** | 1,620,837 | 3082,8 | 1,475,309 | 2806,0 | 74,412 | 141,5 | 69,838 | 132,8 | 11,744 | 22,3 |
| | | % | (100) | | (91,0) | | (4,6) | | (4,3) | | (0,7) | |
| NL | 1960 | 11,487,000 | 36,550 | 318,2 | 30,342 | 264,1 | 2,380 | 20,7 | 10,353 | 90,1 | 466 | 4,1 |
| | | % | (100) | | (83,0) | | (6,5) | | (28,3) | | (1,3) | |
| | 1978 | 13,898,000 | 69,500 | 500,1 | 48,896 | 351,8 | 2,435 | 17,5 | 15,556 | 112,2 | 736 | 5,3 |
| | | % | (100) | | (70,4) | | (3,5) | | (22,4) | | (1,1) | |
| S | 1960 | 7,480,000 | 434,341 | 5806,7 | 413,802 | 5532,1 | 7,248 | 96,9 | 19,928 | 146,1 | 727 | 9,7 |
| | | % | (100) | | (95,3) | | (1,7) | | (2,5) | | (0,2) | |
| | 1978 | 8,276,000 | 369,327 | 4462,6 | 337,399 | 4076,8 | 12,506 | 151,1 | 12,974 | 156,8 | 843 | 10,2 |
| | | % | (100) | | (91,4) | | (3,4) | | (3,5) | | (0.2) | |
| J | 1967 | 100,243,000 | 4,519,554 | 4508,6 | 4,445,974 | 4435,2 | 41,582 | 41,5 | 31,745 | 31,7 | 15,446 | 15,4 |
| | | % | (100) | | (98,4) | | (0,9) | | (0,7) | | (0,3) | |
| | 1977 | 113,863,000 | 2,638,937 | 2317,6 | 2,563,302 | 2251,2 | 45,952 | 40,4 | 29,681 | 26,1 | ≃14,000≃ | ≃12,3 |
| | | % | (100) | | (97,0) | | (1,7) | | (1,1) | | (≃0,5) | |

* Rel. = judgments per 100,000 population

** Not including Scotland and N. Ireland; incl. non-indictable offences.

*** Including "contraventions"

Source: MschrKrim 63(1980), p.375

**Table 16:** Number of Prisoners in 1977 in all of the European Countries including Turkey and Cyprus (ordered according to ratio of prisoners per 100,000 general population and in comparison to the same statistics for 1932/1936)

| | | Total Absolute Number of Prisoners | | | | Number of Prisoners per 100,000 population | |
|---|---|---|---|---|---|---|---|
| Country | Total Population | total | prison terms | pre-trial d. | pre-trial d. in % | 1977 | 1932/36 |
| 1. Netherlands | 13,000,000 | 3,500 | — | — | — | 27 | 52 |
| 2. Cyprus | 600,000 | 200 | — | — | — | 33 | — |
| 3. Greece | 9,000,000 | 3,050 | 2,500 | 550 | 2 | 34 | — |
| 4. Iceland | 220,000 | 75 | 50 | 25 | 33 | 34 | — |
| 5. Portugal | 9,000,000 | 3,500 | 2,200 | 400 | 11 | 39 | — |
| 6. Ireland | 2,000,000 | 1,350 | — | 50 | 4 | 45 | 19 |
| 7. Norway | 4,000,000 | 1,900 | 1,500 | 400 | 21 | 49 | 57 |
| 8. Luxembourg | 380,000 | 150 | 110 | 40 | 27 | 50 | — |
| 9. Sweden | 8,000,000 | 4,100 | 2,800 | 1,300 | 32 | 51 | 39 |
| 10. Switzerland | 6,300,000 | approx. 3,500 | — | — | — | 55 | 165 |
| 11. Italy | 56,000,000 | 31,500 | 13,500 | 18,000 | 57 | 56 | 126 |
| 12. Denmark | 5,000,000 | 3,100 | 2,000 | 800 | 26 | 62 | 44 |
| 13. France | 52,000,000 | 32,000 | — | — | 42 | 62 | 56 |
| 14. Belgium | 9,900,000 | 6,322 | — | — | — | 64 | 61 |
| 15. Spain* | 36,000,000 | 21,753 | — | — | approx. 60 | 64 | — |
| 16. England & Wales | 52,000,000 | 42,000 | — | — | — | 81 | 30 |
| 17. West Germany | 60,000,000 | 50,000 | 39,900 | 10,100 | 20 | 83 | 157 |
| 18. Turkey | 40,000,000 | 40,000 | 19,000 | 21,000 | 53 | 100 | — |
| 19. Austria | 7,000,000 | 8,000 | — | — | — | 114 | 105 |
| 20. Finland | 4,800,000 | 5,500 | — | — | — | 115 | 232 |
| 21. East Germany** | — | 46,000 | — | — | — | 274 | 157 |
| 22. Poland*** | — | 107,000 | — | — | — | 305 | 151 |
| 23. USSR**** | — | approx. 1,5 Mill. | — | — | — | 350–660 | — |

* For 1980, according to FAZ Nr. 224 vom 28. 9. 1981.

** For 1977, according to a western estimation by *Freiburg,* A.: Kriminalität in der DDR. Opladen 1981, p.57.

*** For 1980, according to an estimation by *Lammich,* S.: MschrKrim 64(1981), p.88.

**** According to *Shtromas,* A.: Review of Socialist Law 1977, p.298; *Umbreit,* M.: U.S. Corrections—A Scandinavian Perspective. Michigan City 1980, p.24; for 1979 *Christie,* N.: Limits to Pain. Oslo 1981, p.32.

***** For the 1930's, according to *Hennings,* E.: The Prison Population of the World. MschrKrim 28(1937), pp.298f.

Source: Allgemein KrimB 1977, 42, 68f.

Some of this information for the beginning of the 1970s was gathered by the United Nations in 1975. The 1979 planned data-gathering was unsuccessful because many of the countries questioned did not respond. Because of this insufficient representation, a longitudinal analysis of prison populations could not be realized. A comparison of prison populations in the 1930s, however, reveals that West Germany occupied a relatively high position "among the European powers" at that time, followed by Poland and Italy, whereas England and Wales, Sweden, Belgium, and the Netherlands had relatively low prisoner ratios. (See Hennings, 1937, pp.298f.; for the present situation, Table 16.)

These findings in fact do support the observation that *the Netherlands' sanctioning system continually has increased in importance as a model* for penal corrections. The low prisoner ratio in the Netherlands is even more surprising, since its crime rate and *development in criminality* is hardly lower than in the other Western European countries. Of course, the more recent lack of information provided by the Netherlands in official government statements, in correctional statistics, and in the relevant literature is apparent, since the last official data were published in 1977. Obviously, the difficulties in the Netherlands also have increased, as can be inferred from the police and court statistics. A relatively higher prisoner ratio probably exists now than in the early 1970s. The Netherlands' model position in corrections probably results from the practice of imposing average prison terms of less than one month, in comparison to three months in Sweden, and 21 months in the United States. In addition, one must consider not only that low prison sentences are imposed in the Netherlands, but also that collective pardons are granted in order to keep the prison population low, and that prisoners are placed on a so-called waiting list until the required "room" in the penal institutions is vacant. These practices are possible, since they are tolerated by the people of the Netherlands.

The importance of popular understanding for these types of practices, particularly for collective pardons, has been illustrated in investigations and discussions in the field of "penal corrections and the public" ("Strafvollzug und Öffentlichkeit"; Kury, 1980). When the general public, because of its rigid value system or fear of crime, is incapable of accepting, or at least of not protesting, correctional policies oriented toward the prisoner's resocialization and self-responsibility, then it is hardly possible to attain low prison ratios. A comparison of attitudes toward collective pardons in the Netherlands and West Germany is supportive of this finding.

In North Rhine-Westphalia during the second half of the 1960s, and in Berlin and Hesse in 1979 and 1980, the attempt also was made in West Germany to impose a "correctional stop" and to introduce pardoning procedures in order to conquer the new problem of prison overcrowding. (See Kaiser, 1980, p.374.) Contrary to the reaction in the Netherlands (see van Dijk, 1981, pp.7,12.), however, these efforts were met with strong protests, with complaints to the state legislatures, and with severe criticism by the judiciary.

Although excessive attempts toward granting pardons have not been made in many countries, such as in West Germany, considerable constitutional problems arise with respect to such practices. Pardoning procedures not only *endanger the principle of equality and constitutionality,* but also contradict *basic attitudes* toward blameworthiness and punishment, and furthermore interfere with security and general crime prevention. Extreme differences exist on an international level in the *evaluation* of these problems. The judgments made in turn affect the type and nature of punishment imposed as well as the prisoner-to-population ratio. *Different levels of criminality* also affect the position taken in any particular country. One, therefore, can never "separate" criminal corrections completely from the crime rate (on this relationship, see Jasiński, 1976, pp.47,50ff.), as is sometimes attempted. (See Christie, 1981, p.33.) The level of punishment, however, is not the only standard for comparative evaluation. Of no less importance in this comparison appears to be the effectuation of constitutionality and judicial controls.

## 1.2 Constitutionality and Protection of Legal Rights

Although the importance of recognizing these two factors in any comparative analysis is clear, the difficulties in evaluating constitutionality are no less than those involved in evaluating the level of punishment. Certain *indicators* can be developed to evaluate the guarantees made to protect basic rights, to provide constitutionally acceptable judicial procedures, and to secure the prisoner's legal rights during the correctional period. These guarantees usually are contained in statutory provisions and other regulations. The extent to which these norms actually are enforced, however, cannot be determined. Interviews of prisoners in the various nations or other empirical investigations of this problem do not exist, and requested government statements are insufficient for evaluation. Furthermore, it appears difficult to make any general determinations on the degree of constitutionality from the number and types of complaints filed and from the resulting judicial procedures. It is feasible that certain pre- or extra-judicial mechanisms, which may be more economical and effective than judicial controls, exist to solve these conflicts. This conclusion has been supported by West German experience with judicial review of correctional administrative files, according to §§ EGGVG, in comparison with practices of the so-called petition boards. (See Kaiser/Kerner/Schöch, 1982, p.58.) The Swedish ombudsman is also an example of an extra-judicial control mechanism, although more recently the possibility of (administrative) judicial review of correctional administration has become available in Sweden. (See Marnell, 1981, pp.131f.) The recognition of basic rights within the correctional system and the legal protection of these rights provided for prisoners, therefore, can offer only an indication of constitutionality.

In addition, the European nations recognize *various means of solving conflicts, as well as different stages of legal support* for these mechanisms. In West Germany, major reliance is placed on judicial review by the penal correctional courts. In addition, an internal administrative complaint procedure exists, which according to an empirical study processes 95 percent of all complaints filed. In other European countries, judicial control of administrative orders within the correctional system is either permitted on a limited basis or not permitted whatsoever. Even nations such as France, Austria, Poland, and Hungary, all of which have correctional courts, allow judicial review only in extremely narrowly defined cases. Minimum Rules for the Treatment of Prisoners No's.36, 56 (2) recognize only a control over the protection provided for the prisoner's individual rights as defined in the law of the nation involved. In order to provide more control over the prisoner's rights and to insure that the minimum conditions for an effective correctional system are being fulfilled, the introduction of review or supervisory organs is being considered as a supplement to occasional interviews with the governments involved (cf. ECCP, 1980, p.11).

Contrary to the Minimum Rules for the Treatment of Prisoners, which attempt to define the minimal conditions for penal corrections, the European Human Rights Convention is concerned generally with *guaranteeing basic rights,* including those of prisoners. Article 25 HRC gives every individual the right to petition directly to the Commission in cases of violations of a recognized right. This access to an organization of international control represents "the actual novelty and epochal aspect of the Convention" (Ganter, 1974, p.175). The control provided, however, is limited by the fact that access is available only if the country involved as respondent actually recognizes the jurisdiction of the Commission. Most, but not all, of the European nations have recognized the Commission's jurisdiction (cf. Mikaelsen, 1980, pp.20f.; France did not recognize the Commission until October 1981, and Greece still has not recognized its jurisdiction.).

By the middle of 1971, more than 5,000 individual complaints had been filed under Art.25 HRC with the *European Commission for Human Rights.* This Commission occupies a key position within the system provided by the Convention for the protection of human rights. Almost 40 percent of these complaints were filed by prisoners (Secretary of the HRC, 1971, pp.1,46). This percentage did not drop significantly until 1979. (Council of Europe: Yearbook, 1979, p.398; see also Table 13.) The Human Rights Commission reviewed these complaints according to the standards set by the Convention, and these decisions contributed to the creation of the European Minimum Rules for the Treatment of Prisoners. Until 1971, only four of approximately 2,000 relevant individual prisoner complaints actually were recognized, which in and of itself must "appear alarming" (Ganter, 1974, p.184). The Commission seldom takes a direct position on factual matters over which the constitutional courts within the individual country have jurisdiction. One cannot maintain, therefore, that essential impulses for the West German correctional reform came from the decisions of this commission, even though prisoner complaints frequently were directed against the West German correctional system until 1971.

More than one-half of these complaints were filed against West Germany at that time (Ganter, 1974, p.188). From the decisions of the European Human

Rights Commission published after 1978, prisoners' complaints appeared to increase against Great Britain during the 1970s. Switzerland was the second most often named respondent (cf. Review on "European Basic Rights" from 1978 to 1981 with pertinent indications). One can conclude that for English prisoners, who rarely have access to any nationally recognized judicial controls, an appeal to the European Human Rights Commission is apparently the most promising means of objecting to interferences in their individual rights. In contrast, West Germany today seldom is named as respondent to a prisoner's complaint.

Apparently in West Germany, the general improvement of conditions within the correctional facilities, the clarification of prisoners' legal rights in the new Corrections Code, and the case decisions made by the correctional courts had both milder and more stabilizing results. In addition, the requirements of the West German Corrections Code appear to exceed those demanded by the European Minimum Standards. (See, Ganter, 1974, pp.94ff.,188.) Appeals to the European Human Rights Commission, therefore, usually come into question only for individuals confined in psychiatric clinics or placed under pretrial detention.

Regardless of their importance, constitutionality and the protection afforded prisoners' rights offer only one aspect for judging a correctional system in addition to the level of punishment discussed above. One also must consider the potential for socialization and humanization within the correctional system.

## *1.3 Socialization and Humanization*

Indicators of the preparedness and potential of a correctional system to assist the prisoner in his social reentry, i.e. socialization, can be found primarily in the stated goals and responsibilities of the correctional system, in the nation's acceptance of the European Minimum Rules for the Treatment of Prisoners, and in the actual construction of the correctional facilities.

One striking factor is that the Minimum Rules for the Treatment of Prisoners are recognized both in Europe and in the world in general. This *recognition of a minimum standard for corrections* certainly has not been merely verbal but also has been attempted in practice, although with considerable limitations in some nations. The strongest impetus for the further humanization and unification of corrections appears to lie in this acceptance, which supersedes even the political division existent in Europe.

*Nevertheless,* the philosophy of corrections, or expressed more precisely, the concretely desired *correctional goal,* remains *problematic.* If the main goal of corrections is to prepare for the prisoner's release, as observed in Scandinavia, the Netherlands and Hungary, then the question immediately arises as to why one sends the criminal to prison. If he were not confined, then release preparations would not have to be undertaken. The avoidance of damages from confinement and the assimilation of the outside world within the correctional system would be superfluous. This paradox has not been resolved convincingly and it appears to be an expression of the general crisis in freedom-depriving correctional systems. Although this theoretical debate seems to be basic and penetrating, in practice general agreement exists as to the purpose of corrections and the appropriate direction for its reform.

When Sweden argues for the opening of penal institutions and an expansion of the prisoner's contact with the outside world through measures such as prison vacation leaves, it is striving for an important and normal contribution to the improvement of confinement conditions and the humanization of prisons. (See ECCP, 1980, pp.93f.) The Prison Commission for Belgium and Luxembourg, on the other hand, sees prison vacations as a part of individual treatment, since they are a means of permitting the prisoner to have contact with the outside world. Accordingly, this commission has proposed as an addition to Minimum Rule No.67 that treatment include contact with the outside world and that for this purpose vacation be seen as a means of treatment (ECCP, 1980, p.88). As the above examples reveal, factual differences, even regarding correctional reform, do not exist, but rather the labels used in the various countries are different. What one refers to as "treatment" is called by another "humanization." (See too, Christie, 1981, p.48.)

Our comparison reveals that *investments and efforts made in the construction and expansion of correctional facilities* for similarly sized correctional populations are *extremely different.* The correctional staff in the Netherlands, for example, is almost twice as large as it is in Switzerland for approximately the same number of prisoners. Even in Switzerland, with 55 prisoners to 100,000 population, the prisoner ratio is not particularly high. Although Switzerland does have a few excellent penal institutions, internationally it is viewed incorrectly as a model for a future-oriented correctional system. Even in the field of penal corrections, advertisement, image building, and the ability to sell oneself appear to play an important role.

If one compares Sweden or Denmark to the Netherlands, the Scandinavian countries cannot compete with respect to either the prisoner-to-population ratio or the size of the correctional staff. On the other hand, open correctional facilities are used more in Sweden and Denmark than in any other European nation, and voluntary workers supplement the work done by the smaller official correctional staff.

A particularly relevant and *unsolved problem,* not only in Europe but also in the entire world, is the *treatment of recidivists.* Attempts toward solving or reacting to this problem are manifold, but advancement and success is very limited (cf. Ichikava et al., 1980, pp.1ff.). In evaluating a correctional model, this factor certainly also must be considered, although penal corrections can contribute only minimally to crime control. In light of the successful program of crime control practiced in Japan and the socialist countries, however, it seems inappropriate to ignore this factor completely (as does Christie, 1981, p.33).

*Special problems* also confront penal corrections. Narcotic usage presents considerable difficulties almost everywhere in Western Europe, both within and outside the correctional system, and appears not to have any convincing solution. Not only narcotic users and terrorists, but also foreigners and minorities, as well as juveniles, the mentally ill, and the aged pose distinctive problems for corrections. These types of problems often are left unaddressed, perhaps because they are not included within the Minimum Rules for the Treatment of Prisoners or because general correctional problems are so massive that lower level special problems are forgotten. The relationship between corrections and criminality, the provision for confining criminals in psychiatric clinics (see here, and on the violation of Art.5 HRC, Trechsel, 1980, pp.526f.), and correctional programs for the aged and foreigners all are fields that remain unmentioned in reports and discussions of penal corrections.

## 2. Longitudinal Analysis

Publications on comparative corrections over the past thirty years reflect completely *different viewpoints and* correctional *needs.* In 1950, Hugueney mainly concentrated on determining the state of penal corrections after World War II in order to support new reform efforts, whereas fifteen years later, Conrad provided impressionistic travel notes on deficiency profiles, phantasies, and experiments in European correctional systems. Conrad's horizon of expectations was determined essentially by the treatment ideals of the 1950s and the U.N. standard minimum rules. Conrad (1965, pp.169ff.) summarized his observations at that time as follows:

> "We have traversed far and wide and found standard correctional practice in many forms: . . . They are working in institutions which are mostly obsolete, improvised, overcrowded, and inconveniently situated. The administrative structure is cumbersome and bureaucratic, hard-pressed to keep things going. Maintenance of present services keep the staff busy; there is little inclination and less time for innovation. People, buildings, organization charts. They are for the control of hundred of thousands of grand and petty offenders. Deterrence, retribution, incapacitation, and even treatment may be the objectives expected by the administration of criminal justice. But the essence of correctional practice as now administered throughout the world is control. Within this framework much else may be done. Much else must be done, if only in the name of humane standards of behavior by the state toward its citizens."

*What has changed* since then? One must conclude that both major and minor changes have occurred. The optimism of the correctional reformers and sociologists either has been abandoned or radically distorted into utopia (e.g. the demand to abolish the correctional system). The comparative inventories of Wicks/Cooper, Ward/Schoen, Shorts and the ECCP, which all appeared between 1979 and 1981, reflect the particular needs of criminal corrections in the late 1970s, after correctional philosophy had been altered by scepticism concerning the treatment ideal. The *main problem areas* now appear to be long-term confinement, secure confinement of dangerous criminals, overcrowding in prisons, as well as the necessity of more intensive regard for the minimum standards and the protection of prisoners' rights, and the special problem of narcotics consumption. Although corrections has lost quantitative relevance in countries such as West Germany, it has gained qualitatively when seen on a longitudinal basis. Increased attention now is being paid to the evaluation of freedom and freedom-deprivation and to the protection of human rights.

Several United Nations' investigations of the recognition given the Minimum Rules for the Treatment of Prisoners reveal this new orientation. Investigations conducted in 1967, 1974 and 1979 reveal that correctional systems throughout the entire world are fulfilling minimum humane, constitutional and administrative demands on an increasing level. The results of these investigations, however, are drawn from the information provided by the various national governments and, therefore, are probably somewhat too "favorable." Random investigations of correctional staff members and prisoners probably would lead to considerable modifications of these findings. The fact that mechanisms for international supervision of the enforcement of the Minimum Rules are being considered could be the result of conditions that do not meet up to the standard expected (ECCP, 1980, p.16). In addition, some nations' refusals to answer or to answer completely the questionnaires given (only one-third of all the countries questioned gave sufficient answers) provide no more information than the total lack of information available for the unreported nations.

Our balancing of debits and credits in European penal corrections reveals that not only larger nations are innovative and willing to experiment. On the contrary, small nations, independently from the Netherlands or the Scandinavian countries, have achieved *great accomplishments* and have developed several model institutional forms, e.g. Mittersteig in Austria and Saxerriet or St.Johannsen in Switzerland. Within the socialist countries, Hungary also offers a good example for penal corrections. For this reason, Jescheck's comment in 1959 that West Germany could learn from the smaller European nations is still true today.

The question now arises as to *whether the West German correctional system has provided any model institutions* or whether Conrad's (1965, pp.146ff.) biting criticism is still applicable today. This latter assumption obviously would be incorrect, even if an independent "German model" could not be found. The opening and relaxation of West German penal corrections is being practiced widely, although this practice is nothing new. Although the socially therapeutic experiments being conducted are not innovative, they are still completely different in their prerequisites for application and conditions of execution from those carried out in the earlier model institutions in Denmark and the Netherlands. The fields in which West Germany comes closest to being a model is in that of securing prisoners' rights through statute and judicial control. This superiority becomes particularly obvious when one views the complaint systems in Austria, Switzerland, France, England, and even in Scandinavia. Only during the past few years has this field been considered intensively or commented upon by the courts of these nations, e.g. Sweden.

Seen in its *entirety,* our comparative analysis reveals that the *concept, form, and practice of penal corrections* vary considerably among the different European countries. Certain *common profiles,* however, emerge in both *West and East Europe.* One variation is obvious from the prisoner-to-population ratio, which fluctuated during the 1970s in the Western European nations from 20 to 120 prisoners per 100,000 population, with West Germany located in the upper 50 percent of these countries. Contrarily, according to the information available, this ratio was considerably higher in Eastern Europe with 270 to 660 prisoners per 100,000 population. The real reasons for this difference cannot be explained merely from the practice of stationary confinement as opposed to open corrections, but rather are the result of particular uniquenesses within the total system of social controls according to statutes, punishment levels, correctional planning, and attitudes of the general public toward penal corrections and criminality. Accordingly, one also can differentiate the concepts and styles of some of the western European systems as following either the "Scandinavian Model" or the "Dutch Model," depending upon whether or not, in addition to favoring short prison terms, institutional treatment is preferred. Countries such as England and Italy, in which penal corrections seem to be facing a crisis, represent an opposite extreme. The countries in middle Europe, which do not favor short prison terms but which emphasize conditional release and treatment within the correctional system, are more moderate. The widespread increase in criminality in Western Europe, however, has led to more severe and longer prison sentences and thereby to an increase in the number of confinees with all its accompanying problems. In comparison, the Eastern European countries still impose longer prison terms, although shorter and average length terms are being replaced by conditional releases and monetary fines. The prisoner's improvement or resocialization is still the main goal of penal corrections in the socialist nations.

# VII. Conclusions and Predictions

**Citations:** Mittelstädt, O.: *Gegen die Freiheitsstrafen. Ein Beitrag zur Kritik des heutigen Strafensystems.* 2nd.ed. Leipzig 1879; id.: *Für und Wider die Freiheitsstrafen.* ZStW 2(1882), pp.419–449; Klug, U.: "Abschied von Kant und Hegel." In: *Programm für ein neues Strafgesetzbuch. Der Alternativ-Entwurf der Strafrechtslehrer,* ed.by J. Baumann. Frankfurt/M. 1968, pp.36ff.; Hassemer, W. et al.: "Soziale Reaktion auf Abweichung und Kriminalisierung durch den Gesetzgeber." In: *Sozialwissenschaften im Studium des Rechts.* Vol.3 Strafrecht, ed.by W. Hassemer et al. Munich 1978, pp.1ff.; Kaiser, G.: "Kriminalpolitik ohne kriminologische Grundlage? Die Zukunft des Strafrechts und die Wandlungen kriminologischen Denkens." In: *Gedächtnisschrift für H. Schröder,* ed.by W. Stree et al. Munich 1978, pp.481ff.; Sack, F.: "Probleme der Kriminalsoziologie." In: *Handbuch der empirischen Sozialforschung,* ed.by R. König. Stuttgart 1978, p.386; Jescheck, H.-H.: *Die Krise der Kriminalpolitik.* ZStW 91 (1979), pp.1037–1064; Jung, H.: "Kriminalpolitischer Stellenwert und Problematik der kurzen Freiheitsstrafe." In: *Materialdienst der Evangelischen Akademie Bad Boll* 15(1979), pp.4–14; Müller-Dietz, H.: *Grundfragen des strafrechtlichen Sanktionensystems.* Heidelberg et al. 1979; Schneider, H.-J.: *Crime and Criminal Policy in Some Western European and North American Countries.* International Review of Criminal Policy 35(1979), pp.55ff.; id.: "Behandlung des Rechtsbrechers in der Strafanstalt und in Freiheit." In: *Die Psychologie des zwanzigsten Jahrhunderts.* Vol.XIV. Zürich 1981, pp.899–935; Strasser, P.: "Forensische und therapeutische Kriminologie als 'Etikettierungswissenschaften'." In: *Reformen des Rechts. Festschrift zur 200-Jahr-Feier der Rechtswissenschaftlichen Fakultät der Universität Graz.* Graz 1979, pp.281ff.; Anttila, I., Törnudd, P.: "Reasons for Punishment." In: *Crime and Crime Control in Scandinavia 1976–1980,* ed.by N. Bishop. Stockholm 1980, pp.48ff.; Conrad, P., Schneider, J.: *Deviance and Medicalization: From Badness to Sickness.* St.Louis 1980; Heijder, A.: *Can we Cope with Alternatives?* C&D 26(1980), pp.1–9; Murbach, F.: *Das medizinische Modell der Delinquenz.* Zürich 1980; Nelson, A.: *Crime and Responses to Crime.* Stockholm 1980; Roxin, C.: *Zur Entwicklung der Kriminalpolitik seit den Alternativ-Entwürfen.* JA 12(1980), pp.545–552; v.Trotha, A.: "Gesellschaftlicher Wandel, Theoriebildung und Fallstricke im Umgang mit der Kriminologie." In: *Seminar: Abweichendes Verhalten IV—Kriminalpolitik und Strafrecht,* ed.by K. Lüderssen et al. Frankfurt/M. 1980, pp.92ff.; Christie, N.: *Limits to Pain.* Oslo 1981; Fogel, D., Hudson, J. (Eds.): *Justice as Fairness. Perspectives on the Justice Model.* Anderson Publ.Co. 1981; Gassin, R.: *La criminologie et les tendences modernes de la politique répressive.* RSCrim 1981, pp.265–279; Heinz, W.: *Entwicklung, Stand und Struktur der Strafzumessungspraxis. Eine Übersicht über die nach allgemeinem Strafrecht verhängten Hauptstrafen von 1882 bis 1979.* MschrKrim 64(1981), pp.148–173; Ortner, H. (Ed.): *Freiheit statt Strafe. Plädoyer für die Abschaffung der Gefängnisse.* Frankfurt/M. 1981; Quensel, S.: "Stigmatisierung durch Resozialisierung? Probleme einer Behandlungsideologie." In: *Stigmatisierung durch Strafverfahren und Strafvollzug,* ed.by W. Haesler. Diessenhofen/CH 1981, pp.161ff.

What can we conclude from our analysis? Perhaps one would say that the idea of treatment is "dead," since resocialization in the correctional systems here and elsewhere hardly is practiced. Would one conclude that we have reached an "end to the penal institution" in light of the fact that European correctional systems again are suffering from overcrowding? Should one decide to abandon further efforts in criminal corrections because they are pointless? Certainly these are not the answers.

The *treatment concept,* partially influenced by the "défense sociale nouvelle," took priority in international discussions of the 1950s and 1960s. The idea of punishment, however, appears to have experienced a renaissance (cf. Kaiser, 1978, pp. 490ff.; Jescheck, 1979, p.1050; Schneider, 1979, p.63; Anttila et al., 1980, p.49; Roxin, 1980, pp.21ff.). Since the Scandinavian "retreat from the treatment ideology" was adopted as a slogan in the West German literature, the question seems legitimate as to whether one still should maintain the treatment goal, which finally found its way into correctional legislation (Müller-Dietz, 1979, p.137). Of course, one must remember that the treatment concept is still supreme on a worldwide basis, regardless of the criticism attached thereto. The international retreat from the treatment concept, which has been claimed in some Scandinavian and American literature, therefore, is limited to only a few nations. Although this type of change is being discussed in these countries, the measurable corresponding *practical* effects are either unclear or non-existent. This claim also contradicts a trend that began here one and one-half centuries ago with the "farewell to *Kant* and *Hegel*" (Klug, 1968, pp.36ff.):

> It is high time to finally retreat from the criminal theories of *Kant* and *Hegel* with their irrational, contemplative lyrical excesses and in all their epistemological, logical and moral questionability.

Nevertheless, today we are not experiencing a simple return to old ideas or moving in an outdated direction. The development of an innovative criminal policy concept, however, also is not taking place.

More recent criticism, formulated under the "justice model," is directed, as was Mittelstädt's (1882) one hundred years ago, against the "brutal practice" and prevaricated rhetoric in the name of rehabilitation (cf. Fogel et al., 1981, pp. ivff.). It is argued that in practice correction results in the unemployment of more than one-half of prison inmates. The total lack of any meaningful treatment programs or medical care and the racial segregation practiced during admissions keeps a rehabilitative correctional system far behind its self-set goals. One certainly should not abandon resocialization, but participation therein should be voluntary. One should neither expect too much of resocialization nor forget the prisoner's legal rights. The limitation, structuring and reviewing of administrative judgments, is seen to be one of the essential elements of the "justice model."

Nothing can be said against this type of *criticism,* which obviously does not reject a model of resocialization or treatment. On the contrary, it should be supported. Nevertheless, two of the above objections must be examined more closely. One of them maintains that the prisoner's basic rights and the constitutionality of correctional procedures are being jeopardized, whereas the other states that treatment is nonsense because of its ineffectiveness.

The latter-mentioned *criticism claiming ineffectiveness of treatment* is hardly applicable to West German corrections, since treatment in the real sense of the word did not exist, with some few exceptions, before the early 1970s. Inventories and situation analyses reveal that treatment research, both here and in the United States, has not surpassed its initial test phase. One cannot determine, therefore, exactly which concrete treatment methods are the best for which group of prisoners during which period. Nevertheless, both foreign and domestic observations, experiences, and insights have been made in treatment processes on criminals. The information gathered was almost completely unknown earlier, although it is essential to the orientation and improvement of criminal corrections. In the meantime, empirical research has indicated that directed use of therapeutic measures combined with social assistance and supportive correctional measures could be promising. The more recent criticism, therefore, offers no convincing reason for resignation and retreat from treatment and treatment research. On the contrary, its development is necessary and urgent. Treatment in the absence of consent, however, is neither sensible from a therapeutic point of view nor clearly permissible from a constitutional standpoint. Only the individual who agrees to the application of treatment is suitable for this treatment (cf. §9 StVollzG). The problems resulting in the selection of suitable prisoners for treatment within the correctional system, of course, cannot be overlooked.

The *concern expressed for basic rights,* however, places the permissibility of any form of treatment in question. For this reason, one should never overlook the danger involved in extending a prison term for the purpose of more effective treatment. This danger is particularly precarious in countries in which prison terms of undetermined length are statutorily permissible and actually applied. Since undetermined sentences are not within the West German adult correctional system, this concern is superfluous. The juvenile sentence of undetermined length continually has decreased in frequency over the past twenty-five years. Both this type of sentence and adult security custody, which could be seen as a hidden form of undetermined prison sentence, have almost no practical relevance in West Germany today. Furthermore, with the exception of the provisions contained in §65 StGB, no intent has been expressed to provide inherently ineffective treatment to prisoners against their free will, but instead efforts have been made to offer the possibility of receiving treatment. For this reason, the legislature should not rely on §65 StGB, but rather on the so-called corrections solution in §§9,123 StVollzG.

Although the argument is logical and persuasive that the various treatment and assistance measures (cf. §7 [7] StVollzG) can be applied only to the extent they support the goal of corrections, one should not overlook the possible disciplinary nature of treatment measures, such as the denial of day or vacation leaves. For the individual who wants to remain unchanged, who sees the goal of corrections as meaningless, and as a result, who does not participate in treatment, the granting and denying of vacations and other correctional relaxations can be a means of exerting positive and negative sanctions. For this individual, the previous system of privileges and punishments continues to exist under another name. The question then becomes whether it would not be better and more honest to admit that this situation exists than to try to justify it through irrational treatment attempts. The concept of treatment, furthermore, should be protected from perversion.

This situation and the problems involved therewith are in no way new. One hundred years ago, Mittelstädt vehemently turned against the "improvement purpose of confinement" and "every form of forced rehabilitation in the prisons" (1879, p.64). He was of the opinion, as are many critics today, that "the old formulas and optimism which supported this reasoning were things of the past . . ." (p.88). "Does one of the possible improvement measures offered under the modern form of prison rehabilitation exist which offers any guarantee of success and proof of value?" he asked impatiently and directly (p.28). He saw the results of his analysis to indicate "the obvious bankruptcy of the entire modern punishment system with the exception of its denials of freedom!" (p.57). "The results of treatment will not improve because they cannot possibly be better. My criticism is directed exclusively against a stystem that unreasonably strives toward unattainable goals and employs irrational means for the purpose of such unattainable goals" (p.58). "The state penal authority . . . is invested with neither the responsibility nor the power to improve or rehabilitate, neither with respect to the individual nor the entire society . . . In any event, deterrence and deterrence alone, or punishment as negative and as punishment alone, is the only effective means of at all maintaining the existing legal order and, if one please, the moral order in our national unity'' (p.61). Such were Mittelstädt's conclusions, as are many of the conclusions of his modern colleagues in the United States and Scandinavia today. For these reasons he demanded: ''the return to other types of punishments that make confinement possible; the last positive goal to be strived for'' (p.74.).

So far, so good, but what did the ''positive concepts,'' with which Mittelstädt (p.87) ''wanted to confront the existing punishment system'' (p.87) concretely look like? Firstly, ''the simple, direct, final destruction of the most extreme criminal branches of society . . . the whole purpose of the death penalty. Only after ax and guillotine have performed their duty 'sans phrase' for some time again can we begin to reconsider the entire question with healthy nerve, firm imperturbability and open conscience to determine rationally the permissible forms and limits of this ultima ratio earthly justice'' (p.77). Furthermore, the ''reintroduction of corporal punishment, more corporal punishments and less deprivations of freedom, so is the national postulate'' (p.81). ''Our penitentiaries need only be reopened a few years under the regime of hunger and cudgel and the now disappeared feeling that punishment is shame will become alive again'' (pp.83f.). These were Mittelstädt's ''positive concepts'' with which he wanted to critically confront the ''existing penal system,'' concepts that even then were not future-oriented, not to mention one hundred years later.

It is not only in West Germany that more sentences are being awarded and more prison terms given now than a decade ago. Today, almost as many persons are confined as in the middle of the 1960s. Again prisons are overcrowded, and prisoners are being confined under degrading circumstances. The courts again are condemning this type of confinement and the Justice Department must alter its correctional policies anew. During such a period, it is clear that the concept of treatment is difficult to maintain. But do other better strategies exist?

Ambulant sanctions cannot be applied to multiple recidivists. For the same reasons, sanctioning forms applied in other countries, such as community service or community prevention, also are inapplicable. The model of short prison terms hardly appears acceptable for multiple recidivists and dangerous criminals (cf. Jung, 1979, pp.14ff.), even though it is recommended and legitimized with reference to Hegel (cf. Heijder, 1980, pp.3f., 8). The mere lengthening of prison terms for the purpose of deterrence and prevention not only leads to a higher prisoner ratio but also contradicts the principles of social justice and coresponsibility. So viewed, no alternative to treatment exists. Inspired from and rejuvenated through critical essays, however, comparative surveys on the development of a sanctioning system occasionally led to the notion that a ''therapeutic state'' were developing (v.Trotha, 1980, pp.99ff.). In other words, it is being assumed that past punishment forms increasingly could be replaced by forms of treatment as an expression of active social control. Although hardly any concrete support for this type of assumption exists in Europe or elsewhere, it is maintained that an increasing "medication of deviance" (Sack, 1978, p.386; Schneider, 1979, p.63; Strasser, 1979, pp.281ff.; Conrad et al., 1980; Murbach, 1980; Quensel, 1981, p.161) exists with corresponding consequences for the criminal law. The concept of "treatment," however, does not necessarily imply a concept of medical therapy in either content or method. If one considers that at most only two percent of all registered criminals have had even forensic medical contact, and that of these prisoners only a fraction underwent medically directed therapy, then the putative tendencies of a *"medicalization of criminal law"* or a "therapeutic state" appear to be empty magical formulas, and in this case, *unfounded.* Contrarily, the expressions "treatment by training" (Müller-Dietz, 1979, p.137), and "social training," seem to illustrate a concept of treatment with its goal and method aimed toward the social integration of the criminal actor. The prepared labeling approach and the critically radical criminological antiposition to the principle of individualization, i.e. theories opposed to personality orientation and actor-directed treatment, however, cannot meet the needs of criminal corrections today or in the near future. Criminal corrections, in the absence of differentiation, offers of socialization, and treatment, is in fact dehumanization and regression (see Jescheck, 1979, p.1053; Roxin, 1980, p.224).

One of course cannot question the existence of a legal concept of illness, of psychiatric hospitals, and medically directed detoxication clinics. It is also true that in addition to "criminalization" other constructions of reality and definitions of the problem exist, such as "pathological," "psychological," and "sociological." These concepts, in combination with crime analysis, have unquestionably inspired penology and at least have assisted in defining the limits of criminal legal intervention, in expanding upon the protection of human rights, and in furthering the process of rationalization. No serious objections can be made, however, to the increased contributions made by doctors or psychologists to crime legislation or penal corrections, as long as constitutional security is guaranteed and legal policy principles and voluntariness of treatment are maintained.

In fact, we are confronted with an *actualization of pragmatic theories of action,* which always have affected criminal legal discussions and the enforcement of criminal law, quite independent from theory. Only in this way can one explain that treatment goals and retributive concepts occasionally exist simultaneously and are pragmatically unified, as in the Netherlands, or that theories and strategies of legitimization vary but practices remain the same (as in Scandinavia) or seriously decline (as in England and Wales).

Whereas the *Dutch practice* of short prison terms is supported theoretically by Hegel's concept of retribution (Heijder, 1980, pp.3f., 8), the *Scandinavian prac-*

*tices* are attributed to general prevention (Anttila et al., 1980, pp.48ff.; critically, Christie, 1981, pp.41ff., 45ff.). When taken literally and no longer as secondary rationalizations, however, both of these efforts to provide theoretical support for existing practices are not convincing in light of the situation in these countries. Neither the concept of retribution nor of general prevention is clearly sufficient to support awarding short prison terms, executing these terms in open institutions, or granting extensive prison leaves. Particularly the Dutch practices of extremely selective sentencing and of placing those individuals sentenced on a so-called waiting list because of overcrowded prisons cannot be derived from the idea of retribution. With the exception of the Danish institution Herstedvester, correctional practices and the number of prisoners in Scandinavia have not changed significantly over the last decade despite some avid theoretical discussions (cf. also ECCP, 1980, pp.63,66,93f. on Sweden). What in Scandinavia is considered to be "humanization" or an expression of the "concept of justice" is considered here to be "treatment," in correspondence generally with the U.N. Minimum Rules for the Treatment of Prisoners (see §§7 [2],10f. StVollzG). To decide that these two concepts are mutually exclusive would be completely arbitrary. A review of the situation in Scandinavia reveals that the system draws upon the principle "in dubio pro libertate," the principle of necessity, and the prohibition of excessiveness. On the contrary, nothing can be said against drawing upon these and other legal policy principles. Finland is particularly interesting in this respect. The so-called treatment ideology was never employed in Finland, and the prisoner-to-population ratio there has been more than twice as high over the past fifty years as it has been in any of the other Scandinavian countries. Accordingly, many regard the treatment ideology to be an important humanization factor regardless of its inherent deficiencies.

The *situation in the United States* is completely different. The considerable increase in officially registered crimes, the extremely high prisoner-to-population ratio—wherein blacks are overproportionately represented—and the erection of large penal institutions all indicate that the idea of treatment hardly can be considered promising, especially in light of the low use of monetary fines here in relation to western Europe. Exactly this aspect indicates the necessity of more closely connecting the possibility of intervention through the prison term with general sanctioning practices.

Similar to the development in other European nations (cf. Table 15), we see in West Germany that short prison terms decreased considerably during the 1970s, and that longer prison terms again increased (cf. Heinz, 1981, pp.148ff.). The diverse strategies responsible for this development probably are related to the various criminal sub-groups involved, viz., first offenders and occasional criminal actors as opposed to dangerous, intensive criminals. This assumption is supported by the worldwide practice of replacing short- and middle-length prison terms with *conditional sentences and parole assistance,* interalia. During the past two decades, conditionally suspended sentences were granted more frequently than prison terms, both in Western Europe and in the United States. During the 1950s, this development began at a time of general acceptance of the treatment concept, and apparently has not yet reached its culmination.

The *political-economic assumption* that nations impose more prison terms during periods of higher unemployment and more suspended sentences during periods of low levels of unemployment (Hassemer et al., 1978, p.40) cannot be supported by the post-war sanctioning practices in Europe. The development in West Germany from the post-war period to the 1960s reveals that the number of prison terms imposed to socially integrated and thereby non-dangerous criminals, actually increased during this period of economic growth. Any political-economic assumptions along this line, therefore, appear to be too undifferentiated to record and explain the complexity of sanctioning practices.

Furthermore, the comparative analysis of sanctioning statistics indicates, with some reservations, that the *monetary fine has prevailed* as an expression of the punishment concept. Socialist countries, on the one hand, and Western nations such as France and Switzerland, on the other (cf. Table 15), reveal that the use of differing sanctioning methods has not necessarily met with less success. West Germany, England and Wales, Japan and Sweden make wide use of the monetary fine, but they also permit individualized payment plans and have diverse practices in awarding substitute prison sentences in the case of inability to make payments. This diversity has not led to any recognizable problems in penal sanctioning and corrections. The question then becomes particularly relevant to the *necessity of employing a system of sanctions and their practice.* The development of deviance and its recognition by the general public, of course, cannot be disregarded, since the effect these factors have on possible "feedbacks" with criminality and consequences for the effectiveness of criminal law are still unclear. This confusion is necessitated by the fact that conditions and mechanisms separate from those inherent in the criminal legal system, such as urbanization, industrialization, public awareness, minority integration, social mobility and migration, etc., play significant roles in this complex problem.

*Nowhere,* however, can "developments in other nations" be seen as "examples" of the fact "that a *society* can exist *without prisons*" (contrarily, Ortner, 1981, p.12, but without convincing support). The demand for abolishing penal corrections always will find some listeners, but only very few will be convinced that this goal can be attained during their lifetime. As great as the scepticism of the prison sentence is and as widespread as the calamities of penal corrections appear to be, an "end to prisons" (Schneider, 1981, p.927), which is more postulated than concretely proposed, still is not in sight.

# INDEX

# INDEX